CHRISTIANS AND MOORS IN SPAIN

Volume II
1195-1614

Colin Smith

Aris & Phillips Ltd — Warminster — England

British Library Cataloguing in Publication Data
Christians and Moors in Spain.
    Vol. 2: c.1195–1614
       1. Spain. Christian church. Relations with
Islam, history. 2. Spain. Islam. Relations with
Christian church, history
       I. Smith, Colin, 1927- II. Series

ISBNS   0 85668 447 3 (cloth)
         0 85668 448 1 (limp)

ISSN   0953 797 X

Reprinted 1998

The publishers gratefully acknowledge the financial assistance of the Dirección General del Libro y Bibliotecas of the Ministerio de Cultura de España with this translation.

Printed and bound by CPI Group (UK) Ltd, Croydon, CR0 4YY

CONTENTS

INTRODUCTION

There is little to be added to what was said by way of introduction to volume I. As one moves forward in time the dates of texts and events become more secure, but some of our texts deal with 'events' which knew no greater reality than that conferred on them by their authors' brains and their readers' receptivity (38, 55, 60, 70), a reality surely as strong as that conveyed by descriptions of battles or saintly apparitions. The legal texts are in a slightly different category, perhaps, but even such as 53 or 59 are available for 'deconstructive' or other kinds of analysis taught by modern criticism. Even the most seemingly factual account, such as 58, is no more than a distant perception composed long after the event on the basis of memory and fragmentary early accounts. The three texts united in 61 are offered precisely in order to provide an exercise in comparison of diverse perceptions.

An effort has been made to do justice to most parts and languages of what eventually became Spain. There are two texts by outsiders (39, 66) and several from within Muslim lands. Portugal is excluded, since texts from there could well make an independent volume, but Muslim North Africa is present (38, 49, 59, 67) for reasons which need no justification, and the sea itself has a part to play in the drama (70).

A volume could readily have been made of exclusively military accounts, but these have been limited here to a few of the most important episodes (37, 40, 42, 58, 61) and balanced by several passages about peace-making (46, 57, 59) and by one wry view from the alternative society (39). Warfare, even if blessed by the Pope and dignified by the name 'Crusade' was eventually seen to be not the only means with which to confront and subdue Islam: the new orders of mendicant friars in the 13th century sought to win souls by peaceful conversion, often in perilous circumstances (41) but with better prospects after due preparation (48, 51). Juan Manuel's serene consideration of the problem is notable (56). If blind prejudice and misinformation continued surprisingly late (52), one quite amazingly independent assessment of Islam could be made and sent in an eloquent document to John II of Castile; but this was by a dangerously deviant Christian and was to be buried in secrecy until our own times (62). In other texts Christians rubbed shoulders with Muslims at all kinds of levels in both Christian and Muslim lands (44, 49, 50, 54, 57, 59, 60, 64, 72), and sometimes more than shoulders were at least wishfully involved (55). Chroniclers' pens recorded what regal eyes appreciated in Muslim agricultural (45) and building (47) skills; the royal gaze was naturally acquisitive in part, but surely full of genuine admiration too. With texts from 65 on we enter an area which is almost akin to modern politics and which is certainly capable of arousing strong passions among historians and among Spaniards of the present day. It seemed that no

harm could be done by letting Cervantes have the last word, though the translation probably does not adequately represent his ironies and ambiguities.

In conclusion, the editor/translator hopes that even the specialist historian or scholar of Spanish will find something new here. It is a source of wonder and regret that so many of the texts from which extracts have been taken are little known or available only in a very large university library. Short extracts although chosen for their value as detachable pieces may not properly represent the qualities and fascination of the complete texts. While every Hispanist knows the *Abenámar* ballad and Cervantes, texts such as 38, 41, and 62 are probably unknown to many, not so much because they are in Latin as because they have not been offered in modern or semi-popular editions. The mid-15th century chronicles in Spanish so well edited by Juan de Mata Carriazo in the 1940s (texts 61, 63, 64, 65) are rare items today and hence much less known than they should be. There is work here, one feels, for many editors in Spain and abroad. For readers who do not command the original languages, it is hoped that the materials offered will prove rewarding, and these volumes are specially designed for them.

BOOKLIST

To the items listed in volume I may be added:

Rachel Arié, *L'Espagne Musulmane au temps des Nasrides (1232-1492)* (Paris, 1973)

Fr Robert I. Burns, *Moors and Crusaders in Mediterranean Spain: Collected Studies* (London, 1978)

Louis Cardaillac, *Morisques et Chrétiens. Un affrontement polémique* (Paris, 1977)

Charles-Emmanuel Dufourcq, *L'Espagne Catalane et le Maghrib aux XIIIe et XIVe siècles* (Paris, 1966)

Salvador de Moxó, *Repoblación y sociedad en la España cristiana medieval* (Madrid, 1979)

James Muldoon, *Popes, Lawyers, and Infidels: The Church and the Non-Christian World, 1250-1550* (Liverpool, 1979)

R. Douro

● COIMBRA

R. Tagus

Guadalerza

Alenquer

Piedrabuena

R. Guadiana

● LISBON

Cara

Andú

CORDOVA

R. Guadalquivir

Carmona

● Ecija

● SEVILLE

Sant

Lebrija

Antequera ●

Jerez

Alora ●

Puerto de Santa María

Coín ●

MÁLAC

CADIZ

Marbella

Algeciras

Tarifa

Gibraltar

0

Ceuta

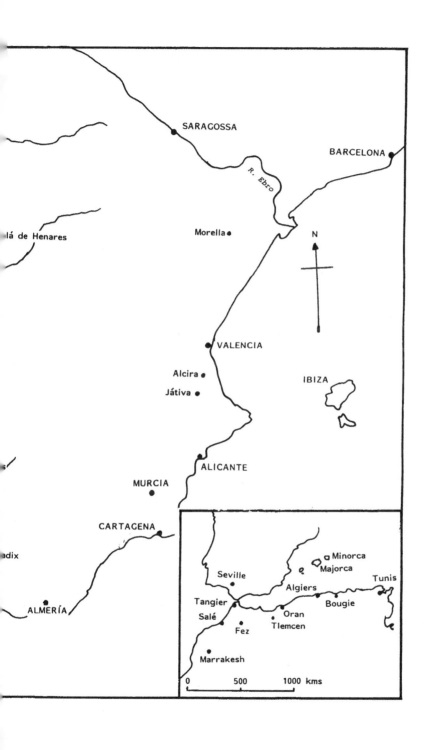

SARAGOSSA

BARCELONA

R. Ebro

Morella

lá de Henares

N

VALENCIA

Alcira

Játiva

IBIZA

ALICANTE

MURCIA

CARTAGENA

adix

ALMERÍA

Minorca

Majorca

Seville

Tunis

Algiers

Tangier

Bougie

Salé

Oran

Tlemcen

Fez

Marrakesh

0   500   1000 kms

2

37. The aftermath of Alarcos (1195-96)

After the fall of Jerusalem to the Muslim forces of Saladin in 1187, Pope Clement III (1187-91) wrote to the Archbishop of Toledo urging him to try to resolve the differences among the monarchs of Christian Spain so that they could unite in a campaign against al-Andalus. There was a general fear that Islam was again on the offensive on all fronts. In the East the Third Crusade attempted to resist this. In Spain, as a consequence doubtless not intended by the Pope, Alfonso VIII of Castile tried to assert his hegemony. He made a peace treaty with Navarre and in April 1188 invaded León; by June Alfonso IX of León (1188-1230) was suing for peace, and at Cortes in Carrión the same month the Castilian monarch was able to retain his territorial gains and force Alfonso IX to kiss his hand in sign of vassalage, at the same time arming the young man knight. The papal legate secured a further treaty (Tordehumos, April 1194) by which Castile handed back certain castles to León.

On 1 June 1195 a huge Muslim army, commanded by the Almohad Caliph Ya'qub I (in our text Almiramomelim, Almiramamolin: Arabic amir al-mu'minin, 'commander of the faithful') resident in Marrakesh, crossed the Strait. Alfonso VIII and the Castilian army met them at Alarcos near Ciudad Real, suffering a grave defeat on 19 July, with the consequences outlined in our text. The armies of León and Navarre had been moving to join the Castilians, apparently with the genuine intention of fighting at their side, but either they were slow or Alfonso VIII was over-confident and joined battle prematurely. The disaster to the Christians sent waves of alarm throughout Western Europe; yet it was exploited, in ways frankly stated by our text, by the Leonese and

Predictus rex Maurorum spolia diripuit, castra quedam cepit, scilicet turrem de Guadalferza, Malagon, Beneuentum, Calatraua, Alarcos, Caracuel, et sic in terram suam reuersus est.

Rex uero Legionis, qui ibat in auxilium regis Castelle, uenit Toletum et consilio quorumdam satellitum Sathane conuersus est in arcum prauum querens occasiones quibus discederet ab amico et de amico factus est crudelissimus inimicus, nempe manebat alta mente repositum quod ei contingerat in curia, de qua supra facta est mentio, in Carrione celebrata.

Recessit igitur de Toleto a rege glorioso indignans quia quedam castra, que petierat, ei dare noluerat, gratulabundus et gaudens de infortunio quod acciderat Castellanis.

Confederatus est statim regi Marroquitano et, accepta pecunia ab eodem et multitudine militum armatorum, guerram mouit regi Castelle, ita quod anno sequenti, eo tempore quo reges solent ad bella procedere, cum Almiramomelim terram, que est ultra serram, uastaret et Toletum ciuitatem diebus multis quasi obsessam teneret.

Idem rex Legionis intrauit in regnum Castelle per terram de Campis cum

Navarrese as they took their revenge for hurts recently endured at the hands of the now weakened Castilians.

The account is that of the Latin Chronicle of the Kings of Castile, almost certainly the work of Juan, Bishop of Osma in Castile and distinguished servant of the Crown; he died in 1246. The work embraces the reigns of Alfonso VIII, Henry I, and Ferdinand III. Historians think this account of Alarcos superior to those of Lucas de Tuy (1236) and Rodrigo Jiménez de Rada (1243). The extract is from the edition by Luis Charlo Brea, Crónica latina de los reyes de Castilla (Cadiz, 1984), pp. 15-17.

Alfonso VIII was not without spiritual support in his desperate situation. In a bull of 31 October 1196 from Pope Celestine III addressed to the Archbishop of Toledo and Primate of Spain, the Leonese King and his henchman Pedro Fernández de Castro (who had fought on the Almohads' side at Alarcos) were to be excommunicated if they did not abandon their alliance with the Moors, and their vassals were to be relieved of their allegiance to these lords. In a further bull of 10 April. 1197 the Pope granted crusading indulgences to all who fought against the King of León. A peace was patched up late that year, sealed by the marriage of Alfonso IX to Princess Berenguela of Castile. Pedro Fernández continued to serve the Almohads at intervals, eventually dying in Morocco in 1214. Castilian feelings against León and especially against the traitor Pedro Fernández of the hated Castro clan seem to have motivated some attitudes in the Poema de mio Cid *(Colin Smith, The Making of the 'Poema de mio Cid' (Cambridge, 1983) pp. 177-78, following Lacarra; see also text 24).*

The aforementioned ruler of the Moors took his spoils and captured the following fortresses: Guadalferza, Malagón, Benavente, Calatrava, Alarcos, and Caracuel, and then he went back to his land.

Then tne King of León, who was going to the aid of the King of Castile, reached Toledo, and on the advice of certain accomplices of Satan changed into a weapon of evil [Psalms 77.57], seeking opportunities by which he might separate himself from his ally, and from friend he became a most cruel enemy; to be sure, there remained in his mind the memory of what had happened to him at the Cortes, mentioned above, held in Carrión.

He therefore left Toledo, angered with our glorious Monarch because he had refused to hand over certain castles he had asked for, and overjoyed about the disaster which had befallen the Castilians.

He at once allied himself to the Sultan of Morocco and, after receiving from him money and a large number of soldiers, declared war on the King of Castile; then, the following year, in the season when monarchs are wont to make war, he ravaged the land beyond the mountains [Trasierra] in the company of the Almiramamolin and for some time virtually besieged the city of Toledo. The King of León invaded the kingdom of Castile through Tierra de Campos with the

Maurorum multitudine supradicta, qui, uelud inimici crucis Christi, multa enormia in contumeliam et dedecus christiane religionis in ecclesiis et ecclesiastica supellectile comitebant.

Peruenit autem usque Carrionem ubi uisus fuit purgare dedecus, quod sibi credebat illatum quando manum regis Castelle fuit osculatus.

Eadem tempestate rex Nauarre Sancius, qui regi Castelle attinebat in secundo gradu consanguinitatis ex utraque parte, hedificauit castrum quoddam iuxta uineas de Locronio, quod uocauit Coruum; regnum et Castelle cepit ex illa parte uastare, cum ullam iustam causam belli crederetur habere.

Sic igitur Christiani cum Mauris colligati colligatione impietatis in desolationem regis Castelle conspirasse uidebantur, mala quecumque poterant atrociter toto regno undique inferentes, adeo quod nusquam in toto regno uel angulus unus inuenire posset, in quo quisquam securus esset.

Ignis ascensus uidebatur in furore Domini et elationem animi, si quam conceperat rex nobilis ex gloria precedenti, deprimere uidebatur, ut intelligeret rex prudens et nobilis quoniam regnum filiorum hominum in manu Dei est et cuicumque uoluerit dabit illud.

Rex autem gloriosus, utpote qui non multum frangebatur aduersis nec nimis extollebatur in prosperis, accinxit se uiriliter ad defendendum regnum suum, ponens spem suam et fiduciam in uirtute Domini nostri Iesu Christi, cuius fidem semper firmissime credidit et contra hereticam prauitatem defendit.

aforementioned army of Moors and these, as enemies of Christ's Cross, committed many atrocities in churches and to church furnishings, to the disgrace and dishonour of the Christian faith.

He reached Carrión determined to erase the blot of shame he thought had been placed upon him when he kissed the hand of the King of Castile.

At the same time Sancho [VII, 'el Fuerte'], King of Navarre, who was related to the King of Castile in the second degree of consanguinity on both sides, built a castle – which he called Corvo – close to the vineyards of Logroño; and he began to ravage that part of the Kingdom of Castile, believing that he had a just cause for war.

Thus Christians allied to Moors in an impious alliance seemed to conspire for the destruction of the King of Castile, barbarously inflicting all possible harm in the whole kingdom, to the extent that not in a single corner of the realm could anyone feel safe.

The fire of God's anger seemed to increase and to affect adversely the exalted state of mind which our noble King had perhaps acquired from his earlier achievements, in order that our wise and illustrious monarch should realize to what extent the realm of the sons of men is in God's hand, and that God may give it to whom He will.

However, our glorious King, as one neither much broken by adversity nor too uplifted by success, prepared himself manfully to defend his kingdom, placing his hope and trust in the strength of our Lord Jesus Christ, faith in whom he always most firmly maintained and defended against all manner of heretical evil.

38. Ovid in an unexpected setting (1199)

The following extraordinary tale is included by the English historian Roger of Howden (Hoveden) in his Chronica, *completed in 1201. He wrote it on a spare page at the end of his account of events of the year 1190, though it relates to events around 1199 (this being the date of the death of Sultan Ya'qub I: 23 January): evidently the tale reached the chronicler at a late stage in his work but was too good to disregard, and he squeezed it in where he found space. Howden's chief concern was with English affairs, but he shows himself well-informed about some Peninsular and Mediterranean matters; there is a short paragraph preceding our extract about Peninsular rulers in the period 1191-99, but after it Howden turns to other matters, so he did not know – and we do not know – what conclusion the episode may have had.*

The persons involved are Sancho VII of Navarre, 'el Fuerte', reigned 1194-1234; Ya'qub I, Sultan of Morocco and al-Andalus, 1184-99, and his son Muhammad, aged 17 at his accession, who succeeded him, 1199-1213; and the Muslim princess, daughter of Ya'qub and sister of Muhammad, who is unnamed. History of the more mundane kind knows nothing of the tale which follows, alas. It seems that Sancho VII was indeed on good terms with the Almohads and received an annual subvention from them (and for this and other reasons he was excommunicated by Pope Celestine III in late 1197). When on 20 May 1198 Alfonso VIII of Castile and Peter II of Aragón met at Calatayud and resolved to partition Navarre, invading it later that year, Sancho went in desperation to Morocco to seek Almohad aid. He seems to have stayed there for two years, his name being absent from the documents of Navarre between February 1199 and March 1201. The invaders annexed large parts of his kingdom, a situation which Sancho accepted in treaties made in 1207 and 1208. Rodrigo Jiménez de Rada (who was Navarrese) says in his De rebus Hispaniae *of 1243 (VII.32) that Sancho with a few companions went for a time to al-Andalus and sent messengers to negotiate with the Sultan in Morocco; but he does not mention the love-story. A few years later, at the battle of Las Navas in 1212 (our text 40), Sancho commanded the right wing of the allied Christian forces in their decisive victory over the Almohads.*

Processu vero temporis, filia Boyac Almiramimoli, imperatoris Africanorum, audita per communem famam probitate Sanctii regis Navarrae, fratris Berengerae reginae Angliae, dilexit eum in tantum, quod vehementer adoptavit eum sibi in maritum. Et cum ipsa propositum suum diutius celare non posset, indicavit patri suo imperatori quod ipsa seipsam laqueo suspenderet, nisi Sanctius rex Navarrae eam sibi in uxorem duceret. Cui pater respondit: 'Quo modo potest hoc fieri, cum tu sis pagana, et ille Christianus?' Cui filia respondit: 'Parata siquidem sum fidem Christianorum suscipere, et secundum legem illorum vivere, dummodo

We do not know Howden's source for the story, but to judge by its position in his manuscript, he received it rather than himself inventing it. Gascony was Angevin territory and had a common border with Navarre along the Pyrenees; Eleanor of England was Queen of Castile (wife of Alfonso VIII); Sancho's sister Berenguela had married Richard I of England and after his death in 1199 lived in Gascony; Bishop García of Pamplona went to England in 1201 to resolve problems concerning the dowry of widowed Queen Berenguela; priests and ambassadors passed to and fro, and northern crusaders en route for the Holy Land often touched at Peninsular ports; by any one of these means the story could have reached Howden. Its beginnings may have lain in popular rumour in Navarre (why has Sancho gone to Morocco? ... cherchez la femme? ...) which tempted somebody, most likely a priest with literary leanings, to write the episode up with Ovidian embellishments, elegant even if nonsensical in the mouths of a Muslim Sultan and his daughter, a further element of unreality being added when the Sultan describes his daughter as a 'pagan'. One might guess also that when King John of England met Sancho at Chinon on 14 October 1201 to make an alliance, Sancho in his cups had a tale to tell about his recent experiences in Morocco, and that this was recorded by some secretary and passed on to Howden. Nothing of this kind greatly surprises at the end of a century which had seen the flowering of 'courtly love' ideals in Provence and throughout Europe, so many infidel princesses defying conventions and their fathers when in love with Christian warriors in the chansons de geste, *the amorous triumph of Charlemagne in infidel Toledo (alluded to in our text 8, introduction), the romanticizing of the story of Sa'ida (text 21), and in real life Richard I of England, no less, offering his own sister to Saladin. Some may care to savour the potential operatic notes which can be heard not too distantly here: surely the Sultan's 'Nescio quid faciam' anticipates a hypothetical aria, 'O ciel! Che farò ...?' in Rossini's* Il navarrese in Algeri?

The text is taken from the edition of the Chronica *by W. Stubbs in the Rolls Series, 51 (London, 1868-71, 4 vols), III, pp. 90-92. Stubbs helpfully identifies the Ovid passages. He comments in a note on the astonishing speed of 'the process of the circumstantial elaboration of a myth'. There is a rambling discussion of the episode in: Luis del Campo Jesús,* Sancho el Fuerte de Navarra *(Pamplona, 1960), pp. 100-61.*

As time went on, the daughter of Ya'qub I. Emperor of the Africans, having heard by popular report of the outstanding qualities of Sancho, King of Navarre, brother of Berengaria Queen of England, fell so deeply in love with him that she passionately wished to have him as her husband. When she was no longer able to keep this notion to herself, she told her father the Emperor that she would hang herself unless Sancho of Navarre would take her as wife. Her father answered her: 'But how can this be achieved, when you are a pagan and he is a Christian?' To this the daughter replied: 'I am ready to adopt the

8

praedictum regem Navarrae in maritum habeam; quod per te, pater mi, de facili potest fieri. Nam omnia te metuunt, et ad te sua brachia tendunt; blanditiis tamen opus est, terror furorque absint; preces et munera mitte viro, ut sic eum mihi compares.

    Crede mihi, res est ingeniosa dare.

Mitte etiam matri et sorori, et aliis familiaribus suis, munera larga manu, ut ipsi eum in tuos conatus alliciant. Fit cito per multas praeda petita manus.'

    Cui pater respondit:

    Donec eras simplex, animum cum corpore amavi,

    Nunc mentis vitio laesa figura tua est.

Nescio quid faciam, angustiae enim mihi sunt undique, quia nisi rex ille Navarrae in amorem tuum conversus fuerit, tu te laqueo suspendes; illum ergo precibus variisque muneribus aggrediar tentans, si cum modo quolibet tibi in maritum adquirere possim. Mallem tamen, ut tibi virum de gente nostra sumeres.'

    Cui puella respondit:

    'Devorer ante precor subito telluris hiatu,

    Aut rutilo missi fulminis igne cremer,

quam aliquem habeam virum praeter illum regem Navarrae.' Imperator igitur Africanorum misit nuncios suos ad Sanctium regem Navarrae, per quos mandavit illi, ut ipse veniret ad eum filiam suam in uxorem ducturus, et ille daret ei tantam pecuniam quantam vellet, et insuper totam terram quae dicitur Hispania Saracenica, videlicet, totam terram quae est a finibus terrae regis Portugalensis usque ad montem de Muneian, qui dividit terras paganorum, qui sunt in Hispania, a terra regis Arragoniae.

    Dum autem rex Navarrae iret ad eum, mortuus est ille Boiac Almiramumoli, Africanorum imperator. Cumque praefatus rex Navarrae venisset in Africam, invenit imperatorem mortuum, et filius imperatoris defuncti adhuc minimus erat, et nondum aptus ad regni gubernationem, et erant ei in imperio multi adversantes. Cum autem rex Navarrae ad eum venisset sperans se accepturum sibi in conjugem praefatam puellam, dixit ei puer qui regnaturus erat, quod si vellet juvare eum, et servire ei ad terram suam obtinendam, ipse daret ei sororem suam cum promissis patris sui, sin autem, poneret eum in captionem, de qua nunquam exiret. Ipse autem videns se in arcto positum, elegit magis servire ei quam poni in captione, juxta illud Augustini, 'Qui murorum ambitu, ne fugiat, clauditur, ibi se praecipitet ubi murus brevior ingeritur'.

Christian faith, and to live according to their Law, provided that I have the King of Navarrre as my husband; and that, dear father, can easily be achieved through you. Everybody goes in awe of you, everybody stretches out arms towards you [Ovid, *Amores* I.2.33]; send him requests and presents, and you will secure him for me.

Believe me, giving is an artful business.

[*Amores* I.8.62]

Send presents generously too to his mother and his sister, and other relatives, so that they too should be drawn into helping your efforts. If a lot of people are reaching out for the loot, it is quickly won' [*Amores* I.8.92].

Her father replied:

'When you were innocent, I loved your soul and body,
Now your beauty is ruined by evilness of mind.

[*Amores* I.10.13-14]

I don't know what to do; troubles beset me on all sides; unless the King of Navarre can be made to fall in love with you, you'll hang yourself; so, trying to work on him with pleas and all manner of presents, I will see if I can win him as a husband for you. But I would prefer you to take a man from our own people.' To this the girl replied:

'I rather beg to be swallowed up by some sudden fissure in the earth,
Or burnt up by the glowing fireball of a thunderbolt from on high,

[*Heroides* III.63-64]

than to have any man other than the King of Navarre.' Thereupon the Emperor of the Africans sent messengers to the King of Navarre, asking him to come and marry his daughter, promising him that he would give him all the money he wanted, and in addition all of al-Andalus, that is to say, all the land which lies between the frontier of the King of Portugal and Mount Muneian [var. Muncian: unidentified; possibly Morella, inland from Peñíscola, a fortress on the frontier at the time, taken by the Aragonese in 1234], which marks off the lands of the pagans in Spain from the territory of the King of Aragón.

Then, while the King of Navarre was on his way to him, Ya'qub, Emperor of the Africans, died. When the King of Navarre reached Africa, he found the Emperor dead, and the son of the deceased very young, and not yet ready to take on the governance of his realm; moreover, in his empire he had a lot of enemies. Since the King of Navarre had arrived hoping to be accepted as the spouse of the princess, the young man who was to succeed to the throne told him that if he wished to help him, and serve him in the task of recovering his land, he [the Emperor] would give him his sister according to the promises of his father; but if he refused to help, he would hold the King in captivity and he would never escape from it. The King, seeing himself in a dilemma, chose rather to serve the Emperor than to be held captive, for as St Augustine says, 'He who is shut up inside walls so that he should not escape, will rush to that

Domino igitur concedente, et Sanctio rege Navarrae laborante, filius Almiramimoli subjugavit sibi infra triennium omnes adversarios suos; et factus est imperator. Interim Aldefonsus rex Castellae, et rex Aragoniae, invaserunt terram dicti regis Navarrae, unus illorum una parte, et alter illorum altera parte, ita quod Aldefonsus rex Castellae cepit super eum vigintiquatuor oppida, et praedictus rex Aragoniae cepit super eum octodecim oppida.

point at which the walls are least high.' Consequently as the Lord granted, and with King Sancho toiling in his service, the son of Ya'qub subdued his enemies within three years, and then became Emperor in the full sense.   Meantime Alfonso [VIII] of Castile and the King of Aragón invaded the lands of the King of Navarre, one from one side, the other from the other side; Alfonso of Castile took twenty-four towns from him, and the King of Aragón eighteen.

39. Preparations for the Crusade: an alternative view (1212)

The troubadour Guilhem Adèmar was born about 1175 at Meyrueis near Nîmes. He was a gentleman but, lacking resources to maintain that status, turned to verse. He was poetically active from about 1195 to about 1217. According to a later biographical account, he eventually became a religious in the Order of Grandmont (and perhaps did penance for the sentiments of the text which follows).

The poem from which the extract is taken belongs to the early months of 1212. The King of Aragón, Peter II, went to see Raymond VI, Count of Toulouse, on behalf of Alfonso VIII of Castile, the motive being to seek help

(5)   Mas eras ai a bon port de salut,
Fe qe vos dei, mon navei aribat
Et ai lo plom e l'estaing recrezut
E per fin aur mon argen cambïat;
Ç'autrejat m'a una de las gensors
Dompnas del mon – a jes no-m descove –
Qe-m des s'amor e d'un baisar m'estre;
Et es tant pros c'us reis i for'honratz.

(6)   E per aisso mi teing per ereubut
E non envej el mon nuill home nat,
Si-m vol midonz tener vestit o nut
Un ser lonc se en luoc de moillerat.
Anc no fon faig al mieu par tals honors
Cum a mi er, si-naissi s'esdeve
Qe-l sieu blanc cors gras, escafit e le
Remir baisan ni teng'entre mos bratz.

(7)   Si-l reis n'Amfos, cui dopton li Masmut,
E-l mieiller coms de la crestïantat
Mandavon ost – puois ben son remasut –
E nom de Dieu, farion gran bontat
Sobre-ls pagans sarrazins traïtors,
Ab qe l'us d'els menes ensems ab se
Marit seignor qi-nclau e ser'e te;
Non ant pechat no lor fos perdonatz.

for the campaign which culminated at Las Navas in July 1212 (text 40). If a crusading contingent was raised in Toulouse it would enlist and remove from the scene the husband of the lady of Narbonne (Bïatriz, Beatrice?) with whom Guilhem was in love. It is this Count who is alluded to in the second line of stanza 7.

The poem's first line is 'Non pot esser sofert ni atendut'. It consists of seven stanzas and an envoi, stanzas 5-7 being reproduced here from the edition by Kurt Almqvist, Poésies du troubadour Guilhem Adémar (Uppsala, 1951), pp. 130-33; with commentary on pp. 26-31. See also Carlos Alvar, La poesia trovadoresca en España y Portugal (Madrid, 1977), pp. 117-20.

(5) Now, by my faith, I sailed my ship into the goodly harbour of salvation, giving up lead and tin and changing my silver into pure gold. For one of the loveliest ladies in the world has promised – to my enormous pleasure – to grant me her love and to give me a kiss; so noble is she that a king would be honoured by that.

(6) And so I count myself very fortunate and would not envy any other man alive, if one evening my lady would receive me in the place of her husband, dressed or naked, stretched out at her side. Never would so much favour be done to a man of my station if it were granted to me, while kissing her and holding her in my arms, to gaze on her white, rounded, willowy, smooth body.

(7) If King Alfonso, whom the Almohads fear, and the best Count in Christendom, mobilize their forces – since they have not yet set out – in the name of God, they would perform a great service against the pagan treacherous Saracens, provided that one of them takes with him the lord her husband, who keeps [my lady] shut away in his possession; they have not so far sinned in any way which could not be forgiven them [by such a goodly act].

40. Las Navas de Tolosa (1212)

This battle, fought on the southern slopes of the Sierra Morena near the village of Santa Elena, was the most important single action ever fought on Spanish soil. After the defeat at Alarcos, years of effort were required by Alfonso VIII to restore the position of the Castilians. By 1206 peace had been made with León and Alfonso was beginning to prepare a major campaign against the Almohads. The Pope proclaimed a Crusade and from 1206 the bull was being read in Spain by (St) Domingo de Guzmán, founder in that year of the Dominican Order. At papal urging a large army was raised by bishops and others north of the Pyrenees, and the Kings of Aragón and Navarre came in person with contingents (the Leonese hesitated, eventually sending a force which arrived too late to take part). In Rome in 1212 there were processions, and services of intercession were held.

In the spring of 1212 the armies concentrated in Toledo, the mass of men creating immense problems of supply and payment, as our text frankly shows. These problems and worse, those of indiscipline and violence by the non-Spanish troops against Christian and especially Jewish civilians, dogged the whole campaign, although on these the present letter is judiciously restrained. The battle was fought on Monday, 16 July, and the royal report to the Pope, whose interest had been keen and practical, must have been written a few days later. Since Alfonso can hardly have had a command of Latin, his text must have been dictated to a scribe who translated it; or perhaps it was redacted by the Archbishop of Toledo, Rodrigo Jiménez de Rada, who was with the army at all stages and who carried the Virgin's banner into the battle. He later wrote his own account in his De rebus Hispaniae *completed in 1243 (chapters 1 to 14*

Sanctissimo patri ac domino Innocentio, Dei gratia summo pontifici, Aldefonsus, eadem rex Castellae et Toleti, cum osculo manuum atque pedum, salutem. A Sanctitate vestra credimus non excidisse propositum impugnandi sarracene gentis perfidiam, uobis per nostros nuntios deuote et humiliter intimasse, in omnibus tanquam patris et domini uestrum subsidium expetentes, quod sicut a patre pio nos recognoscimus benigne et pie pariter impetrasse.

Quocirca cum litteris uestris nuntios nostros, quos ad hoc exsequendum idoneos reputauimus, ad partes Francie non distulimus destinare, addentes etiam ut omnibus militibus uenientibus ad bellum et omnibus seruientibus, prout decebat, expensas uictu[i] necesarias largiremur, quibus possent commode sustentari. Unde fuit quod, audita remissione peccatorum quam uos uenientibus

of Book VIII), and this very full account was adopted in the Primera crónica general. *It is noticeable that Rodrigo palliated the unpleasant aspect of the Christian campaign – the defection and treachery of the* ultramontanos, *the non-Spaniards – and further exaggerated the number of Muslims killed, which he puts at 200,000. For other accounts and for a good general survey, including important notes on the difficulties of the terrain which posed such problems, see Huici Miranda, pp. 219-37. The present text is taken from Julio González,* Alfonso VIII *(Madrid, 1960, 3 vols), III, pp. 566-74. In this volume the following text is the letter which Alfonso's Queen, Berenguela, sent to her sister Blanca (Blanche), wife of Louis VIII of France, also a report on the battle.*

There can be no doubt that the figures of casualties (and of the original army) on the Muslim side are exaggerated, and those of the Christian losses minimized. However, with regard to the latter, it has been suggested that '20 or 30' is perhaps not unreasonable if it refers to those of knightly class only, no account being taken – the case would hardly be unique – of the commonalty of foot-soldiers.

Why did the ultramontanos *defect? Because of the terrain and the heat, says Alfonso diplomatically. The facts seem to have been otherwise. The* ultramontanos, *in advance of the Spanish forces, took Malagón on 25 June, and slaughtered its garrison. Calatrava surrendered on terms to Alfonso on 1 July: all lives were spared and the garrison was allowed to depart. It was this act, by Alfonso and his commanders, counselled by clerics and entirely normal in Spain, which outraged the non-Spaniards who had come to kill infidels and take booty; and it was this total difference of attitude which led the French and others to abandon the campaign and return to Toledo (bereft of its own fighting-men) with the intention of sacking it. Moreover, the Pope had forbidden deals with the infidel of the kind which secured the surrender of Calatrava, so that again Alfonso (or his scribe) had to keep this aspect quiet and devise another explanation when reporting to the Pope.*

To the most Holy Father Innocent, Pope by the Grace of God, Alfonso, King of Castile and Toledo by the same, sends greetings, kissing your hands and feet. We know that your Holiness has not forgotten that we planned to do battle against the perfidy of the Saracens, and we reported to you humbly and devotedly by our messengers, begging your help in all things pertaining to a father and a lord, which help we recognize we have obtained in kindly and compassionate fashion from our loving Father.

For this reason we did not delay in sending our heralds (whom we thought most suitable for carrying this forward) out with our letters to certain parts of France, adding that we would provide, to the extent that could reasonably be sustained, the necessary costs of provisioning all those knights coming to join the campaign, and for all their serving-men to the degree that was fitting. Hence it

indulsistis, uenit magna multitudo militum de transmontanis partibus, necnon et archiepiscopi Narbonensis et Burdegalensis, et episcopus Nannetensis. Fuerunt qui uenerunt usque ad duo millia militum cum suis armigeris, et usque ad decem millia seruientium in equis, et usque ad quinquaginta millia seruientium sine equis, quibus omnibus nos oportuit in uictualibus prouidere. Venerunt etiam illustres amici nostri et consanguinei rex Aragonum et rex Nauarre cum potentatu suo in fidei catholicae auxilium et iuvamen. Quibus, nobiscum aliquanto tempore apud Toletum facientibus moram, expectabamus quippe homines nostros qui uenturi erant ad bellum, omnia necessaria, prout per nuntios nostros promisimus, non defecimus ministrare, licet expense essent propter sui multitudinem nobis et regno nostro fere importabiles et onerose. Non enim solum in iis que promiseramus, verum etiam in pecuniis specialiter et in textrariis, quibus fere omnes tam milites quam seruientes pariter indigebant, nos oportuit prouidere. Sed Deus, qui multiplicat incrementa frugum iustitie, ministrauit nobis abunde secundum sue gratie largitatem, et dedit omnia posse perficere perfecte pariter et abunde.

Congregata itaque nostra et suorum multitudine, uiam Domini cepimus proficisci, et uenientes ad turrim quamdam, que Malagon nuncupatur, satis munitam, ultramontani antequam nos peruenerunt per unum diem, et illam cum Dei auxilio impugnantes in continenti ceperunt.

Licet autem nos eis in omnibus necesariis largissime provideremus, ipsi tamen attendentes laborem terre, quae deserta erat et aliquantulum calida, uoluerunt acepto proposito retroire et ad propria remeare. Tandem, ad magnam instantiam nostram et regis Aragonum, processerunt usque ad Calatravam, que non distabat a praedicto castro nisi per duas leugas, eamque nos ex parte nostra et rex Aragonum ex sua et ipsi ex sua in Dei nomine cepimus expugnare. Saraceni autem qui intus erant, attendentes se Dei exercitui non posse resistere, disposuerunt uillam nobis tradere, ita quod persone eorum salve discederent, ueruntamen sine rebus; cumque nos istud nulla ratione vellemus aceptare, rex Aragonum et transmontani habentes super hoc consilium uiderunt uillam esse munitam muris et antemuralibus, profundis fossatis et excelsis turribus, et quod non posset capi nisi suffoderentur muri et sic ruerent, quod cederet in graue damnum fratribus Salueterre, quorum fuerat, et non posse, si necessitas incumberet, retinere. Unde apud nos institerunt firmissime et uilla salua et integra cum armis et magna copia uictualium que ibi erant, quibus satis indigebat exercitus, nobis redderetur, et persone saracenorum uacue et inermes recedere permitterentur. Nos autem, attendentes eorum in hoc firmam uolentatem, uotis eorum annuimus, ita quod medietas omnium eorum quae intus habebantur cederet in partem regis Aragonum et alia medietas in partem ultramontanorum,

was that, when people heard of the remission of sins which you granted to those coming to join us, there arrived a vast number of knights from the regions beyond the Pyrenees, including the Archbishops of Narbonne and Bordeaux and the Bishop of Nantes. Those who came numbered up to 2,000 knights with their squires, and up to 10,000 of their serving-men on horseback, with up to 50,000 serving-men on foot, for all of whom we had to provide food. There came also our illustrious friends and relatives the Kings of Aragón and of Navarre in support of the Catholic cause, with all their forces. We did not fail to provide for all of them, as we had promised through our heralds, while delaying for a time at Toledo as we waited for some of our men who were due to present themselves for the campaign, and it must be said that the costs for us and for our kingdom were extremely heavy on account of the huge numbers involved. We had to provide not only what we had promised, but also money and clothing, for almost everybody, both knights and serving-men, was in need. However, God, who gives increase to the fruits of justice, provided abundantly for us in accordance with the generosity of His grace, and gave us all that could be desired equitably and richly.

When both hosts were assembled, we set out on the road God had chosen for us, and coming to a certain fort named Malagón, amply defended, the French, who got there one day ahead of us, at once stormed and took it with God's help.

Even though it had fallen to us to provide them generously with all necessities, they [the French] became too concerned with the difficulties of the terrain, which was empty and rather hot, and they wished to turn back and go home. At length, after much pressure from us and the King of Aragón, they continued as far as Calatrava, which was only some two leagues from the aforementioned fort, and we all – Castilians and Aragonese and French, each from his own side – began to attack it in God's name. The Saracens inside, realizing that they would not be able to hold off this army of God, negotiated about surrendering the place to us, on condition that they should be allowed to leave unharmed, although without their belongings. We were unwilling to accept any such arrangement. The King of Aragón and the French held a council about it, and knew that the place was strongly fortified with walls and outer defences, deep ditches and lofty towers, so that it could not be taken unless the walls were undermined and made to collapse; but this would be much to the detriment of the Friars of Salvatierra, to whom it had earlier belonged, and by whom it would not be tenable (the walls being razed) in case of need. For this reason they most earnestly urged that the place should be handed over to us whole and undamaged with the weapons and all the great stores of food that were in it, and that the Saracens should be allowed to leave empty-handed and without weapons. So we, paying heed to their firm wishes in this matter, assented to their proposals, the conditions being that a half of all that there was inside should go to the King of Aragon and the other half to the French, no part of it being retained by our-

et nec nobis nec nostris aliquid uoluimus retinere. Ipsi autem, propositum repatriandi apud se retinentes, licet dominus Deus nobis exhiberet gratiam et honorem, et nos uellemus omnibus eis sufficientissime necessaria ministrare, desiderio patrie coacti, omnes pariter, signo Crucis relicto, cum archiepiscopo Burdegalensi et episcopo Nannetensi, licet certitudinem de bello saracenorum haberemus, ad propria redierunt, exceptis admodum paucis, qui remanserunt cum archiepiscopo Narbonensi et Tibaldo de Blazon, qui naturalis noster erat, cum suis et quibusdam aliis militibus, qui erant de Pictavia; et ii omnes qui remanserunt uix erant inter milites et seruientes centum quinquaginta; de peditibus autem eorum nullus remansit.

Cumque rex Aragonum apud Calatrauam moram faceret expectando quosdam milites suos et regem Navarre, qui nondum ad nos peruenerat, nos cum nostris processimus et peruenimus ad quoddam castrum eorum, quod Alarcos dicitur. Illud castrum, licet bene munitum esset, cepimus, et alia tres castra, quorum unum dicitur Caracouia, aliud Benauentum et aliud Petrabona.

Inde procedentes peruenimus ad Saluamterram, ibique peruenerunt ad nos rex Aragonum, qui de suis hominibus non duxit in exercitum nisi tantum milites generosos, et rex Navarre, qui similiter uix fuit in exercitu de suis plus quam ducentis militibus comitatus.

Et, quia rex saracenorum in uicino erat nobis, Saluamterram noluimus expugnare, sed, procedentes contra saracenorum mulitudinem, peruenimus ad quedam montana, in quibus non erat transitus aliquis nisi in certis locis. Cumque nos essemus ad pedem illius montis ex parte nostra, saraceni uenientes ex parte alia obtinuerunt summitatem montis, uolentes nobis transitum impedire. Sed milites nostri ascendentes uiriliter, quia adhuc pauci saraceni ad locum illum peruenerant, eos cum Dei auxilio uiriliter expulerunt, ad castrum quoddam munitum, quod propter transitum impediendum saracenorum rex construxerat, ceperunt, quod Ferrat dicitur. Quo occupato, exercitus Domini secure potuit ad cacumina montis ascendere, ubi multum laborauit propter defectum aquarum et loci ariditatem. Saraceni autem, uidentes quod transitum illum occupare non possent, alium transitum qui erat in descensu montis, arctissimum et inuium occuparunt; talis quippe erat quod mille homines possent defendere omnibus hominibus qui sub celo sunt; et iuxta transitum illum ex altera parte erat totus saracenorum exercitus et sua tentoria iam fixa.

Cumque nos ibi facere moram ob defectum aque non possemus, nec procedere propter transitus dificultatem, quidam ex nostris consuluerunt quod iterum ad pedem montis descenderemus et aliam transitum ad duas uel tres dietas quereremus. Nos autem, attendentes fidei periculum et persone nostre dedecus, noluimus huic parere consilio, eligentes potius in difficultate transitus mori pro fide quam faciliorem transitum querendo qualitercumque in fidei negotio retroire.

Cumque iam quidem propositum firmassemus, ad indicium cuiusdam rustici, quem Deus nobis ex imperato misit, in eodem loco alium transitum satis facilem

selves or our men. The French – still keen on the idea of going home, even though the Lord God was showing us grace and favour, and even though we were willing to go on providing them all with necessities in a generous way – driven as they were by the urge to go home, all together abandoned the Cross, together with the Archbishop of Bordeaux and the Bishop of Nantes, even though there was certainly going to be a battle with the Saracens; and they went off, except a very few who stayed on with the Archbishop of Narbonne and Tibaldo de Blazon, who was one of our liegemen, and also his men and certain other knights of Poitou. Those who remained, knights and serving-men, amounted to scarcely 150; and of their foot-soldiers, none at all remained.

Since the King of Aragón was waiting at Calatrava for certain knights of his and the King of Navarre, who had still not joined us, we set out with our men and arrived at a certain enemy castle called Alarcos. We took this castle, well defended though it was, together with three others, Caracuel, Benavente, and Piedrabuena.

Going forward from there we reached Salvatierra, where the King of Aragón joined us, he having brought only a small number of noble knights in his army; and the King of Navarre, who similarly was accompanied by a force of scarcely 200 knights.

Since the Sultan of the Saracens was close to us, we resolved not to attack Salvatierra, but, advancing towards the Saracen host, we reached a mountain range which was impossible to cross except in certain places. Since on our side we were at the foot of the range, the Saracens advancing from the other side were able to occupy the crest, seeking to bar our passage. But our men went up bravely, because up to that time only a few Saracens had reached that area, and our men vigorously drove them off, with God's help; and they took a fort called Ferral, which the Saracen ruler had built in order to bar our way. Once this was taken, the army of the Lord was able to go on up to the mountain peaks in safety, but it was hard going because of the lack of water and the barrenness of the place. The Saracens, seeing that they could not block that pass, occupied another passage on the downward slope, exceptionally narrow and difficult; it was such, indeed, that a thousand men could readily defend it against the greatest army on earth. At the far end of it lay the whole Saracen army with their tents already pitched.

Since we could not stay there because of the lack of water, nor advance because of the difficulty of the pass, certain of our men advised that we should go back down the mountain and look for another pass some distance away. But we, concerned for the danger to the faith and disgrace to our person, refused to accept this advice, preferring to die for the faith on the difficult terrain of the pass rather than to seek an easier way, or to back down from an affair which concerned the faith, in whatsoever fashion it might be.

When we had thus strengthened our resolve, our barons – who were to strike the first blows in the battle – heard of the suggestion of a certain

magnates nostri, qui primus ictus in bello habituri erant, inuenerunt; et in quodam loco exercitui eorum uicino, licet aridus esset et siccus, saracenis hunc transitum ignorantibus, tentoria posuerunt. Quod cum saracenorum exercitus attendisset, processit ut mansionem illam impediret. Nostri autem, licet pauci essent, se uiriliter defenderunt.

Nos autem et rex Aragonum et rex Navarre, armati cum militibus nostris in loco prime mansionis, que erat in summitate montis, expectauimus, donec totus exercitus Domini peruenit secure ad locum ubi anteriores nostri castra metati sunt; et ita, dante Domino, factum est quod, licet uia esset inuia et inaquosa, lapidosa et nemorosa, nihil de nostris amisimus. Hoc autem factum est die Sabathi, XVIII kalendas mensis Augusti. Circa serotinam uero horam sareceni, attendentes quod omnia tentoria nostra tute fixeramus, dispositis aciebus suis, uenerunt ante loca castrorum et ibidem quedam preludia belli in modum torneamenti cum nostris exercuerunt.

Sequenti autem die Dominica summo mane uenit saracenus cum infinita multitudine, dispositis aciebus suis. Nos autem, uolentes considerare multitudinem gentis sue et dispositionem et statum et qualiter in omnibus se haberent, habito prudentum uirorum consilio et in his exercitatorum, expectauimus usque ad sequentem diem Lune. Ipsis autem sic existentibus, posuimus milites nostris cum peditibus ut extremos agminis nostri non possent in aliquo molestare quod quidem diuina operante gratia sic euenit.

Sequenti die, scilicet, secunda feria, omnes in Dei nomine armati processimus dispositis aciebus, cum eis pro fide catholica pugnaturi. Ipsi autem promontoria quedam obtinuerunt ualde ardua et ad ascendendum difficilia propter nemora que inter nos et ipsos erant et propter alueos torrentium profundissimos que omnia nobis erant magno impedimento, ipsis uero maximo expedimento. Verumtamen ille, a quo omnia, in quo omnia, per quem omnia, fecit mirabiliter, et direxit manus sui exercitus contra inimicos suos; et anteriores nostri, necnon et medii, multas acies eorum que in minoribus promontoriis existebant in uirtute Crucis dominice prostauerunt. Cum autem peruenissent ad extremam aciem eorum, infinite siquidem multitudinis, in qua rex Carthaginis erat, ibidem difficillimos conflictus militum, peditum et sagittariorum inuenerunt, quos sub maximo periculo et uix, immo etiam, iam non poterant tolerare. Nos autem, attendentes bellum illud eis omnino importabile, impetu equorum processimus, signo Crucis dominice preeunte et uexillo nostro, in quo erat imago beate Virginis et Filii sui, in signis nostris superposita. Cumque nos iam pro fide Christi mori constanter eligeremus, attendentes Crucis Christi et imaginis suae Matris ignominiam, quas lapidibus et sagittis irruere impetebant, in armas furentes aciem illorum infinite multitudinis diuisimus, et, licet ipsi essent constantes in bello, et firmi super domino suo, Dominus illorum infinitam multitudinem Crucis sue gladio trucidauit. Et sic rex saracenorum cum paucis in fugam conuersus fuit. Sui autem impetus nostros interim sustinebant, sed statim

shepherd, whom God by His command sent to us, that in that very spot another relatively easy passage existed.   In a certain place close to the enemy camp, although barren and dry, they pitched camp, since the Saracens did not know of this pass.   When the Saracen army realized what was happening, they advanced in order to stop the camp being established.   Our men, even though few, defended themselves bravely.

We and the Kings of Aragón and Navarre waited, fully armed, with our men in the place where we had first halted, which was on the crest of the mountain, until the whole army of the Lord safely reached the spot where our advance patrols had marked out the camp.   Thanks be to God, it happened that although the way was difficult and waterless, also rocky and wooded, we lost none of our men.   This was Saturday, 14 July.   Late that day the Saracens, observing that we had safely erected all our tents, drew up their battle-lines and approached our camp, indulging in skirmishing rather as in a tournament, as a prelude to battle.

Very early next day, Sunday, the Saracens came up with their huge army arrayed in battle-lines.   We, wishing to study the numbers of their men and their disposition and attitude, and to find out how they behaved in all circumstances, took advice from our expert and seasoned men, and resolved to wait until the following day, Monday.   In these circumstances, we posted cavalrymen and foot-soldiers so that the enemy should not in any way be able to attack the ends of our line, and this, thanks to God's grace. did not happen.

The following day, Monday, we all armed and set out in God's name, in full array, to do battle with them for the Catholic faith.   The enemy occupied certain eminences, very steep places and difficult to climb by reason of the woods which lay between us and them, and by reason of some very deep gorges cut by streams, all of which formed a major impediment to us and was a great help to the enemy.   Then indeed He by whom, and in whom, and through whom, all things are miraculously done, directed His army against His enemies; and our front ranks, and some of the middle ranks, by virtue of the Cross of the Lord, cut down many lines of the enemy who were stationed on the lower eminences. When our men reached the last of their lines, consisting of a huge number of soldiers, among whom was the King of Carthage, there began desperate fighting among the cavalrymen, infantrymen, and archers, our people being in terrible danger and scarcely able to resist any longer.   Then we, realizing that the fighting was becoming altogether impossible for them, started a cavalry charge, the Cross of the Lord going before and our banner with its image of the Holy Virgin and her Son imposed upon our device.   Since we had already resolved to die for the faith of Christ, as soon as we witnessed the shame being suffered by the Cross of Christ and the image of His Mother when the Saracens assailed them with stones and arrows, we broke their line with its vast numbers of men, even though the Saracens resisted bravely in the battle, and stood solidly around their lord.

post maximam stragem suorum reliqui in fugam conuersi sunt. Nos autem insequentes eos usque ad noctem, plures tamen insequendo interfecimus quam in bello.

Et sic bellum Domini a solo Domino et per solum Dominum est feliciter consummatum. Deo autem honor et gloria, qui Cruci sue dedit uictoriam per Iesum Christum, dominum nostrum.

Fuerunt autem milites saraceni, ut postea vera relatione· didicimus a quibusdam domesticis regis saracenorum, quos captiuos cepimus, CLXXXV millia; peditum uero non erat numerus.

Occubuerunt autem in bello ex parte sua centum millia armatorum et amplius secundum estimationem saracenorum quos postea cepimus. De exercitu autem Domini, quod non sine grandi gratiarum actione recitandum est, et quod incredibile est, nisi quia miraculum est, uix viginti quinque Christiani aut triginta de toto nostro exercitu occubuerunt. O quanta letitia! O quot gratiarum actiones! nisi de hoc dolendum sit: quod tam pauci martyres de tanto exercitu ad Christum martyrio peruenerunt.

Ut autem magna eorum multitudo credatur, cum exercitus noster in castris eorum post bellum per biduum fecerit moram, ad omnia incendia que necessaria erant in coquendis cibis et pane et aliis non composuerunt aliqua ligna nisi de sagittis et lanceis eorum quae remanserant, et uix potuerunt comburere medietatem. Cumque dicti exercitus propter longam moram factam in locis eremis et incultis deficeret in uictualibus et aliis, ibidem tantam inuenerunt tam ciborum quam armorum, necnon etiam dextrariorum et aliorum iumentorum copiam, quod capientes ad suam unusquisque de iis uoluntatem, plus ibi dimiserunt ex magna abundantia quam ceperunt.

Tertio autem die procedentes uenimus ad quedam castra eorum, scilicet Bilche, Bannos, Tolosa, que in continenti cepimus. Tandem peruenimus ad duas ciuitates, quarum altera dicitur Biacia, altera Ubeda, quibus non erant maiores citra mare preter Cordubam et Hispalim, quarum alteram, scilicet Biaciam, destructam inuenimus, ad altera uero, scilicet Ubedam, quia situ loci et artificio fortissima erat, confugerat multitudo hominum infinita ex omnibus uillis adiacentibus. Cum enim uilla numquam ad imperatore uel ab aliquo regum Hispanie expugnata sciretur uel subiugata, in eadem posse saluare sua corpora se credebant. Sed et hanc in breui divina gratia fauente cepimus, et funditus destruximus quia non possemus habere tantam multitudinem gentium que ad illas populandas sufficere possent, et bene perierunt ibi sexaginta millia saracenorum, quorum quosdam interfecimus, quosdam captiuos duximus ad seruitium christianorum et monasteriorum que sunt in marchia reparanda.

Hec igitur, sanctissime Pater, uobis scribenda decreuimus, pro auxilio tote christianitati impenso gratias quas possumus exhibentes, et humiliter supplicantes

Our Lord slew a great multitude of them with the sword of the Cross. Then the Sultan with a few of his men turned in flight. Others of the enemy for a time bore the thrust of our attacks, but soon, after heavy loss of life, the rest turned and fled. We followed up the pursuit till nightfall, and killed more in that rout than we had in the battle.

In this way the battle of the Lord was triumphantly won, by God alone and through God alone. To God be the honour and the glory, who granted the victory of His Cross through Jesus Christ, our Lord.

The Saracen horsemen had numbered 185,000, as we afterwards learned in a true account from certain servants of the Sultan, whom we took prisoner; the foot-soldiers were uncountable.

On their side there fell in the battle 100,000 armed men, perhaps more, according to the estimates of Saracens we captured later. Of the army of the Lord – a fact not to be mentioned without the most fervent thanksgiving, and one scarcely to be believed, unless it be thought a miracle – only some twenty or thirty Christians in our whole host fell. What cause for joy and thanksgiving! Yet there is one cause for regret here: that so few in such a vast army went to Christ as martyrs.

In order to show how immense were the numbers of the enemy, when our army rested after the battle for two days in the enemy camp, for all the fires which were needed to cook food and make bread and other things, no other wood was needed than that of the enemy arrows and spears which were lying about, and even then we burned scarcely half of them. Even though our army was running short of food and other supplies, because we had spent so long in bare and barren countryside, we found such an abundance of food and weapons, as also of war-horses and beasts of burden, that our men, by taking as many of them as they wished, still left more out of the huge number of animals than those they took.

On the third day we advanced to certain enemy fortresses, Vilches, Baños, and Tolosa, and at once captured them.

Eventually we reached two towns, Baeza and Ubeda, the largest there are on this side of the sea except for Cordova and Seville. We found Baeza already destroyed. A great number of people had fled from all the nearby settlements to Ubeda, because it was exceptionally strong both on account of its situation and on account of its defences. Since the people knew that no other city of that size had been stormed or taken by the Emperor or by any other Hispanic ruler, they thought they would be safe there. However, by God's grace we captured Ubeda in a short time, and, since we did not have enough people to settle it, we razed it to the ground. Some 60,000 Saracens perished there: some we killed, others were taken as captives into the service of the Christians and of the monasteries which needed to be repaired in the border regions.

We ordered all this to be set down in writing for you, most Holy Father, earnestly offering all the thanks we can for the aid of all Christendom, and

ut uos, quem Dominus ad summi sacerdotii gradum elegit, ei cum sacrificio laudis pro salute populi immoletis uitulos labiorum.

humbly asking you whom God has chosen for the highest rank among His priests, with all praise to Him, to offer up a sacrifice for the salvation of our people.

41. The Franciscans try to preach in Seville (1219)

In 1219, a few years after the foundation of his Order, St Francis began to plan missionary work for his friars outside Italy: some were to go to the East, others to Spain and thence to Morocco. Our texts state the aims of the latter group variously: they were to combat heresy in 'Hispania', presumably that of the Albigensians or Cathars which from Southern France spilled over into Aragón, while other friars were intended to proceed to Morocco in order to preach to the Muslims (these also being 'heretics' according to some authorities, as in text 34). The friars in this group originally numbered six: Vitalis, Beraldus, Petrus, Adiutus, Accursius, and Otho. In Aragón Vitalis fell ill and had to be left behind; Beraldus, who spoke Arabic, was presumably the most useful member in practical terms. We next hear of the party in Coimbra; they had, we may assume, travelled by the pilgrim road to Compostela (though this is not mentioned), and were heading south towards Muslim lands. In Portugal they were at first received coldly by the populace and thought heretical themselves because of their strange speech, their clothing, and their barefootedness, but they were fortunate to be befriended by Princess Sancha, as in our text, and also (in another source) by Queen Urraca, wife of King Afonso II of Portugal (1212-33).

It is especially to be noticed that the ruler of Seville at the time (an emir, not properly a 'king', under the Almohad Sultan Yusuf II who resided in Marrakesh) did not in fact carry out his order to execute the friars, and the latter could, had they wished, have returned safely to Christian territory. In Morocco, probably more specifically in Marrakesh (the texts say 'Marochium' for both region and city) they were protected for a time by Pedro Fernandes, brother of Afonso II of Portugal but estranged from him and currently in the service of the Sultan, and when preaching to the Moors in the market-place were merely derided at first; later, the authorities had to take note of their presence and subversive preaching, and the friars were several times expelled from the city but always returned. Pedro Fernandes took them into his house for a while, forbidding them to go out for their own protection; he then took them on a joint Moorish-Christian expedition to put down a revolt and on returning from it, when the force was dying from lack of water in the desert, Beraldus was miraculously able to cause a spring to flow, to the amazement of all. After

Et inde fratres procedentes Alanquerium devenerunt, ubi erat supradicta domina Sancia, regis Sancii bonae memoriae filia, qui est in monasterio Sanctae Crucis de Colimbria tumulatus, et dominae Aldonciae reginae, quae de Aragonia traxit originem. Quae domina Sancia erat virgo honestissima et perfecta, cum qua sancti fratres diu verba Dei loquentes tandem suum sibi propositum

*other vicissitudes, the friars were arrested, given a last chance to recant, and
then tortured and executed by the Sultan in person (16 January 1220). It is
plain from our texts that the friars had sought martyrdom: one declared to
Queen Urraca in Coimbra that 'sciatis enim pro certo, quod nos, quos hic
videtis, pro Christi fide breviter moriemur. De quo valde laetemur, quia
Dominus, qui pro nobis passus est, nos vult in numero suorum Martyrum
computare. Cum autem apud Marochium martyrio finiverimus dies nostros ...'
('You should know for sure that we, whom you see here, shall shortly die for
the faith of Christ. Indeed we rejoice about this, in that the Lord, who
suffered for us, wishes to count us in the number of His martyrs. And when
we end our days in martyrdom in Morocco ...'). There was divine vengeance
for these deaths: our texts say that the Sultan suffered a severe stroke which
paralysed his right side (his right hand having wielded the sword of execution);
his land suffered a three-year drought and then five years of plague. Coimbra
remained associated with the martyrs, for their relics were deposited there and
received an important cult. We hear of seven other Italian friars who tried to
preach in the streets of Ceuta (Morocco) in 1227; they were arrested and
executed.*

*Peaceful conversion of Muslims, and of course of Jews, had been a pious
hope for centuries. When large numbers of Muslims became subject to
Christian rule in the Middle East after the First Crusade, and in Iberia after
the Christian advance of the first half of the 13th century, the practical
possibilities of such conversion were, or at least were thought to be, much
enhanced. Popes gave encouragement, canon lawyers debated the principles and
practical aspects involved, and the new preaching Orders of friars in the early
13th century – Dominicans (text 48) and, as here, Franciscans – went on
hazardous missions into Muslim lands. St Francis's own Rule (Regula non
bullata) for his friars included a whole chapter, 16, on missionary work among
Muslims and other unbelievers. On all this, see Muldoon (1979) and Kedar
(1984). For the reaction of the Muslim authorities to what was, to them,
subversive provocation by madmen, compare text 10.*

The extract is from the set of texts which make up Appendix I to the
Chronicle of the Franciscan Order, *published in* Analecta Franciscana, 3 (1897).
*This section of the Appendix is on pp. 583–85, attributed to a 'Dominus
Franciscus', priest of Lisbon, about whom nothing is known. The main text of
the* Chronicle *contains a somewhat different narration of these events, pp.
15–19.*

Continuing their journey from there [Coimbra], the friars reached Alenquer; here
resided the aforementioned Princess Sancha, daughter of the late King Sancho [I,
1185-1211], he who is buried in the monastery of the Holy Cross in Coimbra,
and of Queen Dulce who came originally from Aragón. This Princess Sancha
was a maiden lady, very pure and perfect in her life, and the friars, in long talks

revelarunt. Ipsa vero eorum approbans propositum, induit eos saecularibus indumentis, quia aliter Saraceni eos non permisissent transire, nec Christiani eos in navi in transitu fluminis recepissent, qui cavebant Saracenorum offensam, maxime mercatorum, qui multa bona portabant et inde lucrabantur. Et ideo, si scirent, eos ire ad praedicandum Saracenis, eos forte impedivissent, quia plus divitias quam Dei gloriam diligebant. Et sic fratres coopertis habitibus Hispalim, quae nunc Sibilia dicitur, intraverunt et ibi in hospitio cuiusdam Christiani per dies VIII latuerunt, depositis tamen illis saecularibus vestimentis. Quodam vero die sancto ferventes spiritu sine alio ductore usque ad principalem mesquitam sive oratorium pervenerunt, ubi sine timore quamcumque tribulationem mundanam contemnentes, in habitu Christiani coram inimicis fidei apparentes Saracenos furor nimis repleverunt. Sancti vero fratres, zelo crescente, templum illius seu mesquitam intrare voluerunt. Saraceni vero indignati eos clamoribus, impulsibus et lignis impetentes eos mesquitam intrare nullatenus permiserunt.

Sancti vero fratres ex hoc non territi, sed quodam dulcore martyrii fortius animati ad invicem dicebant: 'Quid facimus, quid hic sine praedicatione moramur? Oportet, nos pro Christi fide et honore vitam istam corporalem exponere et Christum esse verum Deum coram isto rege infideli audacter confiteri.' Sicque mutuo se invicem hortabantur et usque ad portam regalis palatii pervenerunt. Quos videns quidam princeps regis interrogavit: 'Unde estis?' Responderunt fratres: 'De Romanis partibus sumus.' Et princeps: 'Quid quaeretis et qua de causa venistis?' Qui dixerunt: 'Volumus loqui regi pro sua utilitate et totius regni sui.' Et ille: 'Defertis litteras vel certitudinem aliam vestrae legationis?' Responderunt: 'Nostram ambasciatam deferimus non chartis, sed mentibus atque linguis.' 'Dicatis', inquit princeps, 'mihi vestrum negotium et ego illud regi fideliter reserabo.' Qui dixerunt: 'Nos primo debemus loqui regi et tu postea, et non antea, scies totum negotium nostrum.'

Tunc princeps ille ad regem accedens sibi omnia per ordinem enarravit. Rex vero sanctos fratres fecit ad se venire. Quos statim interrogavit: 'Unde estis et quis misit vos et ad quid venistis?' Sancti vero fratres ad omnia per ordinem intrepide responderunt: 'Nos Christiani et de Romanis partibus sumus; ad te vero mittimur a Rege regum, Domino Deo nostro, pro tuae animae salute, et relicta superstitiosa secta vilissimi Machometi, credas in Dominum Iesum Christum et eius baptismum accipias, sine quo salvari non potes.' Rex vero furore repletus dixit: 'Maligni et perversi homines, dicitis ista mihi soli, vel toti populo meo?' Illi vero constanter et vultu hilari responderunt: 'Scias, rex, quod sicut cultorum tam iniquae legis per deceptorem illum Machometum plenum maligno spiritu

with her about religious matters, eventually revealed the object of their journey to her. She, approving of this, provided them with ordinary dress, since otherwise the Moors would not allow them to cross into their territory, nor would the Christians allow them to board their boat to cross the river, for they were concerned not to offend the Moors and especially the merchants who handled a lot of goods and grew rich on the proceeds. These merchants, seeking profits rather than the glory of God, would probably have stopped them if they had known that they were going to preach to the Moors. So the friars with their dress concealed entered Seville – whose older name was Hispalis – and there hid for a week in the house of a certain Christian, leaving off, while there, their civil dress. Then one day, aflame with the Holy Spirit and without a guide, they went to the chief mosque or house of prayer and there fearlessly and regardless of worldly suffering, in the habit of their Order and in the presence of the enemies of the Faith, they began to fill the Moors who were standing about with anger. Then the holy brothers, with growing zeal, tried to enter the mosque itself; the outraged Moors with shouts and pushing and wielding sticks barred their way into the mosque by all possible means.

The brothers, by no means fearful at this, but rather strengthened by the cherished notion of martyrdom, said to each other: 'What shall we do? We must not die here without preaching. We must offer up this bodily life of ours for the sake of the faith and honour of Christ, and in the presence of the infidel ruler himself boldly proclaim that Christ is the true God.' Encouraging each other in this way, they reached the gate of the royal palace. Seeing them, one of the chief court officials asked: 'Where are you from?' The brothers replied: 'We come from Christian lands [Italy].' The official asked: 'What are you seeking and for what reason have you come?' The friars replied: 'We wish to speak to the King for his own benefit and for that of his whole kingdom.' He inquired: 'Are you carrying letters or some authentication of your mission?' They replied: 'The embassy we bear is not on parchment but in our minds and on our tongues.' 'Tell me', said the official, 'what your business is and I will report it faithfully to the King.' They answered: ' First we must speak to the King; later, not earlier, you shall know the whole of our business.'

Then the official went to the King and gave him a full account. The King ordered the brothers to be shown into his presence. He at once asked them: 'Where are you from, who sent you, and why have you come?' The friars fearlessly made their answer to all points: 'We are Christians, from Christian lands [Italy]; we have been sent to you by the King of Kings, by our Lord God, for the good of your soul, so that, abandoning the superstitious sect of the utterly vile Muhammad, you should believe in the Lord Jesus Christ, and receive baptism; without this you cannot be saved.' Then the King said angrily: 'Are you, so evil and perverse, saying this to me alone, or to all my people?' They replied, firmly and cheerfully: 'You should realize, your Majesty, that since you are the head of the adherents of that most evil religion spread by Muhammad, a deceiver

promulgatae es caput, sic inter malos peior est et gravior tibi poena in inferno servatur. Quare tibi ista principaliter dicimus, ut te et tuos ad viam ducamus veritatis, qua finaliter valeatis salvari.' Ad quae verba rex ira plenus capitibus eos truncari iussit.

Fratres vero vultu laetissimo ab eius conspectu amoti ad invicem dixerunt: 'Eia fratres, invenimus quod quaerebamus; simus constantes et mori pro Christo minime timeamus.' Quibus princeps ait: 'O miseri, cur sic viliter mori vultis? Sed audite consilium meum. Revocate quae contra legem nostram dixistis et Dei nuntium Machometum et accipite Saracenismum et vivetis et multa bona habebitis in hoc mundo.' Sancti vero responderunt: 'O miser, si scires, qualia bona pro ista morte in aeterna vita speramus, ista temporalia nobis non praesentares.' Post hoc filius regis videns eos, misericordia motus dixit prudenter patri suo: 'Quomodo sic definivisti, pater? Quomodo istos sine causa occidere iubes? Inspice leges, interroga seniores et quod iustum fuerit iuxta ipsorum consilium iudicabis.' Ad cuius verba rex temperatus iubet, fratres in quadam summitate turris includi. Illi vero Sancti Spiritus igne succensi, magnis vocibus de turris altitudine ingredientibus et egredientibus curiam fidem Christi praedicabant legem Maurorum et eius observatores damnantes. Quod audiens rex eos praecepit in fundo turris carceralis includi; et iterum fecit eos coram se praesentari. Quibus et dixit: 'Miseri et insani homines, numquid adhuc sunt corda vestra a tanta turpitudine revocata?' Qui responderunt: 'Corda nostra sunt solidiora continue in fide Domini nostri Iesu Christi.' Tunc rex, vocatis senioribus et sapientibus ad consilium, adductis coram omnibus sanctis fratribus et veram fidem constanter confidentibus, dixit eis: 'Vultis ad terram christianorum reverti, vel ire Marochium?' Responderunt fratres: 'Corpora nostra in tua sunt potestate, animabus nocere non potes. Idcirco ubicumque nos mittere volueris, ire parati sumus et subire quamcumque mortem dictaveris propter Christum.'

imbued with a devilish spirit, among the damned there is a worse and more awful punishment reserved for you in hell. So it is to you that we principally speak, in order that we may lead you and your people to that path by which you may at the end be saved.' At these words, the King in fury ordered their heads to be struck off.

The brothers with cheerful countenances were removed from his sight and said to each other: 'Well now, brethren, we have found what we were looking for. Let us be firm and not fear in the least to die for Christ.' The court official said to them: 'You wretches, why do you want to die in this shameful way? Now listen to my advice. Take back what you said against our Law and Muhammad the messenger of God, adopt Islam, live, and receive many good things in this life.' But the holy brothers replied: 'You, poor wretch, if only you knew what good things we hope for in the life everlasting as reward for this death, would not offer these merely earthly things to us.' Then the son of the King saw them and, moved to pity, said discreetly to his father: 'Why did you decide the issue in that way, father? How can you order that these men should be killed for no reason? Study our laws, consult the elders, and you will issue a judgement about them which will be truly just.' At these words the King, now calmer, ordered the brethren to be shut up at the top of a certain tower. But there, aflame with the fire of the Holy Spirit, they began to preach the faith of Christ and to attack that of Muhammad and his followers by loud shouting from the top of the tower to all those entering or leaving the court. When the King heard of this he ordered them to be shut away in a dungeon at the base of the tower. He then had them again brought into his presence, and asked them: 'Why, you wretched madmen, have your hearts not drawn back from this shameful behaviour?' They answered: 'Our hearts are stronger day by day in the faith of our Lord Jesus Christ.' Then the King, having called his elders and wise men to a meeting, brought the friars before the whole assembly – they constantly proclaiming the true Faith – and said to them: 'Do you want to go back to Christian lands, or go to Morocco?' The brethren answered: 'Our bodies are in your power, but you cannnot harm our souls. Therefore, wherever you wish to send us, we are prepared to go, and for Christ's sake we will undergo whatever kind of death you decree.'

42. A famous victory against great odds (1231)

In times of turmoil in al-Andalus as Christian pressure continued, Ibn Hud, descendant of a famous line of rulers of Saragossa, used his base in Murcia to extend his command over much of remaining Muslim territory from 1228. In the west, in what is now Extremadura, the Portuguese and Leonese achieved successes against him in 1229-30. The Castilian expedition whose final stage of operations is told in the following text was clearly trying to exploit this weakness of the Muslims in 1231, but had gone dangerously far into the

(1043) Abenhut commo quier que los cristianos poca gente eran, reçelandolos et non los teniendo en todo tan en poco, fizo acabdellar sus azes et fueron las azes de los moros siete, que en la que menos auie eran de mill et quinientos caualleros arriba, et en tal dos mill et en tal mas; lo que los cristianos no podien de si todos fazer vna sola, la mas pequenna que en las siete de los moros auie, pero que era y con llos fi del rey de Baeça – ca el rey de Baeça era uasallo del rey don Fernando, et desque sopo que el infante entraua en caualgada, enuiol su fijo con dozientos caualleros que fuesen con el, et con bien trezientos omnes a pie – et freyres de Santiago et de Calatraua et de las otras ordenes venieron y otrosi. Mas todo era nada contra el poder de los moros. Tel Alfonso et Ruy Gonçalez de Ualuerde eran y en esta batalla, et fueron y buenos. Mas por quantos ser podien en esta batalla, non pasauan por todos por mill los caualleros, con toda la otra gente a cauallo; et los de pie de dos mill et quinientos arriba, et non lo eran. Quando los cristianos vieron tan gran poder de gentes contra si, et el suyo tan pequenno, si miedo ouieron, esto non me demande ninguno. Era y vn rey que traye sieteçientos caualleros de alaraues, que veniera en ayuda de Abenhut; et estos los començaron, en llegando, a çercar en derredor, et exetandolos de mala guisa et muy fiera. Grant era el peligro et la coyta en que los cristianos estauan, ca a la mar non se podien acoger nin aca tornar, ca les estaua el agua fonda de la vna parte et la gente de los moros de la otra. Don Aluar Perez que fieramiente los estaua esforçando, amonestandoles começo a dezir tantas buenas cosas et de tantas guisas, que les fizo cobrar esfuerço et coraçones, et perder todo miedo, asi commo si diez tantos que los moros fuesen. El infante tenie la çaga et traye y quinientos moros catiuos que desa caualgada tomaron, et enbiol don Aluar Perez dezir, que traya la delantera, que fezies descabeçar los catiuos todos; et fezieronlo asi. Don Aluar Perez ouo su conseio con los omnes buenos de la hueste, et acordaron que toda la gente de pie que la apartasen de los caualleros, commo la de los moros estaua; et asi fue fecho; et non fezieron de si az, mas todos tropel fechos, ca non se ueyen conpanna de que az de si se atreuiesen fazer. Et don Aluar Perez mando llegar las azemilas et las otras bestias todas en vno; et mando sobir peones en ellas, et fizoles fazer tropel del mayor alardo que de si fazer podieron; et a estos mando acostar contra la presa, commo por guarda. Et las bozes et los alaridos de los

extreme south-west (the region of Jerez), was remote from any aid, and was in any case too small in numbers to face Ibn Hud with any confidence. The commanders were Prince Alfonso de Molina, brother of King Ferdinand, and Alvar Pérez de Castro, jointly. The divine aid of St James, so frequently needed over preceding centuries, seems to have assured the victory over great odds. The victory broke Ibn Hud's power in the region and opened the way for further Christian successes.

The passage consists of chapters 1043 and 1044 of the Primera crónica general, *for which see text 1.*

(1043) Even though the Christians were few in number, Ibn Hud feared and did not belittle them, so he drew up his men in seven battle-lines, in the weakest of which there were upwards of 1,500 horsemen, and in others 2,000 and perhaps more; but the Christians all together could not make more than a single line, equal in numbers to the weakest of the Moorish lines. However, they had with them the son of the King of Baeza, for this ruler was the vassal of King Ferdinand, and when he learned that Prince Alfonso was starting the campaign, he sent his son with 200 horsemen to accompany him, together with 300 infantry; also, knights of Santiago and Calatrava and the other military orders came too. But all this was as nothing compared with the power of the Moors. Tello Alfonso and Ruy González de Valverde took part in the battle, with distinction. Even when all were added together, the knights numbered not more than 1,000, even including all the other men who were mounted, and the infantry scarcely reached 2,500. When the Christians saw such a mighty force ranged against them, and their own army so small, if they felt fear let nobody dare to ask me. There was one commander present with 700 Arab horsemen, who had come to help Ibn Hud, and as soon as these arrived they began to encircle the Christians and to challenge them in every possible way. The Christians were in great danger and difficulty, for they could find no refuge on the sea, where the water was deep, and they could not turn aside because the Moors were blocking the way. Don Alvar Pérez put new heart into them and raised their courage in many ways, to the extent that they lost all fear, as though they had ten times the numbers of the Moors. The Prince held the rearguard and was responsible for 500 Moorish prisoners who had been taken on the raid earlier; Alvar Pérez, who commanded the front ranks, sent to tell him to behead all the prisoners, and this was done. Alvar then consulted the army leaders. It was agreed that all the infantry should be separated from the cavalry, as was the case in the Moorish army, and this was done. They did not form up in a battle-line, but made a single troop, for they realized they did not have enough men to do otherwise. Alvar Pérez ordered that all the pack-animals should be placed together, and mounted by foot-soldiers, these to make the largest demonstration of their strength that they could; and they were to stand guard over the booty. The shouts and war-cries of the Moors, and the noise from their drums and trumpets

moros, et los roydos de los atanbores et de los annafiles eran tan grandes que semeiaua que çielo et tierra todo se fondia. Ese dia se uistio don Aluar Perez vna falifa delgada, et tomo vna vara en la mano; et con tales armas entro en la fazienda muy loçano et muy alegre et muy esforçado, acabdellando sus gentes et diziendoles muchos bienes, et dandoles grandes esfuerços; dando a entender que el poder de Abenhut tenia en poco. Los cristianos fueron todos confesados, los que podieron auer clerigos, et los que non, unos con otros. Don Aluaro ante que en la fazienda entrase, fizo cauallero ese dia a Garçi Perez de Vargas, et deste contara adelante la estoria qual comienço ouo en su caualleria, et de qual fue depues adelante. Mas desque los cristianos fueron todos confesados et perdonados et acomendados a Dios, don Aluaro enbio dezir al infante, que estaua en la çaga, que se veniese et se feziesen todos tropel; et commo lo auia ordenado, asi lo fizo.

(1044) El infante don Alfonso desque fue pasado de la çaga a la delantera et fueron fechos todos tropel, don Aluaro los començo a esforçar andando de vna parte et de otra acabdellandolos et mouiendolos much ordenadamiente, deziendoles palabras con que les fazia perder el espanto. Et fueronles ferir, llamando todos a vna uoz 'Sanctiago!', et a las vezes 'Castiella!' Et començaron a entrar por medio de las azes de los moros, quebrantando luego la primera, desi la segunda et la terçera, desi todas, asi vnas en pos de otras, fasta que todas siete las pasaron, matando et derribando et faziendo grant estruyçion en ellos. Et asi se començaron de mezclar et de reboluer de vna parte et de otra, que non pudo auer acuerdo en los moros de tener vnos con otros. Et dizen, asi commo los moros mismos afirmauan depues, que paresçio y Santiago en vn cauallo blanco et con senna blanca en la mano et con vn espada en la otra, et que andaua y con el vna ligion de caualleros blancos; et aun dizen que angeles vieran andar sobre ellos por el ayre; et que estos caualleros blancos les semeiaua que les estroyen mas que ninguna otra gente. Et aun pieça de cristianos uieron esta uision. Los moros començaron luego a derramar et foyr, et dexaronse uençer, boluiendo espaldas el que ante podie. Et los cristianos començaron a yr en alcançe con ellos, matando et catiuando; et fezieron en ellos tan grant mortandat, que las gentes de pie que en el alcançe yuan non podien pasar nin salir adelante, ante el grant enbargamiento de la muchedumbre de los muertos que ante si fallauan; fasta que los metieron por las puertas de Xerex, et alli fue la mortandat en ellos muy grande ademas; tan grande era la priessa de la entrada, et tan pocos se fazian los que por la puerta podian entrar al grant gentio que eran, que vnos a otros se matauan. ¿Que uos diremos? Asi dolauan en ellos, como farian en sennos maderos, sin se defender de ninguna defension; la plaça fue mucho ayna librada de los moros, los vnos muertos, los otros catiuos, los otros foydos. En esa fazienda fue muerto el rey de los gazules, et otros muchos onrrados et poderosos moros de grant cuenta. En la muerte dese rey de los gazules, cuenta la estoria por afirmamiento de los que se y açertaron, se onrro mucho el nouel cauallero Garçi Perez de Uargas – que y don Aluar

were so loud that it seemed heaven and earth were about to collapse. That day Alvar Pérez took up a slender spear and a rod, and with these weapons went into the fray very proudly and cheerfully and bravely, leading his men and giving them every kind of encouragement, making everyone think that he had a poor opinion of Ibn Hud's strength. The Christians all made their confession, to priests if they could, to each other if they could not. Don Alvar, before he went into battle, knighted Garci Pérez de Vargas that day, and our story will tell later on how he began and continued his knightly career. Then, once the Christians had all made their confession and commended themselves to God, Alvar sent to tell the Prince, who was at the rear, to come forward so that all could form up as one troop; and this was done.

(1044) After Don Alfonso had come forward from the rear and a troop had been formed, Don Alvar went from side to side giving everyone all possible encouragement and making them lose their fear. Then they rode forward, with everyone shouting in unison 'St James!', and at times 'Castile!'. They began to pierce the Moorish ranks, shattering the first, then the second and third, and then all one after the other, killing and rolling back the enemy and causing great loss of life. Then they started to fight to each side, the Moors being unable to make any sort of stand. It was said – and the Moors themselves averred the same afterwards – that St James appeared there on a white horse with a white banner in one hand and a sword in the other, together with a regiment of knights dressed in white; also that angels were seen to fly through the air above them; and that it seemed as though these white knights were causing greater havoc than any other body of men. Many of the Christians saw this vision too. Then the Moors began to scatter and flee, turning their backs as quickly as they could and confessing defeat. The Christians started to pursue them, killing some and capturing others. The slaughter was so great, that the infantry in their pursuit could not go forward after a time because they found the piles of the dead an obstacle to their progress. Eventually the Christians forced the enemy back against the gates of Jerez, where the slaughter was also very great: the press of men was so tight in the gateway, and so few were able to enter compared with the huge mass that they formed that they were killing each other. What more can one say? Our men whittled them down as a carpenter whittles a beam of wood, and the Moors offered no kind of defence. The field was quickly cleared of them, some being dead, others prisoners, the rest fugitives. In the fray the leader of the Gazuls was killed, together with many other Moors of high rank. The text we are following says, in confirmation of what was stated by those present, that the new knight Garci Pérez de Vargas, whom Alvar Pérez had

Perez, entrada desa lid, fizo cauallero – el comienço de la su caualleria: ca sin
falla ese dize que lo derribo et lo mato. Et ese rey de los gazules fue el que
llegara con los sieteçientos caualleros alaraues que de suso dixiemos; et commo
quier que los de suso la estoria 'alaraues' nombre, ante los llamauan bien a ese
tiempo 'gazules', et por ese nombre dellos llaman a ese 'rey de los gazules'; et
auie pasado de allen mar, commo en rromeria, en seruiçio de su Mahomad. Et
desque ese rey fue aca pasado, diol Abenhut Alcala, a que agora llaman 'de los
gazules'; et por el nombre de los gazules llamaron depues aca a ese 'Alcala de
los Gazules'. Abenhut non se atreuiendo a fincar en Xerex en quanto en las sus
gentes asi dolauan et destroyen, fuese escolando con la conpanna que pudo, et
alço las uelas et alçose contra do meior guarda sopo. ¿Qui uos podria dezir et
contar las ganançias que alli fueron fechas et ganadas aquel dia, nin quan
grandes fueron las bienandanças que Dios a los cristianos fizo y? Los cristianos
començaron de robar el canpo, et tanto fallauan y yazer por el canpo, que ya
enoiados eran de lo tomar. Pues de lo que en las tiendas fallaron, esto non auia
cuenta, nin es qui lo preçiar podiese. Desque los cristianos ouieron el canpo
robado, fueron desçender en las tiendas de los moros, et fallaron las tiendas tan
pobladas, que non ouieron mester tomar afan de enbiar a otra parte por lo que
mester ouieron; et dizen que en quanto y estodieron que non quemaron fueras
astas de lanças quebrantadas. Et esas sogas et esos tramoios, que para ellos eran
fechos, fueron llenos de aquellos que para ellos los auien fechos. [...]

knighted before battle was joined, did himself honour at the start of his career, for it was he who unhorsed and killed that leader of the Gazuls. He it was who had come up with the 700 Arab horsemen mentioned earlier; and even though our text calls them 'Arabs', they were earlier and still at that time called 'Gazuls', and on account of that name the man was called 'leader of the Gazuls'. He had come from overseas as it were on pilgrimage, in Muhammad's service. When he arrived in al-Andalus, Ibn Hud gave him Alcalá, the one now known as 'Alcalá de los Gazules' [province of Cadiz]. Ibn Hud, not daring to stay in Jerez while the Christians were so strongly on the attack, made his way to the coast with as many men as he had, and set sail for a place of safety. Who could ever manage to tell how great was the booty taken that day, and the extent of the favours which God heaped upon the Christians? Our men began to search the battlefield, and found so much lying about that they wearied of picking it up. As for what they found in the tents, it was uncountable and beyond any man's reckoning. After they had searched the field they began on the Moorish tents, and found them so richly stocked that they had no need to send elsewhere for what they needed; and it is said that while they remained there they had all the wood they needed for their fires from the shafts of shattered lances. And the nooses and the gallows which had been prepared for them were filled with the bodies of the Moors who had made them. [...]

38

43. Miracles of St Dominic of Silos (1232, 1277, 1280)

For St Dominic and Grimaldo's early Vita, *see text 19. The cult of the Saint extended throughout Castile and into León and Navarre, and was evidently at its height in the 13th century, particularly that aspect of it which concerned the Saint as miraculous liberator of captives held in Moorish Granada. Gonzalo de Berceo, who wrote from about 1225 to 1250, used Grimaldo's* Vita *as a basis for his* Vida de Santo Domingo de Silos, *in 'cuaderna vía' verse: stanzas 352–75 of this tell how the Saint in life, by the power of prayer, freed from Moorish captivity a local youth, also called Domingo, after his relatives had been unable to raise the sum required for a ransom. For Berceo the Saint is he who 'quebrántalis las cárceres' (374c). From 1232 to 1293 a monk of Silos, Pero Marín, recorded numerous miracles of the Saint, each precisely dated, nearly all narrating such aid to captives. We know from one of these texts that these joyful events were celebrated in the monastery. A captive so freed was expected to present himself at Silos. When he came, the bells were rung, and the community went in procession to the Saint's shrine to give thanks and praise; if, as often happened, he carried his fetters, these were presented and hung nearby (for a time, at least: one text records that a 'ferrero', a metal-merchant, came to buy what was perhaps a regularly massive amount of iron). Although the captives' own words are quoted at times, each account is hardly verbatim, since the recorder's accounts have a substantial formulaic basis; even so, the narration is an inspiring one, and is still of great interest in sociological and other*

(2) Era de mil docientos setenta annos, Sabbado en la noche ante del Gallo, ocho dias de Mayo, salió Mahomat Adalil de Cordova con grant companna de Moros, & iba correr à Anduiar à tierra de Christianos, & el passando por la puente Dalcolea, dos leguas aquent de Cordova, encontrò en medio la puente un ome con mui grant claridat, & dixo el Moro en latin, qui va y? Dixol la claridat: Yo so Santo Domingo de Silos. Dixo el Moro, dò vas? Dixo Santo Domingo, vo à Cordova à sacar Cativos. El Moro fizo tornar la companna, & venno à Cordova ante que fues de dia: & tenia en una carcel quince Christianos, & metiòlos à todos en el cepo de pies, & las cadenas à las gargantas, & las esposas à las manos, & echòse sobre la carcel con su companna: & à quantos Moros sopo que tenien Cativos, embiòles à decir, que los guardassen, que Santo Domingo era en la Villa. Et ellos guardaronlos con mui grandes prisiones. Quando fuè el dia [fueron à ver] los quince Cativos que tenie el Moro, cataron la carcel, & non fallaron y ninguno, ni los fierros. Et embiòlo à decir à los otros, & cataron los suyos, & non fallaron ninguno. Et contaron, que fallaron esse dia menos cient & cinquenta & quatro Cativos, que sacò Santo Domingo de Cordova.

Acabo de dos annos que esto contesciò, veno este Moro sobredicho con las parias al Rey don Fernant à Burgos, & preguntò al Rey Don Fernant, què Santos havia en su Reino? Dixo [à èl el] Rey, havemos Santiago, Sant Fagunt, & otros

ways. The scale of the ransoming operation may be judged from the fact that Abbot Juan III of Silos, over a period of four years late in the 13th century, secured the release of 250 captives from Granada.

The texts of Grimaldo and Pero Marín, with other materials, were published at Madrid in 1736 by Sebastián de Vergara, who had been Abbot of Silos from 1723 to 1725. Our texts are taken from this. The section of Pero Marín's texts is headed 'Miraculos romanzados ...', which suggests a translation from Latin; but the heading is doubtless Vergara's, and there is no reason to think that Marín did not originally write in the vernacular, the language in which the captives told their stories, which were presumably to be recited to pilgrims visiting the Saint's shrine. The manuscript used by Vergara is of the 14th century, and the original apparently does not survive; a further edition is being prepared in Spain. There is an excellent study of all aspects of Marín's texts by J.M. de Cossío, 'Cautivos de moros en el siglo XIII', Al-Andalus, 7 (1942), 49–93. For the later period, compare text 64, and on the conditions in which captives were held, text 66. At times the whole matter of the ransoming and release of captives was scarcely separable from the appalling trade in slaves, of both religions, on which, for Aragón in particular, see Dufourcq, pp. 71–82, with full bibliography. Religious Orders were specially founded to ransom captives, the Trinitarians in Marseille in 1198 and the Mercedarians in Barcelona about 1218. These activities were paralleled on the Muslim side in respect of Muslims held prisoner in Christian lands.

(2) One Saturday night before dawn, 8 May of Era 1270 [= AD 1232], Muhammad, a commanding officer of Cordova, went out with a large body of Moors to raid Christian lands as far as Andújar. As he was crossing the Alcolea bridge, two leagues this side of Cordova, he met in the middle of the bridge a man surrounded by an intensely bright light. The Moor asked him in Spanish 'Who goes there?' The bright light replied: 'I am St Dominic of Silos.' The Moor then asked: 'Where are you going?' St Dominic replied: 'I am going to Cordova to rescue prisoners.' Then the Moor ordered his soldiers to turn, and he got back to Cordova before dawn. In one prison in which he kept fifteen Christians, he shackled them all by the foot and throat and hand, and together with his men lay down to rest on the cover of the entrance to the prison. He sent messages to other Moors who had captives telling them to guard them well, for St Dominic was in the city: and they put strong shackles on all of them. When day came they inspected the prison where the Moor's fifteen captives had lain, and found no trace of them, nor of the shackles. The Moor alerted the others, who then inspected their prisons, finding no captives in them. It was said that that day 154 prisoners were released by St Dominic and found to be missing.

Two years after this happened, the same Moor came to deliver the tribute money to King Ferdinand at Burgos, and asked him which saints there were in his kingdom. The King replied: 'We have St James, and St Facundus, and many

muchos. Dixo el Moro, qual es aquel que saca los Cativos? Dixo el Rey: Santo Domingo de Silos. Dixo el Moro: Sennor, esse. Et decirte [e] lo que me contesciò con èl. Una noche salia de Cordova con mi companna, que yba à correr à tierra de Christianos, & passando de noche por la puente Dalcolea, vi mui grant claridat, & preguntè, qui era? Et dixome que era Santo Domingo, que iba à Cordova à sacar Cativos. Et contò el Moro al Rey todo como le contesciò con Santo Domingo, assi como escripto es de suso. Et dixo el 'Rey, mandote, que vayas pora el su Monesterio, & que veyas como Yaz, & toda su casa. Et el Rey diol quil guiasse, & veno el Moro aqui, & entrò en la Eglesia, & viò aquella figura de la Imagen de Santo Domingo, que està sobrel su Altar, & dixo, que en aquella figura le viera la noche quel encontrò en la puente Dalcolea. Et el Rey don Fernant contò todo esto, como gelo dixiera aquel Moro.

(9) Era de mill trecientos & quince annos, Joan de Santillana salliera de Santender con otros companneros en una barca por mar pora Algecira, & levaban panos, & vinos, & otras cosas. Et enderecho del Algarbe salieron Moros à ellos & cativaronlos, & levaronlos allent la mar à una Villa que dicen Arcilla, & metieronlos en carcel, & facianlos moler todo el dia, & davanles muchas penas, & mucha laceria. Et este Johan, & sus companneros, que yacian con èl, Pero Martinez de Siguenza, & Pero de Liebana, & Alvaro de Navarra, Yvanez de Leon, & Johan de Bretanna, rogaban de dia, & de noche à Dios, & à Santo Domingo, que los sacassen daquella pena en que estaban. Ellos faciendo cada dia su oracion, un Sabbado en la noche antes del Gallo vieron toda la carcel alumbrada, que semeiaba de dia, & dixoles una boz: 'Fijos, via fuera, que la virtud de Dios es con vusco.' Dixieron los unos à los otros: 'Forademos esta carcel, & saldremos al muro, & darnos a Dios, & Santo Domingo conseio.' Esforzaronse, & con un fierro pequenno, que estaba en cabo del cepo, comenzaron à foradar, & foradaron tres paredes en una noche, & sallieron fuera de la Villa, & fueron ribera de la mar, & fallaron una barcha con sus rimos, & metieronse en la mar, & comenzaron de rimar: & anduvieron dos dias por la mar, & non ovieron fambre, nin embargo ninguno. Et legaron à la Galea, & à las Naves do estaba la Flota del Rey Don Alfonso. Et vinieronse con sus fierros al Monesterio de Santo Domingo, & legaron 15 dias de Abril en Era 1317 annos.

(22) En la Era sobredicha [1318] vino aqui Gil Perez de Motos, Aldea de Molina, dixo: Que fuera en cavalgada con el Rey Don Alfonso, & con su fijo el Infant Don Sancho quando fueron sobre Granada. Et la noche que entrò Fernant Enriquez en el Arrabal de Granada, estando el Rey, & el Infant en la Vega, Almogavares de Granada cativaron este Gil Perez, & otros muchos con èl; & fuè vendido por ocho doblas & media à Mahomat de Aramila. Et metiòl en la carcel, & yogò preso tres annos, & demandol muchas veces que se redimiesse, & èl dicie, que no havie de què. Sobre esto dabal muchas penas, & muchos azotes,

others.' The Moor inquired: 'Which is he that releases captives?' The King answered: 'St Dominic of Silos.' Then the Moor said: 'That is he. I must tell you what happened with him to me. One night I left Cordova with my men, on a raid into Christian lands, and as I was crossing the Alcolea bridge, I saw a great brightness, and asked what it could be. The answer I received was that it was St Dominic, on his way to Cordova to release prisoners.' The Moor told the King all that had happened to him with St Dominic, as has been set down above. The King said: 'I order you to go to St Dominic's monastery, so that you may see its situation and all its buildings.' The King provided him with a guide, and the Moor came here, and went into the church, and saw the image of St Dominic which stands over his altar; and he agreed that this was the same figure as he had seen the night he encountered him on the Alcolea bridge. King Ferdinand confirmed all this, just as the Moor had recounted it to him.

(9) In Era 1315 [= AD 1277], Juan de Santillana sailed out of Santander in a ship with other companions, heading for Algeciras; they carried cloth, wine, and other merchandise. Off the Algarve they were captured by Moors, who took them beyond the Straits of Gibraltar to a town called Arzila, where they were imprisoned and made to grind corn all day, and they were made to suffer great hardships. This man Juan and his companions, Pedro Martínez de Sigüenza, and Pedro de Liébana, Alvaro de Navarra, Ibáñez de León, and Juan de Bretaña, prayed all day and night to God and to St Dominic, begging them to release them from the hardships they were suffering. As they said their prayers every day, one Saturday night before dawn, they saw the whole of their prison-cell lit up so brightly that it seemed it was day, and a voice said to them: 'My sons, go out, for the power of God is with you.' They said to each other: 'We must bore a hole in the wall of this prison, and get out on to the town wall; God and St Dominic will help us.' They made a great effort, and with a small piece of metal attached to one end of their shackles, they began to bore. In one night they bored through three walls and, escaping from the town, reached the seashore; here they found a boat with oars, and so, putting to sea, they began to row. They rowed for two days, feeling no hunger nor encountering any obstacle. Then they reached La Galea, where King Alfonso's fleet lay at anchor. Then they came to the Monastery of St Dominic with their fetters, arriving on 15 April of Era 1317 [= AD 1279].

(22) In the aforementioned Era [1318, = AD 1280] there arrived here Gil Pérez de Motos, a village near Molina, who told us that he had gone on a raid with King Alfonso [X] and his son Prince Sancho, during the campaign against Granada. On the night that Fernando Enríquez reached the outskirts of Granada, the King and the Prince being in the Vega of Granada, frontier patrols of Granada captured Gil Pérez and many others with him; and he was sold for 8½ doblas to Muhammad of Aramila. This man put him in prison, where he lay for three years. The Moor told him repeatedly to ransom himself, but he said that he had no means by which he could do so. As a result the Moor made him

& demandol sesenta doblas, & dos Aljubas descarlata.   Quando viò que non podie levar dèl nada, sacòl de Granada, para passarle allent la mar, que le darian allà muchos dineros por èl.   Fueron à Anduiar, & era Viernes en la noche, & su Sennor, & otros Moros cenaban Coneios, & Perdices, & daban à èl que comies della; & dixo, que la non comeria ca era Viernes, & dieronle un poco de pan, & figos.   Et quando ovieron cenado tomaronle, & ataronle manos à çaga, & ataronle la garganta de cannamo à un post, & los pies à las cargas que levaban, & echaronse todos à dormir.   Este Gil Perez fizo su oracion à Dios, & à Santa Maria, & à Santo Domingo, que por la su mercet, que le sacassen daquella pena en que estaba, & que non passasse la mar.   El que se adurmiò, dixol una boz: 'Gil Perez lievate, vete tu via, & tornate pora la tierra que veniste.' Despertò, & fallò las manos sueltas, & la garganta suelta, & tenia unos fierros à los pies, & salliò à media noche con ellos sobre Moros, & puso los pies sobre el uno, & diò una boz; & fallò la puerta abierta de la posada, & de la Villa, & tornos por la carrera que le dixo la boz.   Et grant piesça veniendo por muchos montes, & por logares perigrosos, non sabiendo por dò, quando fuè de dia arribò à Quintana Redonda, Aldea de Baeza.   Segunt que cataba havia andado treinta y cinco leguas.   Esto fuè veinte dias andados de Octubre.   Legò aqui con sus fierros dia de Santa Lucia.

suffer many hardships, and beat him frequently, setting a price of 60 *doblas* and two long-sleeved robes of scarlet as his ransom. When the Moor realized he would get nothing from him, he took him out of Granada, in order to take him across the sea, where they would give a lot more money for him. They went to Andújar. It was Friday night. His master and other Moors were eating rabbit and partridges, and offered him some of these to eat; but he said he would not eat, for it was Friday, whereupon they gave him some bread and figs. After they had supped they took him, bound his hands behind his back, put a rope attached to a post round his neck, and tied his feet to the loads they were transporting; and then they all lay down to sleep. Gil Pérez prayed to God and St Mary and St Dominic, begging them to release him from his suffering and that he should not be taken across the sea. The moment he fell asleep a voice spoke to him: 'Gil Pérez, arise, go your way, and go back to the land from whence you came.' He awoke, and found that his hands and neck were free, but that he still had the shackles round his feet. With the shackles still on, at midnight he climbed over the Moors, stepping on one of them, who gave a cry; then he found the door of the house open, and the city gate open, and went off along the road which the voice had indicated to him. For a long time he travelled through woods and dangerous places, not knowing where he was, and at daybreak he reached Quintana Redonda, a village near Baeza. He estimated that he had walked thirty-five leagues. He arrived at the monastery on St Lucy's Day [13 December], carrying his shackles.

44. A turncoat redeems himself (1236)

A few years before 1236 Lorenzo Suárez Gallinato was banished by Ferdinand III of Castile-León for some misconduct ('malfetrias') and went to serve Ibn Hud, who ruled much of al-Andalus (see text 42). The Primera crónica general has a long account (731.b.23-733.a.25) of how Suárez, adviser to Ibn Hud at his court in Ecija, was sent on a mission to the camp of the Christians then beginning to besiege Cordova (1236), and on his return gave advice about strategy which proved disastrous for the Moors; as a result, Ferdinand III received him back into favour. Suárez does not seem to have been a permanent double agent, but rather one who saw his chance of again ingratiating himself with his original monarch, and took it.

Fablava el Conde Lucanor con Patronio, su consegero, en esta guisa:

'Patronio, un omne vino a mí por guaresçerse conmigo, et commo quier que yo sé que él es buen omne en sí, pero algunos dízenme que a fecho algunas cosas desaguisadas. Et por el buen entendimiento que vos avedes, ruégovos que me consejedes lo que vos paresçe que faga en esto.'

'Señor conde', dixo Patronio, 'para que vos fagades en esto lo que vos cumple, plazerme ya que sopiésedes lo que contesçió a don Lorenço Çuáres Gallinato.'

El conde le preguntó cómmo fuera aquello.

'Señor conde', dixo Patronio, 'don Lorenço Çuárez bevía con el rey de Granada. Et desque vino a la merçed del rey don Ferrando, preguntól un día el rey que, pues él tantos deserviçios fiziera a Dios con los moros et sin ayuda, que nunca Dios avríe merçed dél et que perderíe el alma. Et don Lorenço Çuáres díxol que nunca fiziera cosa porque cuydase que Dios le avría merçed del alma, sinon porque matara una vez un clérigo misacantano. Et el rey óvolo por muy estraño; et preguntól cómo podría esto ser. Et él dixo que beviendo con el rey de Granada, quel rey fiaba mucho dél, et era guarda del su cuerpo. Et yendo un día con el rey, que oyó roydo de omnes que davan vozes, et porque era guarda del rey, de que oyó el roydo, dio de las espuelas al cavallo et fue do lo fazían. Et falló un clérigo que estava revestido.

'Et devedes saber queste clérigo fue cristiano et tornóse moro. Et un día, por fazer bien a los moros et plazer, díxoles que, si quisieren, que él les daría el Dios en que los cristianos creen, et tenían por Dios. Et ellos le rogaron que gelo diesen. Estonçe el clérigo traydor fizo unas vestimentas, et un altar, et dixo ally misa, et consagró una ostia. Et desque fue consagrada, diola a los moros; et los moros arrastrávanla por la villa et por el lodo et faziéndol muchos escarnios. Et quando don Lorenço Çuárez esto vido, commo quier que él bivía con los moros, membrándose cómmo era cristiano, et creyendo sin dubda que aquél era verdaderamente el cuerpo de Dios et pues que Ihesu Cristo muriera por redemir nuestros pecados, que sería él de buena ventura si muriese por le bengar o por le

Don Juan Manuel's Conde Lucanor *was completed in 1335. It consists of
51 'exempla' (moral and entertaining tales) drawn from a wide range of sources
including the author's own experience. Each follows the pattern of the text
selected, tale 28. Don Juan would have known the account in the chronicle
outlined above, but hardly depends upon it. He moves Suárez to the more
prestigious kingdom of Granada – all that survived of al-Andalus in the 14th
century – and bases his story on respect for the Host, in a way which may owe
something to that piety of the Dominican Order which greatly influenced Don
Juan.*

The text is taken from the edition of the Conde Lucanor *by José Manuel
Blecua (Madrid, 1969). pp. 168-71. There is a complete translation in the Aris
& Phillips series by J.P. England.*

Count Lucanor was talking with Patronio, his adviser, as follows:

'Patronio, a man came to me seeking my protection, and although I know
that he is a good man in himself, some tell me that he has done some wrongful
things. From the excellent judgement you have, I beg you to advise me what I
should do in this matter.'

'My lord', said Patronio, 'for you to do what you have to in this, it would
help for you to know what happened to Don Lorenzo Suárez Gallinato.'

The Count asked Patronio to tell him about it.

'My lord', said Patronio, 'Don Lorenzo Suárez had lived with the King of
Granada. After he returned into King Ferdinand's favour, the King asked him
one day how God could show him mercy and whether he would not be damned,
since he had done so many disservices to God on behalf of the Moors, not being
under any compulsion. Don Lorenzo replied that he had never done anything
thinking that God would have mercy on his soul because of it, except once when
he had killed a priest. King Ferdinand thought this most strange, and asked him
how it had happened. Don Lorenzo said that while he was living with the King
of Granada, the King trusted him greatly and made him his bodyguard. One day
when he was out riding with the King, loud shouting was heard, and since he was
the King's bodyguard, he at once set spurs to his horse and rode towards the
noise. There he found a priest in his religious vestments.

'Now this priest was a Christian who had converted to Islam. One day, to
please and amuse the Moors, he told them that if they liked, he would give them
the God whom the Christians believed in and worshipped. The Moors asked him
to do so. Then this treacherous priest made vestments, and set up an altar, said
Mass at it, and consecrated a holy wafer. After the consecration, he handed it
to the Moors, who went around the town with it and dragged it through the mud
and mocked it in every way. When Don Lorenzo saw this, even though he was
living among the Moors, he remembered that he was a Christian, and believing
firmly that the wafer was indeed the body of Christ and that He had died to
redeem our sins, he thought it would be a goodly thing if he were to die in

sacar de aquella desonrra que falsamente cuydava quel fazían. Et por el gran duelo et pesar que de esto ovo, enderesçó al traydor del dicho rrenegado que aquella traycción fiziera, et cortól la cabeça. Et desçendió del cavallo et fincó los ynojos en el lodo et adoró el cuerpo de Dios que los moros trayan rastrando. Et luego que fincó los ynojos, la ostia que estava dél alongada, saltó del lodo en la falda de don Lorenço Çuáres. Et quando los moros esto vieron, ovieron ende gran pesar, et metieron mano a las espadas, et palos, et piedras, et vinieron contra él por lo matar. Et él metió mano al espada con que descabeçara al clérigo, et començóse a defender.

'Quando el rey oyó este roydo, et vio que querían matar a don Lorenço Çuáres, mandó quel non fiziesen mal, et preguntó que qué fuera aquello. Et los moros, con gran quexa, dixiéronle cómmo fuera et cómmo pasara aquel fecho.

'Et el rey se quexó et le pesó desto mucho, et preguntó a don Lorenço Çuáres por qué lo fiziera. Et él le dixo que bien sabía que él non era de la su ley, pero quel rey esto sabía, que fiava dél su cuerpo et que lo escogiera él para esto cuydando que era leal et que por miedo de la muerte non dexaría de lo guardar, et pues si él lo tenía por tan leal, que cuydava que faría esto por él, que era moro, que parase mientes, si él leal era, qué devía fazer, pues era cristiano, por guardar el cuerpo de Dios, que es rey de los reyes et señor de los señores, et que si por esto le matasen, que nunca él tan buen día viera.

'Et quando el rey esto oyó, plógol mucho de lo que don Lorenço Çuáres fiziera et de lo que dezía, et amól et preçiól, et fue mucho más amado desde ally adelante.

'Et vos, conde señor, si sabedes bien que aquel omne que conbusco quiere bevir es buen omne en sí et podedes fiar dél, quanto por lo que vos dizen que, fizo algunas cosas sin razón, non le devedes por eso partir de la vuestra conpaña; ca por aventura aquello que los omnes cuydan que es sin razón, non es así, commo cuydó el rey que don Lorenço fiziera desaguisado en matar aquel clérigo. Et don Lorenço fizo el mejor fecho del mundo. Mas sy vos sopiésedes que lo que él fizo es tan mal fecho, porque él sea por ello mal envergonçado, et lo fizo syn razón, por tal fecho faríades bien en lo non querer para vuestra compaña.'

Al conde plogo mucho desto que Patronio le dixo, et fízolo así et fallóse ende bien. Et entendiendo don Juan que este enxemplo era bueno, fízolo escrivir en este libro et fizo estos viessos que dizen assí:

Muchas cosas paresçen sin razón,
et qui las sabe, en sí buenas son.

avenging Him and trying to rescue Him from the dishonour which the Moors were doing to Him. In the immense grief and pain which he felt, he made for the treacherous renegade who had done this dreadful deed, and cut off his head. Then he got off his horse and knelt in the mud and worshipped the Body of Christ which the Moors had pulled about. As soon as he knelt, the wafer, which was some distance from him, leaped from the mud into the skirt of Don Lorenzo's dress. Seeing this the Moors were outraged, and laid hands on their swords and on sticks and stones, and came up disposed to kill him. Don Lorenzo drew the sword with which he had beheaded the priest, and began to defend himself.

'When the King heard this tumult and saw that they were trying to kill Don Lorenzo, he ordered that they should not do him any harm, and asked the cause of the trouble. The Moors indignantly told him all that had happened.

'The King was much distressed at all this, and asked Don Lorenzo why he had acted as he did. Don Lorenzo said that he well knew he was not of their faith, but reminded the King that he had been fully aware of this, that the King had entrusted his person to him and had chosen him for this believing him to be loyal and knowing that no fear of death would prevent him carrying out his duty; and since the King considered him so loyal, and knew that Don Lorenzo would do this for him who was a Moor, he should ponder what he, Don Lorenzo, would do as a duty, since he was a Christian, in order to protect the Body of Christ, who is King of Kings and Lord of Lords; concluding that if they should kill him for doing his, it would be the finest day of his life.

'When the King heard this, he was greatly pleased with what Don Lorenzo had done and had said to him, and he loved and esteemed him even more from that day thenceforward.

'Now you, my lord, if you know that that man who seeks to live with you is a good man in himself and that you can trust him, whatever others may tell you about wrongful things that he has done, should not dismiss him from your side; for it could be that what others think is wrongful is not so, just as the King of Granada at first thought that Don Lorenzo had committed a crime by killing that priest. What Don Lorenzo did was in fact a most worthy act. But if you should find out that what your man did was badly done in itself, and wrongful, to the extent that he should be put to shame because of it, on this account you would do well not to receive him in your company.'

The Count was much pleased with what Patronio had told him, and acted accordingly and found it was for the best. The Count, understanding that this was a useful example, ordered it to be written in this book and composed the following verses:

Many things seem wrongful,
But when one knows more about them
are seen to be goodly in themselves.

45. King James views Játiva (1240)

James I of Aragón ('the Conqueror', Jaume el Conqueridor) began to rule
as a minor in 1213 and died in 1276, perhaps the most remarkable in a series of
remarkable monarchs of Aragón. He greatly expanded Aragonese territory and
power by conquering the Balearics from 1229 to 1235 and by taking Valencia –
on whose earlier conquest by the Cid see texts 22, 23, and 26 – in 1238. In the
years following this James tried to conquer the area to the south of Valencia in
order to ensure the safety of the capital; as in text 46, by peaceful agreement as
much as by military means. The success of this approach can be gauged from
the fact that Aragón retained a large, peaceable, and hard-working population
of Muslims up to the time of their expulsion from all Spain from 1609.

What follows is taken from the Crónica *or* Llibre dels feits *whose author is,*
after much debate, now generally agreed to have been James himself. It is far

E faem cridar nostra host, e anam-nos-en al vau de Barraga, e allí esperam
nostra host per un dia. E l'alcaid de Xàtiva, sabé que nós veníem sobre ell, e
envià'ns Abenferri, qui era estat de Llíria e era ab ell. E meravellà's perquè nós
feíem açò, que ell havia son cor e sa volentat de fer-nos tot ço que ell pogués
fer per nós ab raó, mas que ells li havien trencada la treuga que nós li havíem
dada, e sobre açò que se n'hac a defendre; e, si mal havia feit, que ho havia feit
per aquella raó. E nós responem-li que, si tort li havia feit negú que el li faríem
esmenar, mas que volíem que de tot en tot nos retés don P. Alcalà ab los
cavallers, que açò no soferríem nós per res, e que el li demanaríem e que els
talaríem; e anà-se'n Abenferri. E nós al vespre dixem a don Rodrigo:
'Hajam tro a trenta cavallers que anc no vim Xàtiva, e volem-la veer.'
E anam llà a aquell coll agut qui és part del castell, e veem la pus bella
horta que anc havíem vista en vila ni en castell, e que hi havia més de
dues-centes algorfes per l'horta, les pus belles que hom pogués trobar, e les
alqueríes en torn de l'horta, moltes e espesses, e veem encara lo castell, tan
noble e tan bell, e tan bella horta, e haguem-ne gran goig, e gran alegre en
nostre cor; e semblà'ns que no tan solament per don P. Alcalà devíem-nos venir
sobre Xàtiva ab nostra host, mas per haver lo castell per crestianisme, e que Déu
hi fos servit; e d'açò no volguem re dir, a don Rodrigo, de nostre cor.

'rom certain that he could write, but in any case the reality of the matter would *have been that he dictated to a scribe, often long after the events concerned. The edition used is that of Ferran Soldevila, Les quatre grans cròniques (Barcelona, 1971), chapter 318 on pp. 123–24.*

The background to the episode is that Pere d'Alcalà had raided down the coast and had been captured, with five other knights and their men, by the Moors of Játiva. James was therefore making a show of strength before Játiva to secure their release. It is plain, however, that he used the opportunity to view the area long known in Moorish lands as 'the paradise of the West', and of course he viewed it as an intending conqueror (proceeding to occupy it a few years later). There is also some genuinely warm appreciation of the landscape here, a perception which is very far from common in medieval chronicles. Münzer in his Itinerarium *(text 66) has many words of admiration for Moorish skill in farming and horticulture as he observed it in 1494.*

We called our army together, and went off to the valley of Barraga. There we waited a day for the troops to join us. The governor of Játiva realized that we were coming against him, and sent out to us Ibn Farah, who had come from Lliria and was now with him. He expressed surprise that we were acting in this way, since his intention was to do all that he could for us within reason, but they [the Christian knights] had broken the truce which we had granted him, and concerning this he had done nothing for which to excuse himself; if he had done wrong, he had done it for that reason. We answered that if anyone had done him wrong we would look into the matter, but our wish was to have Don Pere Alcalà and the knights returned to us at once; we would tolerate no delay in this, and would hold him responsible if there were, and would come and destroy his trees and crops. Ibn Farah returned to the town. That evening we said to Don Rodrigo [Liçana, cousin of Pere d'Alcalà, and much concerned to secure his release]:

'Let us have about thirty knights who have not seen Játiva, and would like to do so.'

We climbed the pointed hill on part of which the castle stands, and beheld the most beautiful area of irrigated farmland which we had ever seen anywhere. There were more than two hundred flat-roofed houses scattered about, the most handsome one could wish to see, and the farmsteads all round the edge of the irrigated land, very numerous and closely set; and the castle stood there most nobly and handsomely overlooking the splendid farmland. Our hearts filled with pleasure and satisfaction at the sight; and it seemed to us that we should come to Játiva with our army not merely on Pere d'Alcalà's account, but in order to take the castle for Christendom, and in order that God should be served thereby. But we said nothing about this intention of ours to Don Rodrigo.

46. The Aragonese grant terms to Alcira (1242)

Algecira, now Alcira, is on the river Júcar to the south of Valencia. James occupied it on 30 December 1242. The text is from the same source as the last, chapters 329–32, pp. 126–27.

There is a vast amount of fascinating material about Christian-Muslim relations in Valencia and its region in the 13th century in numerous studies by Fr Robert I. Burns, some of them gathered in his book of 1978. In this his paper on 'Spanish Islam in transition: Acculturative survival and its price in the Christian Kingdom of Valencia, 1240-1280' (item XIII, at p. 95) records how a

(329) E al tornar que nós faem, lo raiz d'Algezira era eixit d'Algezira per paor que havia de nós, e era-se'n eixit bé ab trenta cavallers, e anava-se'n a Múrcia: e romàs lo poder de la vila en los sarraïns e en lo senyoriu. E enviaren-nos sos missatges que Algezira era bon lloc e honrat, e dels mellors que fossen en lo regne de València: e, si nós ho voliem, que ells s'avenrien ab nós, nós lleixant-los en aquell lloc. E a nós plac-nos molt la paraula que ens enviaren a dir, e dixem-los que els penríem a mercè, e que els retendríem en aquell lloc, e ells que ens donassen poder d'aquelles torres que són a la porta de València. E ells dixeren que s'acordarien e que ens respondrien. E nós demanam-los quan seria la resposta, e ells dixeren que al tercer dia, e plac-nos molt.

(330) E vengren al tercer dia a nós a València, dels vells de la vila dels mellors que hi eren, e foren quatre por tots los altres. E dixeren-nos que ens darien la torre que era major, que és prop del Pont de la Calçada, que era a la porta que nós demanàvem. E nós dixem-los que ens plaïa, car ells tan bé avenien en nostra fazenda, e que els amaríem e els faríem bé. E faeren ses cartes ab nós com romasessen en Algezira ab aquells furs e costumes que eren en temps de los almohades: e que poguessen fer llur ofici en les mesquites aixi com solien, e que tot catiu sarraí que vingués a Algezira que fos alforro, e que nós no el poguéssem cobrar ne null hom per nós: e donaren-nos dia, que a cinc dies que vinguéssem cobrar la torre. E nós dixem-los que hi seríem a aquell dia, e que faessen eixir tots los vells de la vila e l'altre poble, e que ens jurassen feeltat, e que ens serien lleals a nós e als nostres, e als nostres hòmens.

(331) E sobre açò nós vinguem al dia, e eixiren a nós tots los vells, e juraren sobre el llibre de l'Alcorà que ens serien bons e lleials, e que guardarien nostre cos e nostres membres e els nostres hòmens que hi metríem que tinguessen nostre lloc. E, quan nós haguem emparada la torre, pregam-los que ells

*dispute between the Muslim inhabitants and Christian settlers of Alcira was
resolved by King James, 'Visis omnibus et singulis instrumentis [...] viso etiam
instrumento sarracenorum, habito consilio et diligenti tractatu, voluntate et
consensu senium et sarracenorum Aliasire', that is, James regarded himself as
the legal successor of the last Muslim ruler of Valencia, and regarded Muslim
legislation and rulings as still having some effect; moreover, he consulted
Muslim opinion. There is much else on Alcira (and on Játiva, text 45) in Fr
Burns'* Medieval colonialism: postcrusade exploitation of Islamic Valencia,
(Princeton, 1975), passim.

(329) On our return [to Valencia, after a long absence in Aragón] the
governor of Alcira had left the place with some thirty horsemen, out of fear of
us, and had gone to Murcia; power in the town resided with the chief men
among the Moors. They sent us messengers who said that Alcira was a good and
honourable place, among the best in the Kingdom of Valencia; and if we so
wished, they would make an agreement with us on condition that we allowed
them to stay there. We were greatly pleased with this announcement, and told
them that we would take them under our protection, that we would allow them to
stay, and that they should hand over to us the towers at the Valencia gate [i.e.,
the defensive positions at the gate from which the road to Valencia led out of the
town]. They said they would discuss the matter and let us have a reply. We
asked them when this would be, and they said within three days; we readily
agreed to this.

(330) On the third day there came to us in Valencia four elders of the
town, among the most distinguished in the place, to speak on behalf of
everybody. They told us they would hand over to us the tallest of the towers,
the one next to the Pont de la Calçada [bridge which carried the main road],
which stood at the gate that interested us. We told them that this was agreeable
to us, since it showed that they were being cooperative; and we promised to
protect and treat them well. They drew up documents jointly with us to ensure
that they should stay in Alcira and enjoy those rights and customs they had in the
time of the Almohads, that they should continue to worship in the mosques as
they had done, and that any man brought into Alcira as a prisoner should be set
free without our being able to rearrest him or use any man to do it for us. Then
they fixed a date, agreeing that after five days we should come and occupy the
tower. We told them we would come then, and that they should gather all the
elders and the rest of the population outside the town in order to swear
allegiance to us.

(331) We presented ourselves that day, and all the elders of the town came
out, and swore on the book of the Koran that they would be good and loyal, and
would respect our person and our men that we might put there to represent us.
When we had taken over the tower, we asked them if they were willing for us to
occupy the land up to the third tower, we on our side proposing to build a wall

volguessen que ens dessen tro a la tercera torre, e nós que hi faríem un mur, per ço que els crestians no entrassen als sarraïns ni els sarraïns als crestians, e que hi faríem una portella qui eixiria a la Calçada per on entrassen en la vila, e per ço que ells no poguessen dir que dan los vengués de part dels crestians. E ells dixeren que no ens podien respondre menys de consell dels altres moros, e que tro a cinc dies haüt consell nos respondrien. E nós pregam-ne alguns dels sarraïns dels mejors que ho consellassen. E ells dixeren que en tal manera ho farien que nós ne seríem pagats.

(332) E quan venc a aquell dia responeren-nos que els plaïa, e atorgaren-nos-ho. E feem fer nostre mur entre nós e ells de dues parts, e fo així enclòs lo castell e enfortit. E així haguem Algezira, e prenguem les rendes que solia pendre l'Arrais d'Algezira, ço és lo senyor.

in order that the Christians should not interfere with the Moors nor the Moors with the Christians, adding that we would make a gateway in it which would lead out to the Calçada [main road] and give access to the town, all this in order that they should not be able to say that the Christians were given an advantage. They replied that they could not give an answer about this without holding a council of the other Moors, but that they would hold such a council and let us know within five days. We asked several of the distinguished Moors so to recommend to the council, and they answered that they would act in such a way as would satisfy us.

(332) When the fifth day came they replied that they agreed. So we built our wall to separate them from us all round, and in this way the fort was enclosed and strengthened. This is how we acquired Alcira, and enjoyed the rents which the governor – that is the ruler – of Alcira had formerly collected.

47. Seville (1248)

*Although Cordova, taken in 1236, had been the old capital of the Caliphs,
it had been in decline since the end of their line in 1031, and it was Seville
which was the major remaining prize of al-Andalus and the prime objective of
the campaigns of (St) Ferdinand III of Castile-León in the last years of his
reign. The extent of the siege operations and the immensity of the logistics
involved can be appreciated in the text which follows, chapter 1127 of the
Primera crónica general (on which see text 1). The awe of the Christians before
this great city, more splendid than any in the Christian west, can be appreciated
in chapter 1128.*

*According to this text, the siege lasted some sixteen months, but according
to other sources about six. A contingent of Muslim troops from Granada –
whose ruler Muhammad I had been on terms of peace with Ferdinand III since
1246 – fought alongside the Christians. Most of the fighting was in the nature
of skirmishing to the south of the city as the Christians tightened their hold on
the outlying suburb of Triana, with its important fortress. The Christian camp
was in this area, at Tablada, some 2 km to the south of the city proper. The
Christians also launched many river-borne attacks with their fleet, which had
sailed up the Guadalquivir, and they earlier took important places in the region,
such as Carmona. As was normal in such situations, the Sevillians chose not to
suffer the horrors of a final assault, but, once they realized their state was
hopeless, negotiated the surrender of the city on terms which guaranteed them
passage out of it with their lives and any movable property (as recounted in
chapter 1124 of the chronicle: December 1248).*

(1127) En la hueste que el rey don Fernando sobre Seuilla tenie, auie
semeiança de grant çibdat et noble et muy rica. Conplida era de todas cosas et
de todas noblezas que a abondamiento de toda conplida et abondada çipdat
pertenescan. Calles et plaças auie y departidas de todos mesteres, cada vno
sobre si; vna calle auie y de los traperos et de los camiadores; otra de los
espeçieros et de los alquimes de los melezinamientos que auien los feridos et los
dolientes mester; otra de los armeros, otra de los freneros, otra de los carniçeros
et de los pescadores; et asi de cada mester, de quantos en el mundo podiesen
seer, auie de cada vnos sus calles departidas, cada vnas por orden conpasadas et
apuestas et bien ordenadas. Asi que qui aquella hueste uio, podie muy bien
dezir que nunca otra tan rica nin tan apostada uio, que de mayor gente nin de
mayor poder que esta non fuese, nin tan conplida de todas noblezas nin
marauillas. De todas viandas et de todas merchandias era tan abondada, que
ninguna rica çipdat non lo podrie ser mas. Et asi auien arraygado las gentes con
cuerpos et con aueres et con mugeres et con fijos, commo si por siempre ouiesen
y de durar; ca el rey auie puesto et prometido que se nunca ende leuantase en

Ferdinand died in 1252 and was buried in the cathedral of Seville, with texts inscribed on the four sides of his tomb in Latin, Castilian, Arabic, and Hebrew; in the Castilian version, '... e conquiso la çibdat de Sevilla que es cabeça de toda Espanna ...'. His son Prince Alfonso, later Alfonso X 'the Wise', was present at the siege and when monarch made the city a favourite place of residence for his court. One may speculate that chapters 1127 and 1128 of the chronicle, with their exceptional warmth, are by Alfonso's own hand; the royal besieger conquers the markedly feminine personality of the city at the start of chapter 1128 as any courtly lover might (compare text 61b).

Some of the features mentioned in the description of the city can still be seen. The Torre de Oro beside the river (at one end of the walls and a principal bastion of the harbour defences) was built by the Almohad Sultan Yusuf II after Las Navas (1212). The other tower mentioned, 'de Santa María', is better known as La Giralda. It was originally the minaret of the chief mosque (built 1172–82 by the Almohads), its top floor serving also as an astronomical observatory. The 'maçanas' were four gilded globes which fell in an earthquake in 1355. At the time here described, this mosque – said to have been as large as that of Cordova – had simply been rededicated as the Cathedral of St Mary; it stood till 1400, and when construction of the present Cathedral began in 1402, the Giralda was retained as its bell-tower, extra storeys and the crowning figure of Faith being added in 1568.

There is a paper by A.I. Biglieri on the descriptive rhetoric used in these chapters, La Corónica, 16 (1987–88), 67–80 (with an extraordinary error in taking the 'calles et plaças' of chapter 1127 as being those of the city, whereas they are obviously those of the camp of the besieging army, pp. 75–76).

(1127) In the host which King Ferdinand had at Seville, there was a strong similarity to a great, noble, and very rich city. The camp was full of all the things and all the fine attributes which could pertain to such a complete and well-provided city. There were streets and squares allotted there to every craft, each one keeping to itself: there was one street of tailors and money-changers; another for the spice-merchants, and for the druggists who stocked the medicaments that the wounded and the sick needed; another for the armourers, another for the harness-makers, another for the butchers and the fish-merchants; and so on for each craft, for all those that there might be in the world, for each one of them there was a street set aside, all duly measured up and elegant and well-ordered. Anyone who saw that host could well say that he never saw another so richly and pleasingly disposed, or containing finer people or greater power than this, nor so full of all noble and wonderful things. It was supplied with all kinds of food and merchandise, and no wealthy city could have surpassed it. In the camp, people had established themselves with their persons and possessions and wives and children, as if they were to remain there for ever; for the King had stated and promised that he would not depart from there for as

56

todos los dias de su uida, fasta que la ouiese; et quiso Dios, et conpliose su uoluntad et lo que el quiso. Et esta çertanidad de la auer los fazie venir de todas partes tan raygadamiente commo vos dezimos.

(1128) Dizeseys meses la touo çercada a esa noble çipdat de Seuilla ese bienauenturado rey don Fernando, et no lo fazie sin razon de fazer mucho por ella, que es noble çipdat. Et es la meior çercada que ninguna otra allen mar nin aquen mar que fallada nin vista podiese ser, que tan llana estodiese; et los muros della son altos sobeiamiente et fuertes et muy anchos; torres altas et bien departidas, grandes et fechas a muy grant lauor; por muy bien ercada ternien otra villa de la su baruacana tan solamiente. Si quier la Torre de Oro, de commo esta fundada en la mar et tan ygualmiente conpuesta et fecha a obra tan sotil et tan marauillosa, et de quanto ella costo al rey que la mando fazer ¿qual podrie ser aquel que podrie saber nin asmar quanto seria? Et pues de la torre de Sancta Maria todas las sus noblezas, et de quan grant la beltad et el alteza et la su grant nobleza es: sesenta braças a en el techo de la su anchura, et quatro tanto en alto; tan ancha et tan llana et de tan grant maestria fue fecha et tan conpasada la escalera por o a la torre suben, que los reyes et las reynas et los altos omnes que alli quieren sobir de bestias, suben quando quieren fasta en ssomo. Et en somo de la torre a otra torre, que a ocho braças, fecha a grandes marauillas. Et ençima della estan quatro maçanas alçadas vna sobre otra; tan grandes et tan de grant obra et de tan gran nobleza son fechas, que en todo el mundo non podrien ser otras tan nobles nin tales; la de somo es la menor de todas, et luego la segunda que esta so ella es mayor, et muy mayor la terçera. Mas de la quarta non podemos retraer, que es tan grant et de tan estranna obra que es dura cosa de creer a qui lo non viese: esta es toda obrada a canales, et las canales della son doze, et ay en la anchura de cada canal cinco palmos comunales; et quando la metieron en la uilla non pudo caber por la puerta, et ouieron a tirar las puertas et a ensanchar la entrada; et quando el sol fiere en ella, resplandeçe commo rayos muy lozientes mas de vna iornada. Et a otras noblezas muchas et grandes sin todas estas que dicho auemos; villa tan bien asentada et tan llanna non la a en el mundo, villa a quien el nauio del mar le viene por el rio todos dias; de las naues et de las galeas et de los otros nauios de la mar, fasta dentro a los muros, apuertan alli con todas mercadorias de todas partes del mundo: de Taniar, de Çepta, de Tunez, de Bogia, dAlexandria, de Jenua, de Portogal, de Ynglaterra, de Pisa, de Lonbardia, de Burdel, de Bayona, de Çezillia, de Gasconna, de Catalonna, dAragon, et aun de França, et de otras muchas partes dallen mar, de tierra de cristianos et de moros, de muchos logares que muchas vezes y acaesçen. ¿Pues commo non puede ser muy buena et muy preçiada çipdat tan acabada et tan conplida et o tantos abondamientos de bienes a, commo en esta son? El su azeyte solo suele todo el mundo abondar por mar et por tierra, et esto sin todos los otros abondamientos et las otras riquezas que y a, que serie fuerte cosa de contar a qui por todo pasar quisiese. En el su Axaraf auia bien çient mill alcarias, esto sin los portadgos onde muy grandes rentas

long he lived until he had taken the city; and since it was God's will, the King's wish prevailed. This certainty of the King's that he would capture the city made people come from all parts to establish themselves, as we have said.

(1128) King Ferdinand, blessed with good fortune, besieged the noble city of Seville for sixteen months, and he did not do it without realizing that she was worth every effort being expended, for truly the city is a magnificent one. It is the best defended of any city on this side of the sea or on the other that anyone could find or that might be, that is among those that lie on flat ground. Her walls are quite extraordinarily high and strong, and thick too; there are lofty towers well positioned, most beautifully constructed; any other place might consider itself very well defended if it possessed Seville's barbican alone. For example: the Torre de Oro, placed next to the water and so elegantly built with such subtle and wonderful work, who would ever be able to know or guess how much it cost the ruler who built it? Then the tower of Santa María, with its very fine features and its great height: its roof is 120 yards in breadth, and four times that amount in height; so wide and so easy and so masterful is the construction of the stairway by which people go up to the tower, that kings and queens and nobles who wish to go up it on horseback can do so, right to the very top. And on top of the tower is another, 16 yards tall, very richly worked. Above this are four globes one above the other, so large and of such fine workmanship that in all the world there could be none more beautiful: the topmost one is the smallest, the next down is larger, and the third larger still. But the fourth we can hardly describe, for it is so big and so strangely wrought that it is hard for anyone to credit unless he has seen it. This is composed of a structure of grooves, twelve in all, each groove being five ordinary spans in width. When it was brought into the city it would not go through the gates, and they had to pull down the gateway and make the entrance wider. When the sun strikes it, it gleams as if giving off bright beams of light the whole day. Seville has many other splendid things apart from these we have told of. In all the world there is no city better situated or so flat. It is a city to which sea-going vessels come every day, sailing up the river: ships and galleys and other vessels from the sea dock there right inside the walls with merchandise from all parts of the world, from Tangier, Ceuta, Tunis, Bougie, Alexandria, Genoa, Portugal, England, Pisa, Lombardy, Bordeaux, Bayonne, Sicily, Gascony, Catalonia, Aragon, and France, and from many other places beyond the seas, both Christian and Moorish, and from other places too where they happen to be. How could a city so perfect and complete, so abounding in wealth as Seville is, not be reckoned goodly and highly prized? Its olive-oil alone is carried to the whole world by land and sea, not to mention all the other kinds of supplies and forms of wealth which are there; if anyone should try to catalogue them all, it would be impossible to reckon up. In its olive-growing region there were at least a hundred thousand

salien sin mesura. Et segunt lo prueua la estoria, vna fue esta de las mayores et mas altas conquistas que en el mundo todo fue vista nin fecha que se en tan poca sazon feziese; pues por qual razon pudo seer sennor de la el asi en tan poco tienpo auer et ganar, non puede omne entender y al, fueras merçed que fue del Sennor, cuyo seruidor era, quel quiso onrrar et dar ventura buena, porque tan noble sennorio et tan acabado ouiese, et lo al, que es la flor de los acabamientos de todas onrras: la grant lealtad de los buenos vasallos que auie, que rey que en el mundo fuese no los ouo meiores nin tales de su naturaleza, que sabemos que por todas las partes del mundo ouieron sienpre los castellanos prez desto sobre quantas gentes otras son, et mas seruidores de sennor, et mas sofridores de todo afan. Des aqui lieue Dios el su buen prez adelante, a onrra suya et la de su naturaleza.

farmhouses; and the road-tolls charged provided a huge income. As the text tells us, this conquest of Seville was one of the greatest and noblest that was ever seen or accomplished in the whole world, and it was achieved in a very short time; and one cannot understand how King Ferdinand could take and conquer it in such a short time, unless it were the act of God, whose servant King Ferdinand was. God clearly wished to honour him and give him good fortune, in order that he should acquire a lordship so noble and so splendid. As for the rest, which is the flower of all achievement and of all honour: this was the great loyalty of the good vassals the King had, for none of the world's rulers ever had better ones in his own right, and we know that everywhere in the world the Castilians always had a greater reputation for this than all other peoples, that is for loyalty to their lord and for being able to tolerate labours of all kinds. From now on may God carry their fine reputation forward, for their own honour and for that of their country.

48 The study of Arabic (mid-13th century)

St Raymond of Penyafort in Catalonia (1176-1275) became in 1238 the third Master-general of the Dominican Order (the Friars Preachers). He was said to be the greatest lawyer of Christendom in his time, and as professor of civil and of canon law at Bologna he produced major works such as his Summa de casibus, *and edited the* Decretals *of Pope Gregory IX. He was for long an adviser of the Pope and of James I of Aragón. Whereas the Franciscans (text 41) in their early days had attempted missionary work among Muslims without much preparation (and in the case of the 1219 group were intent on martyrdom), the more intellectual Dominicans believed in proper planning and training. Their attitude to unbelief involved acceptance of the primacy of conscience as elaborated by theorists of the time (Burns, p. 400); hence conversion could not legitimately be forced, but must result from intellectual persuasion by preaching (St Raymond's own* Summa, *I.iv.3). By 1236 their friars in provinces bordering on lands of unbelief – in Europe Germany, Hungary, Spain – were ordered to learn the necessary local languages for this preaching to be effective. In the case of Spain, a* studium, *a proper school for the study of Arabic, had to be created, and at times Hebrew was added to this for work among the Jews. Coll, whose study is mentioned below, thinks the first school was established in Tunis, with which the Aragonese had friendly commercial relations, by about 1245. In 1250, eight specially selected friars, mostly from Aragonese lands, whose names are known, were students there, and others in Valencia. When the Tunis school closed, probably in 1258 when the period of Muslim tolerance there ended, a continuation of it existed in Murcia from 1266 until about 1280. There was a school of Arabic in Játiva, south of Valencia, from 1291 to 1313.*

Studies in these schools would have embraced, in addition to the Arabic language (taught by locally-recruited Muslims, whose conversion was often secured, as in our text), the Koran and such aspects of Christian doctrine as were needed to combat this. For the school which the Franciscans founded in Majorca in 1276, see text 51.

Text (a) is taken from a Vita *of St Raymond, written before 1351; this is anonymous, though attributed by some to Eymeric of Gerona. The period of the activity referred to probably began about 1230. There seems no reason to doubt the general truth of the account, though reservations about the large number of converts claimed are proper. This* Vita *is published in* Monumenta Ordinis Fratrum Praedicatorum Historica, VI, fasc. 1 *(Rome and Stuttgart, 1900), with*

(a)

Infideles etiam Judei videlicet et Sarraceni honestatis ejus excellentiam admirantes et dulci ac racionabili alloquio delectati circa. eum devocionem specialem et reverenciam exhibebant. Pro quorum conversione procuranda totus

our extract on pp. 31-32. Fascicule 2 of the same volume contains (pp. 29-37) the text of a fascinating document, No. XVII, of 1234, in which St Raymond, after approval by the Pope, gives rulings to the friars in Tunis about Christian-Muslim personal relations, trade, and various subtle points of canon law.

On all this see J.M. Coll, 'Escuelas de lenguas orientales en los siglos XIII y XIV', Analecta Sacra Tarraconensia, 17 (1944), 115-38, and 18 (1945), 51-89. See also for the general setting Burns, pp. 353-54, and Dufourcq, pp. 106-9. Chapter 3 of Fr Burns' book Muslims, Christians and Jews in the crusader kingdom of Valencia (Cambridge, 1984), reviews the evidence in detail.

In text (b), Alfonso X establishes a studium of Latin and Arabic in Seville. Latin was a basic requirement everywhere, and courses would have consisted of the usual trivium and quadrivium, but Arabic was a considerable innovation. As to Alfonso's purpose, Vicente de la Fuente in 1884 thought it was to prepare students to study 'física y medicina', in which there was certainly much to be learned in Arabic; but for his scientific works, Alfonso employed Muslim and Jewish savants in Toledo, Seville, etc., masters already of the languages and the subjects. V. Cantarino in his book Entre monjes y musulmanes (Madrid, 1978), pp. 262-63, thinks the purpose was, like that of St Raymond, to prepare missionaries, and he quotes a phrase of Alfonso's about the need to convert Muslims by preaching to them; however, this phrase is not, as Cantarino implies, a part of the 1254 letter, but is from the Partidas (VII.25.2). The clergy were not, of course, to be excluded; in 1260 the Pope allowed all clergy who taught or studied at Seville to keep their benefices while doing so. Cantarino's statement that 'Además, en la carta real de 1254, al expresar su deseo de que se lleguen a traducir los textos sagrados musulmanes y judíos ...' is equally invalid, since nothing of the kind appears in the text. We have to conclude that we simply do not know, and there is no later information. Perhaps Alfonso's intention was resolutely secular, as was his father's when founding the University of Salamanca in 1245 and excluding theology from it; in this case the royal purpose might have been to train Christians as officers of the Crown and the municipalities who would use Arabic in diplomatic, administrative, and commercial fields. The lack of information is sad; one assumes the school did not last long, and it seems to have had nothing to do with the later foundation of the University of Seville.

Alfonso's text is in the Memorial histórico español, I *(Madrid, 1851), p. 54.*

(a)

Unbelievers, both Jews and Muslims, impressed by the high quality of his [St Raymond's] openness and charmed by his gentle and reasonable discourse, showed special devotion and reverence to his person. He was all afire with the

erat caritatis incendiis inflammatus, et super hoc sibi quedam visio mirabilis divinitus est ostensa, in qua sibi est a Domino revelatum, quod per Fratres Ordinis Predicatorum deberet inter gentes infideles multorum conversio ad fidem catholicam procurari; propter quod magis ac magis accensus cum licentia Magistri Ordinis et cum auxilio domini Regis Castelle et domini Regis Aragonum studium lingue arabice fieri procuravit, in quo viginti Fratres Ordinis Predicatorum vel plures in lingua illa per ipsius diligentiam sunt instructi, ex quo fructus maximus est secutus, nam plures quam decem millia Sarracenorum a Fratribus eis predicantibus sunt conversi, et inter Sarracenos de Hispania et etiam in Aphrica divulgata est veritas fidei christiane, et jam taliter approbata, quod multi eorum precipue sapientes dispositi sunt ad suscipiendam fidei catholice veritatem et magistri Fratrum in lingua scilicet arabica fere omnes per ipsorum industriam sunt conversi.

(b)

Conoscida cosa sea a todos los omes que esta carta vieren como nos Don Alfonso por la gracia de Dios [...] por gran sabor que e de facer bien e merced e levar adelante a la noble cibdat de Sevilla e de enrriquecerla, e ennoblecer mas por que es de las mas honrradas e de las meyores cibdades de Espanna, e por que yase hi enterrado el mui honrrado Rey Don Fferrando, mio padre, que la gano de moros, e la poblo de christianos a muy gran loor e grant servicio de Dios, e a honrra e a pro de todo christianismo; e por que yo fui con el en ganarla, e en poblarla, otorgo que aia hi estudios e escuelas generales de latin e de arabigo. E mando que los maestros e los escolares que vinieren hi al estudio, que vengan salvos e seguros por todas las partes de mis regnos, e por todo mio señorio, con todas sus cosas e que non den portadgo ninguno de sus libros, nin de sus cosas que troxieren pora si, e que estudien e vivan seguramiente e en paz en la cibdat de Sevilla. E mando e deffiendo firmemente que ninguno non sea ossado de facerles fuerza, nin tuerto, nin demas, ca qualquier que lo ficiese avrie mi ira e pecharmie en cotto mill moravedis e a ellos todo el danno doblado. Fecha la Carta en Burgos por mandado del Rey, veintiocho dias andados del mes de Deziembre en era de mill e docientos e noventa e dos años [...].

urge to convert them, and concerning this a certain vision was vouchsafed to him from heaven, in which it was revealed to him by the Lord that through the agency of the Friars of the Order of Preachers the conversion of many people among the infidels to the Catholic faith would be secured. Following this, and more afire than ever, St Raymond secured the establishment – with the permission of the Master of the Order and with the help of the Kings of Castile and Aragón – of a school for the study of Arabic, in which twenty or more Friars were taught in that language by his own efforts; from this there followed great benefits, for more than ten thousand Muslims were converted by the brethren who preached to them. Among the Muslims of Spain and also of Africa [Tunis] the truth of the Christian faith spread, and was so widely accepted, that many, especially the more learned among them, were disposed to accept the truth of Christianity, and of the Muslims who taught the friars Arabic nearly all were converted by the efforts of their students.

(b)

Let it be known to all who see this document that I King Alfonso by the grace of God [...], in my great desire to benefit and advance the interests of the noble city of Seville, to enrich it and to ennoble it further – since it is one of the greatest and best cities in Spain, and because my father the most honourable King Ferdinand who took it from the Moors and settled it with Christians for the glory and service of God and for the honour and benefit of all Christendom is buried there; and because I took part with him in conquering and settling it – I grant that there should be established there schools of Latin and Arabic. I order that the teachers and students who go to this college should be able to travel safely through all parts of my kingdom and my realm, with all their belongings, and that they should pay no toll on their books or on whatever they bring for their personal use; and that they should be able to study in safety and in peace in Seville. I absolutely forbid anyone to do them harm or wrong or injustice, and anyone that disobeys this shall suffer the penalties of the law and be fined a thousand *maravedís*, and shall further pay compensation to the victims of twice the value of the damage done. Given in Burgos by the King's order, on 28 December of Era 1292 [= AD 1254]. [...]

49. Prince Henry as mercenary commander (1261-65)

Several of Alfonso X's brothers caused him great grief. In the following extract one of them, Henry, escaped arrest for plotting against the monarch in 1259 and is recorded as an exile and mercenary commander in the service of Tunis from 1261 to 1265. Tunis was then at a high point of splendour and power under its Sultan Abu Abd Allah Muhammad, in part because it had received distinguished and wealthy Muslims who fled from al-Andalus after the loss of Valencia to the Aragonese in 1238, and Henry with his Christian fighting force of vassals and adventurers was evidently effective against N. African enemies of Tunis. Henry survived not only the threat from the lions in the present episode, but long years of fighting and intrigue in Italy and elsewhere, returning to Castile after the death of Sancho IV in 1295 to become, jointly with Queen Mary, tutor to the child-King Ferdinand IV. It is hard to know if one should call Henry a villain in what were villainous times, but he certainly had a knack of survival. As will be apparent from others of our texts, there was nothing exceptional about a Christian nobleman serving a Muslim ruler; Henry was in fact joined for a time in Tunis by his elder brother Fadrique.

En el seteno año del regnado del rey don Alfonso, que fue en la era de mill e docientos e noventa e siete años, e andaba el año de la nascencia de Jesu Cristo en mill e docientos e cincuenta e nueve años, el rey don Alfonso estava en Sevilla e el infante don Enrique estava en Lebrija, e dijeron al rey que el infante don Enrique tenía fecho fablas con algunos ricos homes e caballeros del reino en su deservicio. E por esto el Rey mandó a don Nuño que lo fuese a prender; e don Nuño salió de Sevilla, e llegando cerca de Lebrija, don Enrique sopo commo don Nuño iba a lo prender, a salió a él al campo, e ovieron pelea de consuno, e acaesció que amos a dos se firieron, e don Nuño fue ferido en el rostro e estúvose por vencer, ca don Enrique e los suyos peleaban muy fuerte, e a don Nuño cresció grand compaña que le envió el Rey. E don Enrique e los suyos ovieron a dejar el campo e tornar a Lebrija, e en esta noche partió dende e fue al Puerto de Santa María, e commo quier que el lugar non era aun poblado, estavan y navíos e entró en uno dellos, e fue por la mar a Cáliz, e falló y una nave que iva a Valencia, e fue en ella al regno de Aragón por cuanto estonces era vivo el rey don Jaimes, suegro del rey don Alfonso, e el rey don Jaimes non lo quiso y tener contra voluntad del rey don Alfonso, e mandóle que se fuese del regno. E por esto el infante don Enrique pidióle que le diese navíos en que fuese e que pasaría la mar, e el rey don Jaimes tóvolo por bien. E desde Barcelona pasó a Túnez, e el rey de Túnez acogióle muy bien porque sopo que era fijo de rey, e diole mucho de lo suyo, e moró con él y cuatro años. E en las peleas e contiendas que este rey de Túnez avía con los moros sus vecinos, este infante don Enrique serviale muy bien e avía muy grand fama e ardideza e

Our chronicle errs in saying that Henry sailed from Barcelona to Tunis. He was in London in July 1259, after being welcomed by his brother-in-law Edward of England (later King Edward I; married to Henry's sister Eleanor of Castile) in Gascony. Edward allowed him to fit out ships in Bayonne and Bordeaux, provided he did not use them to attack Alfonso X, and he went from one of these ports to Tunis.

Henry survived as a literary personage in the Conde Lucanor *by Don Juan Manuel, his nephew (see text 45). Tale 9 of this work tells of the horses of two knights in Prince Henry's company in Tunis, and actually concerns the same lion and courtyard as are present in our extract. Doubtless the lion existed; for a good literary precedent compare, however, the lion episode at the start of* Cantar III *of the* Poema de mio Cid *(itself with ample literary precedents). Later, a similar episode figures in* Palmerín de Oliva *(1534) and thence in* Don Quixote II.17.

The text is taken from the Crónica de Alfonso X *(chapter 8) published in the* Biblioteca de Autores Españoles, *vol. LXVI. The chronicle is thought to have been composed by Fernán Sánchez de Tovar (or de Valladolid), a jurist and Chancellor to King Alfonso XI, between 1340 and 1352.*

In the seventh year of the reign of King Alfonso [X], that is Era 1297 or AD 1259, King Alfonso was in Seville and Prince Henry was in Lebrija nearby, when it was reported to the King that Prince Henry was conspiring with certain noblemen and knights to do harm to the King. King Alfonso therefore ordered Don Nuño González de Lara to go and arrest him. Don Nuño left Seville and Prince Henry, realizing he was going to be arrested, went out to face him in the field. They did battle, and both were wounded; Don Nuño was wounded in the face and was about to be defeated, for Prince Henry and his men fought valiantly, even though Don Nuño's forces were augmented by a large company which the King had sent to join him. Prince Henry and his men left the field and returned to Lebrija, and that night he left and went to Puerto de Santa María; the place was not settled at that time, but even so there were ships there, and Prince Henry boarded one of them and went to Cadiz, where he found a ship that was going to Valencia. Prince Henry went in this ship to the Kingdom of Aragón, but King James of Aragón, father-in-law of King Alfonso, was still alive, and, not caring to act against the wishes of King Alfonso, ordered Prince Henry to leave his lands. Prince Henry asked the King to give him ships in which he could depart across the seas, and King James agreed. From Barcelona he went to Tunis, where the Sultan received him well, knowing that he was a king's son; he loaded him with gifts, and Henry stayed four years in his service. In the fights and battles which this Sultan of Tunis had against his Moorish neighbours, Prince Henry served the Sultan well and throughout those lands won great fame

grande prez de caballería en todas aquellas tierras. E los moros del regno de Túnez fablaron con el Rey e dijéronle que aquel infante cobraba mucho los corazones de las gentes de la tierra, e los contrarios que lo avían mucho miedo e que traían muchas gentes de cristianos, e destas cosas tales que se podía seguir muy grand daño e muy grand deservicio a aquel Rey, e que era menester que lo enviase del regno, ca él e las sus gentes eran para amparar e defender la su tierra sin él, e la defendieron otra vez. E commo quier que al rey de Túnez pesaba por esto que le decían del Infante, pero non pudo excusar de creer a los suyos, e cataron manera para lo enviar del regno. E recelaron que si el Rey ge lo dijese o ge lo mandase decir, que pornía algund alboroto en el regno o se iría para sus contrarios con aquellas gentes que allí tenía, e por esto que era bien de tener manera commo lo matasen. E porque non fallaron razón para lo facer, temiéndose de los suyos, que eran muy fuertes caballeros, acordaron que llamase el Rey al Infante a fabla en un corral en que metiesen y con él dos leones que estaban en un apartamiento, e aquéllos que lo matarían. E el consejo avido, pusiéronlo por obra, e luego el Rey mandó llamar a don Enrique a la fabla, e entró dentro en el corral do era consejado que entrase. E todas las gentes suyas que lo guardaban fincaron en otras casas por do iban entrando, que eran muy redradas dende. E el Infante, estando allí con el Rey, díjole el Rey que le esperase allí e que luego vernía allí a él; e salió el Rey de aquel lugar del corral, e por la otra parte salieron los dos leones a fiucia que lo matarían. E don Enrique sacó la espada que él traía consigo, que la non partía de sí, e tornó contra ellos, e los leones non fueron a él. E don Enrique fue a la puerta e salió del corral, e entre tanto que él estaba en esto, los moros prendieron todas las gentes de don Enrique. E desque él fue salido del corral, el Rey non quiso que lo matasen nin le quiso ver, e envióle a mandar que se fuese del regno, e don Enrique pidióle que le mandase soltar sus compañías, e el Rey mandó que soltasen muy pocos dellos, solamente los que avían pasado con él, ca de los cristianos que eran primero e le servían no soltaron ninguno. E don Enrique fuese para Roma a la guerra que avían los romanos contra los reyes de Pulla e de Calabria e el Conde de Provencia.

for bravery and for knightly deeds.

Eventually the Moors of the Kingdom of Tunis told their Sultan that the Prince was winning the hearts of the inhabitants, and those opposed to him said that all went in fear of the Prince, who was always bringing over new Christian fighting-men, from which great harm might come to the Sultan; the Prince should be sent away, since the local Moors were perfectly capable of defending the state without him, as they had done in the past. The Sultan of Tunis was much grieved by what was being said about the Prince, but he could hardly refuse to take seriously what his own men said; so they bethought themselves how they might send him away. They feared that if the Sultan made this known to the Prince, he might stir up some tumult in the state or go over to its enemies together with the men he had with him; so it was better to devise some way of killing him. Since they could find no reason to do this, and feared the Prince's men, who were all extremely hardened warriors, they resolved that the Sultan should invite the Prince to a consultation in a courtyard, and when he was there, they would release two lions kept in an adjoining place, which would kill him. This being agreed, they began to carry it out. The Sultan ordered the Prince to be called to the consultation, and he went into the courtyard as had been suggested. All his men who protected him were kept back in other rooms as they went in, and were as a result some distance from the courtyard. When the Prince had joined the Sultan the latter told him to wait there until he returned; the Sultan left the courtyard, while from another door there emerged the two lions, and everyone thought that they would kill the Prince for sure. Prince Henry was never without his sword, and he drew it, turning to face the lions. The lions did not attack him, and Prince Henry went to the doorway and got out of the courtyard. While he was doing this, the Moors arrested all Prince Henry's men. After Prince Henry got out of the courtyard, the Sultan refused to see him, but also did not care to order that he should be put to death; instead, he sent him a message to say that he should leave his kingdom. Prince Henry asked the Sultan to release his men, but the Sultan ordered the release of just a few of them, those who had originally come to Tunis with the Prince; they did not release those who had been in the country from the start and were in the service of Prince Henry. Henry left for Rome and took part in the wars which the Romans were waging against the rulers of Apulia and Calabria and the Count of Provence.

68

50. Cross-border allegiances (1271-73)

The case of Lorenzo Suárez, who when banished by his Christian monarch and feudal lord went to serve an infidel master (text 44), was hardly unique in respect of an individual, but the following extract describes such a defection or switch of allegiance by a large number of powerful men. Alfonso X's reign was plagued by revolts of the barons, some of them his relatives. As Hillgarth (I, p. 309) summarizes the events which concern our present text: 'In 1271 rebellion broke out, led by another of Alfonso's brothers, Don Felipe. Virtually all the leading nobles of Castile and León were in alliance against the King. They were intriguing with Portugal, Navarre, Granada, and Morocco. It was impossible to placate the rebels, who included a number of bishops.' The motives were the usual ones: complaints about the way royal favour was

(42) [...] Que ante que don Felipe e don Nuño e los ricos omes e infanzones e caballeros que iban con ellos entrasen en Granada, fueron fechas cartas entrellos, una en arábigo e otra en ladino, que decían así:

(43) (i) 'Sepan cuantos esta carta vieren commo nos Alamir Abboadille Mahomad Avenyuzaf Abenasar, rey de Granada, e Amir Amus Lemin, e nuestro fijo e nuestro heredero Alamir Abboadille, facemos este pleyto con el infante honrado don Felipe, fijo del rey don Ferrando, e con el rico ome don Nuño González, fijo del conde don Gonzalo, e con el rico ome don Lope Díaz de Haro, señor de Vizcaya, e con el rico ome don Esteban Fernández, e con el rico ome don Fernand Ruiz de Castro, e con el rico ome don Juan Núñez, fijo del rico ome don Nuño González, e con el rico ome don Diego López, hermano del rico ome don Lope Díaz de Haro, señor de Vizcaya, el sobre dicho, e con el rico ome don Gil Gómez de Roa, e con el rico ome don Ferrand Ruiz, fijo de Rodrigo Alvarez, e con el rico ome Lope de Mendoza.

(ii) E yo el infante don Felipe, el sobre dicho, e estos ricos omes sobre dichos, somos ayuntados sobre esto, que vos facemos a vos, Rey de Granada, e Amir Amus Lemin, e a vuestro fijo Alamir Abboadille, pleito omenaje a buena fe, sin mal engaño que vos lo tengamos, e cuando non vos lo toviésemos, que valiésemos por ello menos contra Dios e contra todos los omes del mundo, commo quien falsa pleito omenaje.

(iii) E sobresto es el pleito e omenaje que vos facemos, que vos fagades a don Alfonso, rey de Castilla, que vos tenga los pleitos e las posturas que vos fizo en Alcalá de Benzaide, e si vos las non toviere, que nos los sobre dichos que vos ayudemos con nuestros cuerpos e con nuestros omes e con nuestro poder en la guerra que oviéredes con él.

(iv) E si sobre esto, don Alfonso, rey de Castilla, vos toviere los pleitos sobre dichos que fueron entre vos e él en Alcalá de Benzaide, que vos el Rey de Granada e vuestro fijo Alamir Abboadille, que le tengades aquellas posturas que posistes con él en Alcalá de Benzaide, sin acrescentamiento ninguno.

distributed; the need to defend seigneurial privileges against the centralizing tendencies of the monarchy; the feeling that the Crown favoured the towns at the expense of the nobility; and so on, with the addition of possible alarm at the monarch's interest in legal reform.

The text is taken from the same source as 49, pp. 32–33. The King of Granada at the time was Muhammad I (1238–73). His title 'Amir Amus Lemin' is a version of 'Almiramomelim' and similar found in our other texts such as 37. At the end of our account the Christian knights in Granada influence the succession to the throne in favour of his son (to whom in this document they had earlier sworn allegiance) as Muhammad II, who was to rule until 1302.

Within both the Spanish and English texts I have inserted numbered subdivisions for greater clarity, as in a modern treaty.

(42) [...] Before Prince Philip and Don Nuño and the noblemen and knights who were with them entered Granada, an agreement was made between them, one copy being in Arabic and the other in Romance, in the following terms:

(43) (i) 'To all who see this agreement: We, Muhammad I, King of Granada, Commander of the Faithful, and our son and heir Al'Amir Abu Adille, make this agreement with the honoured Prince Philip, son of King Ferdinand, and with the nobleman Don Nuño González, son of Count Gonzalo, and with the nobleman Don Lope Díaz de Haro, Lord of Vizcaya, and with the nobleman Don Esteban Fernández, and with the nobleman Don Fernando Ruiz de Castro, and with the nobleman Don Juan Núñez, son of the nobleman Don Nuño González, and with the nobleman Don Diego López, brother of Don Lope Díaz de Haro, Lord of Vizcaya the aforementioned, and with the nobleman Don Gil Gómez de Roa, and with the nobleman Don Fernando Ruiz, son of Rodrigo Alvarez, and with the nobleman Lope de Mendoza.

(ii) I, Prince Philip, the aforementioned, and the noblemen aforementioned, are agreed upon the following: we make to you, the King of Granada, Commander of the Faithful, and to your son Al'Amir Abu Adille, our sincere submission of vassalage, without any deceit; and if we should not hold to this, may we be considered traitors in the eyes of God and all men, as persons who have broken their bond.

(iii) The agreement and vassalage has the following basis: that you should oblige King Alfonso of Castile to keep to the agreements he made with you in Alcalá de Benzaide, and if he does not keep them, we the aforementioned will help you with our persons and our men and our power in the war that you may wage against him.

(iv) And if in this matter King Alfonso of Castile does keep to the agreements made between you and him in Alcalá de Benzaide, you the King of Granada and your son will also keep the agreements you made with him in Alcalá de Benzaide, without any change.

(v) E yo el infante don Felipe e estos omes buenos sobre dichos otorgamos que non fagamos paz nin avenencia ninguna con el Rey de Castilla a menos de vos, e esta avenencia que sea en días de don Alonso, rey de Castilla.

(vi) E yo el infante don Felipe, el sobre dicho, otorgo por mí que tenga este pleito omenaje en días del rey don Alonso e del infante don Fernando e del que fuere su heredero, así commo es nombrado, e el privillegio que fue fecho en Alcalá de Benzaide.

(vii) E yo el infante don Felipe e estos omes buenos sobre dichos otorgamos que vos ayudemos contra todos los omes del mundo, cristianos e moros, en guerra o en paz.

(viii) E nos, el rey de Granada, Amir Amus Lemin, e nuestro fijo Alamir Abboadille, otorgamos que cuando oviéremos menester vuestra ayuda, que vos enviemos con quien podades venir a nuestra ayuda.

(ix) E yo el infante don Felipe, e estos omes buenos sobre dichos, otorgamos todos e somos tenudos que fagamos por vos, rey de Granada, Amir Amus Lemin, e por vuestro fijo Alamir Abboadille, así commo fecimos por el rey de Castilla cuando éramos sus vasallos en todas las cosas del mundo que vos ayades menester mientra fuéremos convusco.

(x) E yo el infante don Felipe e estos omes buenos sobre dichos, otorgamos que vos seamos amigos para siempre jamás, e a vuestros fijos e a vuestros nietos e a los que de vos vinieren.

(xi) E nos Alamir Abboadille Aben Yuzaf Abenasar, rey de Granada, e Amir Amus Lemin, e nuestro fijo Alamir Abboadille, otorgamos a vos el mucho honrado infante don Felipe e a los ricos omes sobre dichos, sobre esto que somos tenudos, e vos facemos pleito omenaje a buena fe, sin mal engaño, si vos tomare el rey de Castilla la tierra que tenedes dél, o vuestras heredades, o vos desaforare, que seamos tenudos de vos ayudar con nuestras tierras, e con nuestros omes e con nuestro poder a guerrealle.

(xii) E si viniéredes a nos, que sea la nuestra guerra una, e si fincáredes en vuestra tierra, que guerreedes vos de vuestro cabo e nos del nuestro, e si acaesciere que vengades a nos, que fagamos contra vos segund ficimos en aquel tiempo cuando venistes a nos.

(xiii) E este pleito e este omenaje tenervos lo emos, e si non vos lo toviéremos, que valgamos menos por ello contra Dios e contra todos los omes del mundo, así commo quien falsa pleito omenaje.

(xiv) E nos el Rey de Granada Amir Amus Lemin, e nuestro fijo Alamir Abboadille, otorgamos a vos, infante don Felipe, e a los ricos omes sobre dichos, que non fagamos con el rey de Castilla paz nin postura a menos de vos.

(xv) E otrosí otorgamos nos el rey de Granada e nuestro fijo que si tomáremos a don Alfonso, rey de Castilla, villas e castillos de hoy adelante, que seamos tenudos de gelo tornar cuando fuere la paz con él.

(xvi) E yo el infante don Felipe e estos ricos omes sobre dichos somos tenudos que si el rey de Castilla vos tomare villas o castillos de hoy adelante, que

(v) I, Prince Philip, and these aforementioned persons agree that we will not make peace nor any pact whatsoever with the King of Castile except with your concurrence; and this agreement is to last for the lifetime of King Alfonso of Castile.

(vi) I, the aforementioned Prince Philip, promise to observe this vassalage during the lifetime of King Alfonso and of Prince Ferdinand and of him who is his heir, depending on whomever is nominated, and for the duration of the agreement made in Alcalá de Benzaide.

(vii) I, Prince Philip, and the aforementioned persons promise to help you against everybody, both Christians and Moors, in war and in peace.

(viii) And we, King of Granada, Commander of the Faithful, and our son Al'Amir Abu Adille, agree that ,when we have need of your help, we shall send for you to come with whatever strength you can command.

(ix) I, Prince Philip, and the aforementioned nobles promise to act for you [...] just as we did for the King of Castile when we were his vassals in all matters needful while we are with you.

(x) I, Prince Philip, and the aforementioned nobles promise to be friends of yours for ever, and to your children and grandchildren and other descendants.

(xi) We, the King of Granada, [...] promise you, most honourable Prince Philip, and the aforementioned noblemen, in this matter [...] in all sincerity [...] that if the King of Castile should take the lands you hold from him, or your estates, or if he should offend you, we will be obliged to help you with our lands, our men, and our power, and to make war on him.

(xii) If you come to join us, let us be as one on our side of the war. If you remain on your lands, you will make war in your region as we shall in ours. If it should happen that you come to join us, we shall act as we did on that earlier occasion when you came to us.

(xiii) We shall observe this treaty of vassalage, and if we do not, may we be considered traitors in the eyes of God and all men, as persons who have broken their bond.

(xiv) We, the King of Granada, [...] agree [...] that we will not make with the King of Castile any peace or pact except with your concurrence.

(xv) We, the King of Granada, and our son further agree that if in future we should take towns and castles from King Alfonso of Castile, we shall be obliged to return them to him when peace is made with him.

(xvi) I, Prince Philip, and the aforementioned nobles agree that if the King of Castile should take from you towns or castles in future, we will persuade him

fagamos que vos los dé cuando fuere la paz.

(xvii) E nos el rey de Granada e nuestro fijo vos otorgamos que cuando quier que ayamos guerra con el rey de Castilla e viniéredes a nos, que fagamos contra vos así commo fecimos este tiempo; e más, otorgamos a vos el dicho infante e ricos omes que vos seamos siempre amigos a vos e a vuestros fijos e a vuestros nietos e a los que de vos vinieren.

(xviii) E nos el rey de Granada Amir Amus Lemin e nuestro fijo Alamir Abboadille, porque sea firme e non venga en dubda, escrebimos en esta carta letra de nuestras manos. E yo el infante don Felipe e los ricos omes sobre dichos posimos en ella nuestros sellos colgados.'

Después que estas posturas fueron firmadas entre el Infante e los ricos omes con el rey de Granada, fueron a Granada, e el Rey e sus fijos saliéronlos a rescebir con muchas compañas, e entraron todos en la cibdad, e diéronles posadas e viandas e las otras cosas que ovieron menester muy complidamente, e moraron y pocos días. E luego el rey de Granada rogóles que fuesen facer mal e daño al arrayaz de Guadix. E el Infante e los ricos omes e los caballeros que fueron y con ellos, tomaron viandas e las otras cosas que ovieron menester, e fueron facer guerra al arrayaz, e llegaron a la villa de Guadix e moraron y un mes talando las huertas e faciéndoles mal e daño. E el arrayaz e los que estaban con él defendianse cuanto ellos podían; así que el mal no era tanto de que el arrayaz se sintiese mucho apremiado; e luego que y llegaron aquellas compañías, el arrayaz se envió querellar desto al rey don Alfonso, e el Rey envió a los ricos omes su mandadero, con quien les envió decir que cuanto dapño ficiesen al arrayaz su vasallo, que de los sus bienes gelo entregaría; e esto excusó gran parte del mal que pudieran facer al arrayaz. E porque el rey de Granada era muy viejo e estaba flaco de dolencia, envióles decir e rogar que se viniesen para Granada, e a pocos días que allí llegaron, finó el rey Abboadille. E los ricos omes de Castilla e de León que eran en Granada ficiéronle mucha honra, ca ellos lo levaron a soterrar, e algunos de los moros non quisieron tomar por rey a Alamir Abboadille su fijo, ca tenían muchos dellos con otro su hermano. E algunos querían tomar uno de los arrayaces de Málaga o de Guadix por los tirar del vasallaje del rey don Alfonso, e los ricos omes de Castilla e de León tomaron su voz de Alamir Abboadille, e ficieron que fuese Rey.

to return them to you when peace is made.

(xvii) We, the King of Granada, and our son agree that whenever there is war with the King of Castile and you come to join us, we will act towards you as we did on that earlier occasion. Furthermore, we promise you the Prince and the aforementioned noblemen to be friends of yours for ever, and of your children and grandchildren and other descendants.

(xviii) We, the King of Granada, and [...] set this down in writing with our own hands, in order that its contents should be secure and not placed in doubt. We, Prince Philip and the aforementioned noblemen, placed our seals upon it.'

As soon as these agreements were signed between the Prince and the noblemen and the King of Granada, they went to Granada, and the King and his sons came out with many of their men to greet them; everybody went into the city, where they were generously provided with lodgings and food and other necessities, and they stayed there several days. Then the King of Granada asked them to go and attack the governor of Guadix. The Prince and the noblemen and knights who were with them took provisions and other necessities and went off to make war on the governor. They reached Guadix and spent a month there chopping down the orchards and doing them every kind of harm. The governor and his men defended themselves as best they could, so that the damage done was not so great that the governor should feel himself greatly harmed. When the company of Christians first reached Guadix, the governor sent a complaint about it to King Alfonso, and the King sent his messenger to the noblemen to say that for however much damage they might do to the governor who was his vassal, he [King Alfonso] would compensate him for it out of their properties. This prevented a good deal of the damage which they might have done to the governor. Since the King of Granada was very old and weakened by illness, he sent to beg them to return to Granada; and soon after they had reached the city, King Muhammad died [22 January 1273]. The noblemen of Castile and León who were in Granada did him great honour, for they carried his coffin to its burial. Some of the Moors did not wish to accept Al'Amir Abu Adille his son as King, for many of them favoured a brother of his. Others again wished to have as King one of the governors of Málaga or Guadix, in order to draw them away from their vassalage to King Alfonso; but the noblemen of Castile and León gave their support to Al'Amir Abu Adille, and made him King.

51. Ramon Llull learns Arabic

It is impossible in a short note to give much idea of the extraordinary life and qualities of Ramon Llull (1235–1316): the man is a whole branch of study in himself. He was born in Majorca of good family and led a worldly early life, being married and having children, and writing troubadour poetry; but one night while writing a love-song to a lady, his eye fell on the crucifix over his bed, and he underwent a dramatic conversion. From that moment his intense preoccupations were the reform of the Church, opposition to the rationalist tendencies of theology, and the conversion of Islam. He travelled tirelessly, bombarded the Pope and any other authority who would listen with plans and proposals, lectured and preached, and wrote – it is said – 243 books on a vast range of topics; some of these were so eloquent and influential that Llull counts as a major formative influence upon Catalán prose. Realizing that to convert

(11) Cumque venisset illuc, relictis ritibus sollempnioribus, quibus usque tunc usus erat, assumpsit sibi vilem habitum de panno quod ipse invenire poterat grossiore, et sic in eadem civitate didicit parum de gramatica, emptoque sibi ibidem quodam Sarraceno linguam Arabicam didicit ab eodem. Deinde post annos novem contigit quod Sarracenus ille, Raymundo quadam die absente, nomen Christi blasphemaret; quod cum reversus cognovit Raymundus ab hiis qui blasphemiam audiverant, nimio fidei zelo motus percussit illum Sarracenum in ore, fronte ac facie. Sarracenus vero rancore nimio inde concepto ex tunc cepit mente tractare, quomodo dominum suum posset occidere.

(12) Cumque ipse clam procurato sibi gladio quadam die videret sedentem dominum suum solum, irruit in eum subito, simul ipsum predicto gladio percussiens, et cum rugitu terribili acclamans: 'Tu mortuus es.' Sed Raymundus, licet tunc ferientis brachium, quo tunc gladius tenebatur, ut Deo placuit, aliqualiter repulisset, vulnus tamen grave, licet non letale, super stomacum ex ferientis ictu recepit; prevalens tamen ipse viribus, illum Sarracenum sibi substravit, gladiumque violenter abstulit ab eodem. Deinde accurrente familia, prohibuit Raymundus, ne Sarracenum interficerent; permisit tamen quod ligatum ponerent in carcere, donec ipse deliberasset apud se, quid de illo foret potissime faciendum; severum namque visum sibi fuit illum perimere, quo docente sibi lingam multum optatam, scilicet Arabicam, iam sciebat; dimittere vero illum vel tenere diutius metuebat, sciens quod ipse non cessaret ex tunc in mortem ipsius machinari.

(13) Perplexus igitur circa istud, ascendit ad abbatiam quandam, que prope erat, orans ibidem Dominum super hac re instantissime per tres dies; quibus completis, admirans quod adhuc in corde suo pretacta perplexitate remanente, Dominus, ut sibi videbatur, ipsius orationem nullatenus exaudisset, mestus ad domum suam rediit; cumque illuc veniens se divertisset ad carcerem, ut suum captivum inviseret, invenit, quod ipse fune, quo ligatus fuit, iugulaverat semet-

Muslims he would need to be able to preach in Arabic, he learned it (as in the text which follows) and founded with papal authorization a religious house and college at Miramar in Majorca, securing funding for thirteen Franciscans to study Arabic and train as missionaries there (1276). Llull himself went to Tunis to preach, in perilous circumstances, and later he went to Bougie, where many believed that he was killed as a direct result of his efforts to preach.

The anonymous Latin Vita *of Llull from which our text is taken concludes in 1311; its materials were, the writer claims, dictated to him by Llull himself. Several manuscripts are extant, and an early Catalán version was made. The Latin text is edited by B. de Gaiffier in* Analecta Bollandiana, *48 (1930), 130-78. For notes on this aspect of Llull, see Norman Daniel,* Islam and the West *(Edinburgh, 1958), passim, with a list of Llull's most relevant works on p. 402; also Kedar, pp. 189-99.*

(11) When he returned from there [Paris], he put aside the stylish kind of clothing which he had up to that time worn and put on a dress of coarse cloth which he had found somewhere. Then, in Majorca, he studied a little Latin and learned Arabic from a certain Moor he had bought [i.e. as a slave]. After nine years it happened that, one day when Ramon was away, the Moor blasphemed against the name of Christ; when on his return Ramon learned about this from those who had heard the blasphemy, he was deeply moved by feelings for his faith and struck the Moor on the mouth, the forehead, and the face. From then on the Moor was very resentful about this, and began to plan means whereby he might kill his master.

(12) After this man had secretly obtained a sword, he saw his master sitting alone one day, and suddenly rushed at him, striking at him with the sword and shouting with a terrible roar: 'I'll kill you!' However, it pleased God that Ramon was able to catch the arm that was wielding the sword; nevertheless, he received a rather serious wound in the stomach. He then was able with his strength to overpower the Moor and to snatch the sword from him. When his family rushed in, Ramon was able to prevent them from killing the man, but he did allow them to carry the man off, bound, to prison, while he debated with himself what could best be done about the matter. It seemed too cruel to him to have the man killed, for Ramon had learned Arabic, so long desired, from him as a teacher; he was nervous about sending him away or keeping him near any longer, knowing that the man would not stop trying to plot his death.

(13) So, perplexed about this, he went to a certain abbey nearby, and there prayed earnestly to God for three days. After that, surprised to find the perplexity still in his mind, and thinking that God, as it seemed to him, had not heard his prayer, he sadly headed for home. Then he turned aside to go and see his slave in the prison, and found that the man had hanged himself with the very

ipsum. Reddidit ergo ʀaymundus gracias Deo, letus, qui et a nece predicti Sarraceni servaverat manus eius innoxias, et eum a perplexitate illa gravi, pro qua paulo ante ipsum anxius exoraverat, liberaverat.

same rope with which he had been tied up.   Ramon therefore cheerfully gave thanks to God, for on the one side he had clean hands in the matter of the Moor's death, while on the other he was free of that grave perplexity about which he had shortly before so earnestly prayed.

52. The education of a prince (1293)

The Castigos e documentos del Rey Don Sancho *are an extensive text, precisely dated at start and end, and have long been known but very little studied. 'Castigos' are 'pieces of advice, counsel', which King Sancho IV of Castile-León (1284-95) ostensibly addresses to his son who was to succeed him as Ferdinand IV (1295-1312). The work thus falls into the well-known category of 'mirror of princes' literature, but in its extent and diversity of materials is more a sort of moralizing encyclopedia. Although King Sancho on many occasions uses the first person, it is hardly likely that the work is truly his; probably, a team of clerics composed it and submitted it for royal approval.*

The basis of the present extracts is the passage of Lucas de Tuy (1236) as adapted for and absorbed into the Estoria de España *of Alfonso X (see text 1). The reference to Muhammad's 'dolencia mala', epilepsy, that is the unhealthy condition of the brain which in part gave rise to his revolutionary religious ideas, may be traced to the same source. The passage said to be taken from 'a chronicle of Muhammad' is found in only one of the surviving MSS and retails*

Otrosy, mio fijo, non quieras contar la mora por muger, mas cuentala por bestia, ca non ha ley ninguna, que Mahomad el su maestro, que les dio mala creençia en que ellos estan por tal de meter mas la gente en aquellas cosas que la nuestra ley da por pecado e por mal vso, es a ellos por saluaçion; e las que nos damos por saluaçion es a ellos por pecado. E los moros non han otra creençia sinon aquel que mas puede soltar la su carrne a los sabores del mundo, aquel tienen por mas saluo.

E por tal de poder mantener la onrra que le fezieron quando lo alçaron por cabdillo e por maestro e por sennor de todas aquellas gentes que fueron de aquella çibdat donde el predicaua. E dezia muchas mentiras e vanidades por consejo del diablo, por tal de los traer a creer la maldat en que oy dia viuen, deziendo que era mensajero de Dios, e era lo contrallo, ca era mensajero del diablo; e que el angel Grauiel lo guiaua e le mostraua todas las cosas que dezia, e era el diablo que le asonbraua, e la dolençia mala que el auia en su cuerpo, la qual adelante declararemos. De lo qual se lee en una coronica suya que un clerigo que ouo muy grant fama de sabidoria ouo de yr a Roma por alcançar onor, lo qual non pudo auer, e fuyo dende muy sannudo e paso a ultramar e començo a fazer infintosamente muy santa vida, symulada e fiera, e desta guisa troxo a sy muy grant gente, en lo qual ouo de auer grant amistança con Mahomad. E dixole: 'Yo fare en guisa que tu seas sennor deste pueblo'. E començo a criar vna paloma, la qual cada que auia de comer ponianle trigo en las orejas de Mahomad, e alli comia fasta que se fartaua, e dende bolaua e

Christian inventions of the usual prejudiced kind. Thus the idea that the Prophet was instructed by a renegade Christian cleric can be traced back to the writings of the very first Christian polemicist against Islam, St John of Damascus, who was born about 670: he wrote of the influence of an Arian monk (Sergius, a Nestorian of Byzantium, in later texts) on Muhammad, probably adapting the early Muslim tradition that Bahira recognized the special genius of the young Muhammad and foretold his destiny. As for the tale of the grains of wheat, this is also in line with other accounts of bogus miracles attributed by Christian adversaries to Muhammad; in other versions, a bull or calf or camel is trained to come at Muhammad's call. Finally, the effort to strengthen prejudice by detailed mention of sexual aspects is all too typical, perhaps almost a constant in popular belief about races and religions viewed in a hostile way: such things pertain more to the social psychologist and anthropologist than to the historian or literary scholar.

The extracts are taken from the edition of Agapito Rey (Bloomington, 1952), pp. 128-30.

Furthermore, my son, you should not consider a Moorish woman as a woman at all, but rather as a beast, for she keeps no law other than that of her master Muhammad; he gave them that evil faith in which they live, in order to plunge them deeper into those things which our Law considers sinful and bad, but which for them counts towards salvation, while what we consider good for our salvation is to them a sin. The Moors have no belief other than that which can best free their flesh for the enjoyment of worldly pleasures, and that is what they most prize.

They do this also in order to maintain Muhammad in that honour which they showed him when they raised him up as their leader and master over all the people who were in the city in which he preached. He spoke many lies and vain things on the advice of the devil, in order to bring them to believe the evil in which they live today, saying that he was the messenger of God, whereas the contrary was true, for he was the messenger of the devil; he also said that the Archangel Gabriel was guiding him and instructing him in what he said, whereas it was the devil who had blinded him, aided by the evil malady he had in his body [epilepsy], as we shall describe later. Concerning this, we read in a chronicle about Muhammad that a cleric who enjoyed a great reputation for learning went to Rome in order to seek preferment, but, failing to obtain this, he departed from there in a rage and went to the Middle East, where he pretended to live a most holy life, making a convincing show of it, and in this way drew to himself a great many people, among whom was Muhammad with whom he formed a close friendship. The cleric said to him: 'I will bring it about that you shall be lord over this people.' The cleric began to train a dove, placing grains of wheat in Muhammad's ears whenever the bird wished to eat, and there it ate until it was sated, when it took flight and went off, returning whenever it felt

iuase, e tornauase quando auia fanbre. E a cabo de grandes tienpos que esta paloma fue costunbrada todavia el clerigo predicaua al pueblo deziendo: 'Yo vos mostrare por graçia del Espiritu Santo al vuestro sennor profeta de Dios, el qual ante vuestros ojos le veredes fablar con el.' E un dia fizoles ayuntar en uno en una muy grand plaça estando faziendo oraçion a Dios que les enviase el su Espiritu Santo en aquella persona santa que fuese su sennor e su cabdillo dellos, para que todos le obedeçiesen e feziesen su mandamiento, asi commo profeta e mensajero de Dios; entre las quales gentes estaua Mahomad asentado. E commo el maldito clerigo vido que estauan todos sosegados e enbeuidos en la su oraçion, solto la paloma, que habia grant gana de comer, e fuese a sentar, commo lo habia acostunbrado, en los honbros de Mahomad, e metiol el pico en las orejas e començo de comer lo que y fallo, commo solia. E desque todo el pueblo vido lo que la paloma fazia, fueron muy marauillados, e el maldito clerigo dixo: 'Amigos, catad aqui vuestro sennor que Dios vos ensenna por la su paloma, que es el su Espiritu Santo, e a el creed de todo lo que vos dixiere.' E luego todos le besaron las manos y los pies e la ropa commo a home santo. [...]

E todas las partes ayunto Mahomad, e fizo el libro que se dize el Alcoran. E las cosas revoluio las vnas con otras, ca por el bautismo del agua santa que los cristianos auemos, sin la qual non podemos ser linpios de pecado, dio el por bautismo vnas palabras que se dizen en algarabia: 'xihedo leylle hirala, xihedo Mahomad arraçorolla', que quieren dezir: 'Non hay otro sinon Dios, e Mahomad, su mensajero'. E mas, que mando que todos se lauasen en agua, espeçialmente quantas vegadas pasare a la muger, tantas vegadas manda que se laue con agua. Eso mesmo dando muchas graçias e solturas a las carnes de deleytes, plazeres. E afirma e dize que los moros todos han de yr a parayso, e han de comer miel e leche e manteca e bunnuelos, e han de auer muchas moças. E bien podemos dezir que si asi fuese, que la vianda que faze distinçion e estiercol, que en tal parayso aura fedor; e pues non es de creer que parayso sea do se faga forniçio e aya fedor. E lo que los cristianos dan por malo e por pecado, dalo el por bueno e por saluaçion; e lo que damos por saluaçion, dalo el por pecado.

hungry. After a long time of training the bird in this way the cleric preached again to the people, saying: 'By the grace of the Holy Spirit I will reveal your lord and prophet of God to you, and you will see the Spirit speaking to him before your eyes.' One day he called them all together in a great square and made them all pray that God would send His Holy Spirit down upon that person who was to be lord and leader over them, in order that all should obey him and do his command, as to a prophet and messenger of God; and among these people Muhammad was seated. When the accursed cleric saw that everybody was calm and absorbed in their prayers, he released the dove, which was extremely hungry, and the bird flew to settle on Muhammad's shoulder, as it had been trained to do, and it put its beak into his ears and began to eat what it found there, as usual. When the people observed what the bird was doing they were amazed, and the accursed priest said: 'My friends, behold here your lord, whom God is pointing out to you by means of His dove, which is His Holy Spirit. You should believe everything that he will tell you.' Then everyone kissed Muhammad's hands and feet and clothing, as those of a holy man. [...]

Muhammad assembled all these elements and made the book called the Koran. He mixed things up, since in place of the baptism with holy water which we Christians have, without which we cannot be free from sin, he gave as his form of baptism words which are, in Arabic: 'xihedo leylle hirala, xihedo Mahomad arraçorolla', which mean: 'There is no God but Allah, and Muhammad is his messenger.' Moreover, he ordered that everyone should wash in water, and in particular that every time a man has intercourse with a woman, he should wash himself with water. At the same time he gave many indulgences for the pleasures of the flesh. He declares that all Muslims will go to paradise, where they will eat honey and milk and butter and cakes, and have many virgin girls. To this we might reply that if things were so arranged, such luxurious foods produce dung, so that paradise would stink; and of course it is not credible that paradise should be a place of fornication and stinks. Those things which Christians consider evil and sinful, he considers goodly and beneficial for salvation; and what we think beneficial for salvation, he considers sinful.

53. The 'Siete partidas'

The famous law-code long attributed in its entirety to a team of experts working from 1256 to 1265 under the direction of Alfonso X of Castile (the initial letters of its seven parts indeed making up the name 'Alfonso') may, according to recent research, have been completed after the monarch's death. However that may be, this and other legal works remain impressive monuments to his urge for reform and logical codification, and it seems to be agreed that the Partidas *largely reflect the code of the* Espéculo *completed under Alfonso in 1255. In many aspects, after revision down the centuries, the* Partidas *form the basis of Spanish law today.*

In Partida II, Title 29 *has several laws concerning captives, clearly a substantial enough group at the time to require legislation. While they are in enemy hands their property at home is to be protected, the rights of a child born to a mother who conceived before her husband was captured have to be considered, and in our extract (II.29.7) other possibilities have to be borne in mind, including the (by no means rare?) case that a man's relatives made no effort to secure his release and that he formed a liaison with a Moorish woman. In* II.30, *laws 1 to 3 define in great detail the important office of* alfaqueque, *the ransomer concerned with cross-border negotiations, who will be seen in*

(II.29.7) Preñada seyendo la muger quando la cativasen, maguer pariese en tierra de los enemigos, quando quier que saliese de poder dellos, el fijo o la fija que allá nasciese debe seer rescebido en los bienes quel pertenescen de su padre o de su madre; et haber en salvo su derecho en todas las cosas bien así como si fuese nascido en su casa dellos. Et si por aventura acaesciese que cativasen marido et muger en uno, et yaciendo en cativo se empreñase ella de su marido, si después desto saliesen de poder de los enemigos de so uno, et el fijo o la fija con ellos, debe haber su derecho en todas cosas también como si fuese engendrado et nascido en tierra de cristianos; et si el fijo saliere de cativo con el uno tan solamente con el padre o con la madre, en los bienes de aquel con quien viene es heredero et le fincan en salvo todos sus derechos en ellos; mas en los bienes de aquel que finca en cativo non ha que veer, fueras ende si después deso saliese el otro de poder de los enemigos et lo conosciesen que era su fijo. Otra manera hi ha aun por que tovieron por bien los antiguos que pudiese el fijo heredar los bienes de su padre: et esto serie quando acaesciese quel que yoguiese en cativo fuese desfiuzado que nol querien sacar ende aquellos que eran tenudos de lo facer, et él con cuita de salir de aquella prisión hobiese fijo dalguna muger de aquella ley quel prometiese sacallo della, si después de la promesa lo sacase et saliese ella con él, et el fijo o la fija con la madre o sin ella, si aquel que salió de la prisión seyendo en su poder lo conosciese por su fijo o por su fija, et le tornase de su ley et mostrase que sus herederos non lo quisieran sacar de cativo pudiéndolo facer. [...]

real-life operation in text 64.

Our other text is from Partida *VII, which concerns what we would nowadays define as the criminal law. Jews and Muslims are inevitably, one regrets to say, included here. Much that is said about Jews living in Christian communities in Title 24 is applied automatically to Muslims in lands of the Castilian Crown in Title 25. Within this latter Title, several laws (after an opening definition of 'moro') deal with aspects of religious conversion, while 9 guarantees the safety of Moorish messengers. Law 10, here reproduced in full, expresses the peculiar horror felt – at least by the guardians of the nation's morals – about sexual contacts across the religious divide. All one can say about it is that presumably the contacts were sufficiently common for a law to be needed, but also that nobody seems to have documented a trial arising out of them in the 13th century, still less any instance of a public stoning.*

The texts are taken from the edition of the Partidas *by the Real Academia de la Historia (Madrid, 1807, 3 vols). On the dating of the* Partidas *in final form to the period 1290-95, see A. Garcia Gallo in* Archivo de Historia del Derecho Español, *46 (1976), 609-70, answered by J.R. Craddock in favour of the traditional dating in the same journal, 51 (1981), 365-418.*

(II.29.7) If a woman is pregnant when captured and gives birth in enemy territory, later being able to return home, the son or daughter that has been born should enter into ownership of the property which is due to come to him or her from the father or mother; and should enjoy his or her rights in all things just as if born in the parental home. If it should happen that father and mother are captured together, and that the woman should become pregnant by her husband while in captivity, and if they afterwards leave captivity bringing their son or daughter with them, that child should have his or her rights in all things too, just as if he or she had been conceived and born in Christian lands. If the child should leave captivity with one parent only, the father or the mother, the child shall inherit the property of that parent with whom he or she is living, and has all his or her rights over such property guaranteed; but the child has no concern with the property of the parent who remains in captivity, unless that other parent later leaves captivity and both parents acknowledge the child as theirs. There remains a further way in which ancient authorities held that the child could inherit his father's property. This is when the man who is held captive comes to believe that those at home who should be trying to secure his release are not making any effort to do so, and he in his desperation to be free has a child by some woman of the other faith who has promised to help him to freedom: if after such a promise she manages to achieve this, and comes home with the man, the son or daughter accompanying her or without her, provided the man so freed acknowledges the child as his and converts him or her to Christianity and is able to prove that the other heirs did nothing to secure his release even though they

(VII.25.10) Si el moro yoguiere con cristiana virgen, mandamos quel apedreen por ello; et ella por la primera vegada que lo ficiere, pierda la meytad de sus bienes, et herédelos el padre o la madre della, o el abuelo o la abuela si los hobiere; et si non los hobiere háyalos el rey. Et por la segunda pierda todo quanto hobiere, et herédenlo los sobredichos herederos si los hobiere; et si non los hobiere, herédelos el rey, et ella muera por ello; eso mesmo mandamos de la vibda que esto ficiere. Et si yoguiere con cristiana casada sea apedreado por ello, et ella sea metida en poder de su marido que la queme, o la suelte, o faga della lo que quisiere. Et si yoguiere con muger baldonada que se dé a todos, por la primera vez azótenlos de so uno por la villa, et por la segunda vegada que mueran por ello.

were in a position to do so. [...]

(VII.25.10) If a Moor should lie with a Christian virgin, he should be stoned to death for it; and she, the first time, should lose one half of her property, this passing to her father or mother, or to her grandfather or grandmother if they are alive; if they are not alive, the property passes to the Crown. For the second offence she should forfeit all that she has, the property passing to the persons aforementioned, if alive, and if they are not, it passes to the Crown; and she should be put to death. The same applies to a widow who acts in this way. If a Moor lies with a married Christian woman he should be stoned to death, and she should be placed in the hands of her husband, who may burn her to death, or set her free, or do with her whatever he wishes. If the Moor lies with a prostitute who makes herself available to all, for the first offence they should be tied together and whipped through the town, and for a second offence they should both be killed.

54. Christian and infidel in alliance (1309)

The last years of the 13th century and early years of the 14th were a time of much military action and of cynically-formed alliances involving Aragón, Castile, Granada, and Morocco. What was at stake was the control of the coastal cities and fortresses from Tarifa and Gibraltar in the west to Almería in the east, or more widely, control of the Strait, since the fortress-city of Ceuta on the Moroccan coast (snatched by the King of Granada from the Sultan of Morocco in 1306) was involved also. The Aragonese were clearly able to play a major part on the military side as in our text with the offer of a naval and cavalry force to be hired out to help the Sultan of Morocco retake Ceuta (in the outcome, the King of Granada rapidly did a deal with the Moroccans by which he surrendered Ceuta to them in exchange for help in other enterprises, 1309). However, their chief concern was to ensure the continuation of good relations with Morocco. While the Castilians were concerned with land, booty, annual tributes, and carrying the crusading war against Islam to North Africa, the maritime and mercantile Catalans who constituted the most active segment of the

I

Al muy alto, e muy noble, e muy poderoso rey Aborrabe, miramomelin de Marruecos, don Jayme, por la graçia de Dios, rey de Aragon, de Valençia, de Serdenya, de Corsega, cuende de Barçelona e de la santa eglesia de Roma senyalero, almirante e capitan general, saludes muchas como a rey que mucho amamos de coraçon, e cobdiçiamos que Dios de mucha de honra, e de buenaventura, e de victoria, contra todos sus enemigos, e quel lexe complir el su deseo e el su plaçer.

Rey noble, façemos vos saber que sobre los fechos tractados entre vuestro hermano, el rey Botebet, a qui fue por su mandadero Bernardo Seguin, amado nuestro, con noes de los quales vos sedes çertificado, segunt nos envio deçir el dicho Bernardo Seguin, e vos plaçe que vengan a buen acabamiento, enviamos a vos el noble e muy honrado e amado consellero nuestro, don Jaçpert viçconde de Castelnou; el qual vos enviamos con pleno poder de tractar e ordenar e firmar todas cosas que nos podiamos façer, como a aquel en quien mucho fiamos, e es çertificado de todo nuestro entendimiento, porque vos rogamos, rey, que lo creades de quanto vos dira de parte nuestra. E porque nos entendiemos por el dicho Bernardo Seguin que vos queriades saber de nos e por nuestra carta quales eran aquellas cosas que eran tractadas, e las quales nos demandavamos ques complissen, mandamos las poner e escribir en esta carta nuestra, segunt se siguen.

1. Tractado es que los reyes sean amigo de amigo e enemigo de enemigo, contra todos los reyes del mundo de moros.
2. Item, que el rey Aborrabe dara por cascuna galea con todo su comp-

people of the Kingdom of Aragón had for long protected and developed their lucrative trading relations with the N. African states, that is with Tunis especially, but also Tlemcen and Morocco, a situation to which the Popes, after repeatedly trying to stop this friendly intercourse with the infidel, were by this time prepared to turn a half-blind eye. Trade treaties extending from 1227 to 1512 are published in the collection mentioned below, often extraordinarily interesting in their details.

The personages concerned are James II of Aragón, 1291-1327; Ferdinand IV of Castile, 1295-1312; Muhammad III of Granada, 1302-09; and the Marinid Sultans of Morocco Abu Ya'qub Yusuf (1286-1307), grandfather of Abu Tabit Amir ('Botebet', 1307-08) and his brother Abu l-Rabi Soliman ('Aborrebe', 1308-9).

The text is taken from M.L. de Mas Latrie, Traités de paix et de commerce et documents divers concernant les relations des Chrétiens et les Arabes de l'Afrique Septentrionale au Moyen Age *(Paris, 1866),* Documents, pp. 297-99. *The background is supplied in the extensive* Introduction historique *to the volume; see also Hillgarth, I, pp. 233 ff.*

I

To the most high, most noble, and most puissant King Abu l-Rabi, Sultan of Morocco: Don Jaime, King by the grace of God of Aragón, Valencia, Sardinia, Corsica, Count of Barcelona and standard-bearer of the Holy Church of Rome, admiral and captain-general, sends greetings as to a ruler we most heartily love, trusting that God will give him honour and victory over all his enemies, and hoping that He will grant him his wishes and desires.

Noble King, we write to inform you about matters discussed with your brother, Sultan Abu Tabit, to whom our beloved Bernard Seguin went as messenger; with other news about which you are already informed, according to what Bernard Seguin has sent to tell us. May it please you that these matters should reach a proper conclusion. We are now sending to you the most noble and honourable and beloved Lord Jaspert, Viscount Castelnou, one of our councillors, who comes to you with full powers to discuss, arrange, and confirm all things on which we might act, as a person whom we entirely trust and who is informed about all our intentions, so we ask you, your Majesty, to believe everything that he has to say on our behalf. Since we understood from Bernard Seguin that you wished to hear from us, by letter, what matters had been discussed, and which we wished to be put into effect, we ordered them to be set down in this letter, as follows:

1. It is agreed that each ruler should be an ally of the allies of the other, and an enemy to his enemies against all the rulers of the Islamic world.

2. Item, that Sultan Abu l-Rabi shall pay 2,000 *doblas* for each galley with its full crew and supplied for four months.

limiento e armada para quatro meses, dos mil doblas.

    3.   Item, pasados aquestos quatro meses primeros, dara mil doblas por galea, de quatro en quatro meses, mientre menester las aura.

    4.   Item, el dito rey Aborrabe dara sueldo para mil cavalleros, para mantener la guerra, entro a tanto que aya acabado su entendimiento de Çepta.

    5.   Item, prometra e jurara en su ley que no aura paç ni tregua nunca con el rey de Granada, sin voluntad del rey de Aragon.

    6.   Item, quando sea presa Çepta, todo el mueble sea del rey d'Aragon, e las personas e el lugar sean del rey Aborrabe.

Dada en Barçelona, tres dias andados del mes de mayo, en el anyo de Nuestro Senyor de mil tresçientos y nueve. – Bernardus de Aversone, mandato regio.

II

(Aço es ço qu'el noble en Jaçpert, vescomte de Castellnou, deu dir al rey Aborrabe, de part del rey d'Arago.)

Primerament, lo saludara de part del dit rey d'Arago.

En apres, li recomptara la gran amor e bona voluntat que fo el temps passat entre la casa de Marrochs e la casa del dit rey d'Arago, e espeçialment en temps de son avi, el rey Abenjacob. Apres la mort del qual rey Abenjacob, lo rey Botebet, volent regonesçer e refrescar la bona amor que avia ahuda son avi ab lo rey d'Arago, trames sos missatges al dit rey d'Arago, ço es, en Bernat Segui e ell veyll Abulabez fill de Gauramet, qui requeseren lo dit rey d'Arago, de part del dit rey Botebet, qui li plagues que fos aquella amor entre ells, la qual era estada entre son avi e ell; encara pregaren, e demanaren que li plagues donar ajuda contra el rey de Granada, senialament de galees per cobrar Çepta del dit rey, qui la li tenia forçada, de la qual cosa ell se tenia fort per minuat, que tant vill rey com aquell fees a ell força; encara retrasqueren los dits missatges al dit rey d'Arago, que gran vergonya li era que tant vill hom con aquell tengues terra prop de tant noble rey com ell, e en sa presençia.

Apres recomptada la missatgeria, complidament e sabia per los dits missatges del rey Botebet, lo rey d'Arago respos, que ver era que tots temps era estada bona amor e pau entre la casa de Marrochs e la sua, e senyaladament en temps del rey Abenjacob, de qui el dit rey d'Arago havia membrança, e que li plahia molt que aquella fos mentenguda entre ells tots temps, e que era apparellat de fer en sos fets tot ço que ell pogues, axi com per amic leyal, guardant pero sa fe e sa leyaltat, la qual tots temps guardaren sos predecessors a tots sos amics. E aço deya per la amor e la convinença que era entre ell e el rey de Castella, la qual era aytal que el rey de Castella, el temps que fou pau ab lo dit rey d'Arago, lo reques e·l prega que volgues que·l rey de Granada fos en aquella pau, axi com a vassayl del dit rey de Castella; e el rey d'Arago otorga ho, per honor del dit rey de Castella.

3. Item, after the first four months he shall pay 1,000 *doblas* per galley every four months while he has need of them.

4. Item, Sultan Abu l-Rabi shall pay the wages of 1,000 horsemen on a war footing until he has carried out his plan with regard to Ceuta.

5. Item, he shall promise and swear according to his Law that he will never make peace or a truce with the King of Granada except with the permission of the King of Aragón.

6. Item, when Ceuta is captured, all the movable spoils shall go to the King of Aragón, while all persons and the place itself remain the property of Sultan Abu l-Rabi.

Drawn up in Barcelona, on 3 May A.D. 1309. Bernard de Aversone, by royal command.

II

(This is what Lord Jaspert, Viscount of Castelnou, should say to Sultan Abu l-Rabi, on behalf of the King of Aragón.)

First, he will greet him on behalf of the King of Aragón.

Then, he will recall to him the alliance and goodwill which existed in times past between the royal house of Morocco and the family of the King of Aragón, and especially in the time of his grandfather Sultan Abu Ya'qub. Following the death of Sultan Abu Ya'qub, Sultan Abu Tabit, wishing to recognize and renew the alliance which had existed between his grandfather and the King of Aragón, sent messages to the King of Aragón, that is, by Bernard Seguin and Abu Labez the elder, son of Gauramet, seeking to restore the alliance as it had existed between Morocco and Aragón. Sultan Abu Tabit further proposed and asked that the Aragonese should give aid against the King of Granada, particularly in the form of ships with which to recover Ceuta from the King of Granada, who had seized it from the Sultan of Morocco, an act which he held profoundly prejudicial to himself, and moreover one done by a ruler as base as the King of Granada was; the messengers sent to the King of Aragón further emphasized how shameful it was for the Sultan of Morocco, so noble as he was, to have such a base person occupying land near his, so close to his presence.

After hearing the message, fully and prudently conveyed by the ambassadors of Sultan Abu Tabit, the King of Aragón replied that it was true that at all times there had existed goodwill and peace between their two royal houses, particularly in the time of Sultan Abu Ya'qub, whom the present King of Aragón remembered well. He would be greatly pleased to have that maintained at all times, and was prepared so to act in all ways as a loyal friend, as his predecessors had always behaved towards their allies. But he had to bear in mind also the alliance and agreement which existed between himself and the King of Castile, according to which the King of Castile, during the time when there was peace with the King of Aragón, had sought to have the King of Granada

E axi, per aquesta raho, el rey d'Arago no podia otorgar la ajuda quels dits missatges demanaven contra el rey de Granada, mas que el dit senyor rey d'Arago, per amor e per honor del dit rey Botebet, e per que pogues satisfer a sa voluntat, e per lo retreyt que li fayen los missatges de part del rey Botebet, se trebayleria de tractar e procurar ab lo rey de Castella quel solves d'aquella covinença. Per la qual cosa, lo dit rey d'Arago trames encontinent un dels maiors de son conseyl al rey de Castella. [...]

included in that peace, since the latter was a vassal of the King of Castile; and the King of Aragón had accepted this for the honour of the King of Castile. For this reason, then, the King of Aragón could not grant the aid against the King of Granada which the ambassadors were requesting. However, the King of Aragón, out of consideration for Sultan Abu Tabit and in order to meet his wishes, and because of the good impression made upon him by the ambassadors from Sultan Abu Tabit, would strive for the King of Castile to release him from that agreement. To this end, the King of Aragón would immediately send one of the most senior members of his council to the King of Castile.

55. An attempted seduction (1330)

To try to give an account in brief form of the Libro de buen amor *of Juan Ruiz, Archpriest of Hita in the diocese of Toledo, would be to court disaster: the reader should consult a recent history of literature and some of the vast bibliography. On one level – that which concerns our extract – it is an 'art of love' in the Ovidian tradition. The major European analogues one needs are provided by the* Roman de la Rose, Boccaccio, *and* Chaucer.

In context, the short episode of the Moorish girl follows that of Doña Garoça, the nun. Her early death after a relationship which may have been 'platonic' or consummated but was certainly passionate has – if only briefly – shattered the poet; he must seek solace, not in religion, but in another affair. Trotaconventos ('procuress of nuns') is the go-between charged with selecting an attractive girl. In the city or region of Toledo with its still large population of Muslims, mudéjares, *and especially in the ambience of very easy-going sexual morality depicted by the poet throughout his work, affairs between Christian and Muslim must have been commonplace, despite the penalties imposed – theoretically? – by the law (see text 53). Trotaconventos by her reference to*

(1508)　Por olvidar la coita, tristeza e pesar,
　　　　rogué a la mi vieja que m'quisiese casar;
　　　　fabló con una mora, non la quiso escuchar;
　　　　ella fizo buen seso, yo fiz mucho cantar.

(1509)　Dixo Trotaconventos a la mora por mí:
　　　　¡Ya amiga, ya amiga, quánto ha que non vos vi!
　　　　Non es quien ver vos pueda y, ¿cómo sodes ansí?
　　　　Salúdavos amor nuevo.' Diz la mora: 'Iznedrí.'

(1510)　'Fija, mucho vos saluda uno que es de Alcalá,
　　　　enbíavos una çodra con aqueste alvalá:
　　　　el Criador es convusco, que d'esto tal mucho ha;
　　　　tomaldo, fija señora.' Diz la mora: 'Legualá.'

(1511)　'Fija, ¡si el Criador vos dé plazer con salud,
　　　　que non gelo desdeñedes, pues que más traer non pud!
　　　　Aducho buen adugo, pues fabladme alaúd:
　　　　non vaya de vos tan muda.' Dixo la mora: '¡Ascut!'

(1512)　Desque vido la vieja que non recabdava y,
　　　　diz: 'Quanto vos he dicho, bien tanto me perdí;
　　　　pues que ál non me dezides, quiérome ir de aquí.'
　　　　Cabeçeó la mora, díxole: '¡Amxi, amxi!'

Alcalá (de Henares) manages to suggest that the lover is a trustworthy local man, and of course wealthy (1510c); his clerical status is for the moment neither here nor there.

The passage is taken from the edition of J. Joset (Madrid, 1974, 2 vols). The brief section which follows this is headed 'Which instruments are not suited to accompany songs in Arabic' and demonstrates – as a previous passage had done more extensively – the poet's musical expertise. This section (stanzas 1513-19) begins 'Después fiz muchas cánticas, de dança e troteras, / para judías e moras e para entendederas', a possibly autobiographical note which shows the extraordinarily rich mixture, in racial and religious terms, of the society of Toledo and other regions of Spain, at the time when the poet wrote. In these circumstances the attempted seduction of one of another race is hardly surprising. The girl, in a variety of ways, says 'No'. The Arabic words and phrases she uses are precisely of the kind which any Christian in Toledo might have known in the 14th century, and should be compared with what the British Army picked up in Alexandria and elsewhere in N. Africa in 1942 and later years; they hardly show that Juan Ruiz knew much Arabic or was in a high degree arabized. The phrases are discussed by Joset and other editors in their notes, and by J. Oliver Asín in Al-Andalus, 21 (1956), 212-14. There is a full English prose translation by Raymond S. Willis (Princeton, 1972).

(1508) In order to forget my trouble, sadness, and grief, I begged the old woman to set me up properly with a girl. She spoke to a Moorish girl, but this girl refused to listen to her; she was quite right, and I wrote lots of songs.

(1509) Trotaconventos said on my behalf to the Moorish girl: 'Dear friend, it's been a long time since I saw you! You hardly show yourself in public: why are you like this? I bring you greetings from a new lover.' The girl said: 'I wouldn't know about that.'

(1510) 'My child, there's a man from Alcalá who sends you warmest greetings, and offers you this blouse together with this love-letter: God is with you, for he's got a lot of this; take it, my lady. 'The girl said: 'No, by Allah!'

(1511) 'My daughter, may God give you joy and good health. Don't scorn these gifts, for I could bring no more; a good present I bring you, so give me a courteous reply. Don't let me leave you in such a speechless state.' The girl said: 'Be quiet!'

(1512) When the old woman saw she was doing no good there, she said: 'I see I have totally wasted my time in talking to you. Since you don't wish to say anything further to me, I take my leave.' The Moorish girl nodded and said: 'Get out! Get out!'

56. Why did God allow Islam to emerge? (1330)

For Don Juan Manuel, see text 44. His Libro de los estados, *composed about 1330, is a discussion of the diverse social 'estates' of mankind, Book I being about secular matters, Book II about the clergy. There is naturally special attention to the duties of high-ranking nobles to God, the monarch, and other men; indeed the work might be placed within the tradition of 'mirror of princes' writing, and has as an alternative title* Libro del Infante *or 'Book of the Prince'. It is structured as a series of answers given to the prince by the King his father, his philosopher-tutor Turín, and especially by Julio, a much-travelled priest who often quotes the views of his friend Don Juan Manuel. Much consists of an adaptation of the story of Barlaam and Josaphat,*

Otrosí a muy grant tienpo después que Jhesu Christo fue puesto en la cruz, vino un falso omne que avia nonbre Mahomad. Et pedricó en Aravia, et fizo crer a algunas gentes nesçias que era propheta enviado de Dios. Et dio en manera de ley muy grant soltura a las gentes para conplir su voluntad muy lixosamente et muy sin rrazón. Et por ende las gentes mesquinas, cuidando que cunpliendo su voluntad podían salvar las almas, creyéndole, tomaron por ley aquellas vanidades que les él dixo. Et tantas fueron las gentes quel creyeron que se apoderaron de muchas tierras, et aun tomaron muchas – et tiénenlas oy en día – de las que eran de los christianos que fueron convertidos por los apóstoles a la fe de Jhesu Christo. Et por esto a guerra entre los christianos et los moros, et abrá fasta que ayan cobrado los christianos las tierras que los moros les tienen forçadas; ca, quanto por la ley nin por la secta que ellos tienen, non avrían guerra entre ellos. Ca Jhesu Christo nunca mandó que matasen nin apremiasen a ninguno por que tomasen la su ley, ca El non quiere serviçio forçado sinon el que faze de buen talante et de grado. Et tienen los buenos christianos que la rrazón por que Dios consintió que los christianos oviesen reçebido de los moros tanto mal es por que ayan rrazón de aver con ellos guerra derechureramente et por que los que en ella murieren, aviendo conplido los mandamientos de Sancta Eglesia, sean mártires, et sean las sus ánimas por el martirio quitas del pecado que fizieron.

Et la secta de los moros, en tantas cosas et en tantas maneras es desvariada et sin rrazón que todo omne que entendimiento aya entendrá que ningún omne non se podría salvar en ella. Et lo uno por esto, et lo ál porque non fue dada por Dios nin por ninguno de llas sus prophetas, por ende non es ley, mas secta errada en que los metió aquel mal omne Mahomat que los engannó.

*a collection of 'exempla' within a frame-story originally concerning the legend
of Buddha, of which via Greek and Latin versions a Spanish one had been made
a few years before Don Juan Manuel wrote.*

*What is especially notable in this extract is the statement that if Islam
would surrender the formerly Christian lands it occupied, there would be no
cause for war between the two faiths; also that there should be no forced
conversion of Muslims by Christians (a standard view of most authorities,
certainly, but one which bore repetition). Meanwhile, since warfare would
inevitably continue, the justification of it as a means for Christians to achieve
martyrdom is clearly expressed, this being part of the divine plan.*

*The extract (Book I, chapter 30) is from the edition by R.B. Tate and I.R.
Macpherson (Oxford, 1974).*

Then, long after Christ was crucified, there arose a false man named
Muhammad. He preached in Arabia, convincing certain ignorant people that he
was a prophet sent by God. As part of his teaching he offered them wholesale
indulgences in order that they could gratify their whims lustfully and to an
altogether unreasonable extent. In this way the lower kind of people, thinking
that by indulging their whims they could save their souls, as long as they believed
in him, took those vain things which Muhammad was telling them as a new Law.
So many people believed him that they took over many lands, including many
that had once been Christian from the time their inhabitants were converted by
the apostles to the faith of Jesus Christ; and they still have these lands today.
That is why there is war between Christians and Moors, and there will be, until
the Christians have recovered the lands which the Moors have occupied; for
neither on account of their faith nor on account of their deviant religion is there
any reason why there should be war between them. Christ never ordered that
anyone should be killed or put under pressure in order to convert, for He does
not wish for any obligatory service, only for that which is given voluntarily and
with a good heart. Good Christian people think that the reason why God allowed
the Christians to take such great harm from the Moors is so that they [the
Christians] should be able to make war justly against them [the Moors], and so
that those dying in such war, having obeyed the commandments of Holy Church,
could be martyrs, their souls being absolved by such martyrdom of the sins they
might have committed.

The religion of the Moors in so many ways is so foolish and unreasonable
that any person of understanding can see that nobody could possibly achieve
salvation by it. This is one argument. The other is that that religion was not
given by God or by any of God's prophets, and so is no sort of faith, but an
erroneous belief into which that evil man Muhammad deceived them.

57. Peace-making leads to an assassination (1333)

Alfonso XI was a noted warrior-king who ruled Castile-León from 1312 (more strictly, 1325, when he came of age) until 1350, when he died of the Black Death while besieging Gibraltar. Tarifa had been taken by the Christians in 1292, at a moment when a new dynastic and military alliance between Castile-León and Aragón produced a somewhat hopeful agreement to partition N. Africa when it should be conquered: Castile was to have Morocco, Aragón the lands to the east. Gibraltar was taken by a Catalán fleet for Castile in 1309. There followed years of rapidly-shifting loyalties among Christian and Muslim powers, with alliances which sometimes crossed the religious divide, but a new force emerged with the accession in 1331 of Abu'l Hassan Ali (the Albohazen of our text) of the Banu Marin (Marinid) dynasty, who ruled from Fez as Sultan of the Maghrib. He was a fanatic for the Holy War, and resolved to prevent the Christians dominating the Strait. Gibraltar itself was retaken by the Moroccans in the summer of 1333. Alfonso undertook a campaign to recover it, but progress was slow, supplies were short, and the season was nearing its end; when he received a report that Don Juan Manuel and other barons were acting treacherously and ravaging the countryside, he was glad to accept the terms offered by the King of Granada, and the two monarchs met to make peace on 16 October 1333. Our text says that in making the offer, the

(147) [...] E el cavallero vino al rrey de Castilla e dixole lo que la otra vez le auia dicho, que el rrey su señor lo queria ver si el lo tuviese por bien. E el rrey, por lo que le auien enbiado a dezir que fazien en Castilla, e otrosi por se non detener alli, dixo que le plazia de se ver con el. E sobresto el cavallero fue al rrey su señor e dixoselo a el e a los moros. E plugoles ende, e el rrey de Granada enbio luego por su alguazil por que fuese a fablar con el rrey de Castilla e las cosas sobre que auien de uer. El tratamiento era que ouiesen tregua e paz entre el rrey don Alonso e el rrey de Granada e el ynfante Abomelique por quatro años; e el rrey de Granada que diese al rrey de Castilla las parias de cada año segund que puso de se las dar al tienpo que el rrey vino sobre Teba; e otrosi que guardase la tregua al ynfante Abomelique e los de su tierra ansi como la deuie guardar al rrey de Granada por las parias que del tomaua; e el rey que les mandase dar de su tierra saca de ganados e de azeyte, pagando ellos los derechos segund que los solian pagar en la otra paz que fue puesta.

E el tracto hecho por esta manera e firmado, el rrey de Granada vino ay al rreal de los christianos a se uer con el rrey de Castilla; e vinieron ay con el todas sus gentes. E el comio con el rrey de Castilla anbos a vna mesa e estando ay muchas gentes de christianos e de moros; e anbos estos rreyes estuvieron grand pieça en vno. E despues que ouieron comido, dio el rrey de Granada al rrey de Castilla de sus joyas las mas nobles que el tenia e pudo auer; espeçial-

*King of Granada acted jointly with Prince Abu Malik (Abomelique), governor
of Algeciras and representative in the Peninsula of his father the Sultan; this
may have been so, but there evidently remained a party which rejected the deal
with the Christians and sought a pretext to kill the King of Granada because of
it. According to one Arabic account, the assassins were members of the Banu
l'Ula clan, who disapproved of the alliance of the Granadine ruler with Sultan
Abu'l Hassan. As our text says, Alfonso himself doubted whether Abu Malik
had been a fully consenting party to the treaty.*

*The King of Granada was Muhammad IV, who had come to the throne in
1325 at the age of only ten.*

The text is taken from the Gran crónica de Alfonso XI, *edited by Diego
Catalán (Madrid, 1976-77, 2 vols), II, pp. 68-71. This, composed in or soon
after 1376, absorbed nearly all the earlier* Crónica *of the same monarch by his
chancellor Fernán Sánchez de Tovar (or de Valladolid), whose narrative extends
to the year 1344; this is used for our text 58. The* Gran crónica *is markedly
superior to the earlier work in much of its detail, for example in recounting the
reasons for the murder of the King of Granada in our extract. Closely related
to these texts is the* Poema de Alfonso XI *written by Rodrigo Yáñez in 1348; this
consists of nearly 10,000 octosyllabic lines, the section relating to the 1333
episode being stanzas 421-66.*

(147) [...] So the knight came to the King of Castile and told him what he
had told him the previous time, that his lord the King [of Granada] wished to see
him, if that was agreeable to him. The King [of Castile], on account of the
report which had reached him about events in Castile, and also to avoid delaying
there, replied that he would be pleased to meet him. Thereupon the knight went
to his lord the King [of Granada] and gave him and the other Moors this report.
They were content, and the King of Granada sent for his chief minister to tell
him to go and confer with the King of Castile, and to inform him of the points
to be discussed. The agreement was that there should be a four-year truce
between the King of Castile and the King of Granada and Prince Abu Malik; also
that the King of Granada would pay to the King of Castile the annual tribute as
it had been agreed it should be paid when the King advanced on Teba; also that
Prince Abu Malik and his people would observe the truce just as the King of
Granada would observe it in respect of the tribute he was taking from him;
furthermore, the King [of Granada] would allow a quantity of cattle and oil to be
taken from his land, the others to pay duties on these just as they had been
accustomed to pay them when the previous truce had been established.

The agreement being made and signed in this way, the King of Granada
went to the Christian camp to meet the King of Castile; and all his people
accompanied him. They dined together at one table, in the company of many
Christians and Moors, and spent a long time together. After dinner the King of
Granada gave the King of Castile some exceptionally fine jewels, in particular a

mente vna espada guarnida la vayna toda cubierta de chapas de oro que auia en esta vayna muchas esmeraldas e rrubies e çafires e pieça de aljofar grueso; e otrosi le dio vn baçinete muy bien guarnido con oro en derredor de la guirnalda auia muchas piedras, espeçialmente auia dos rrubies, el vno en la fruente e el otro ençima del, que eran tamaños como castañas; e otrosi diole muchos paños de oro e de seda de los que labraban en Granada. E otrosi el rrey don Alonso partio con el de sus dones de los que el auie traydo.

E firmado las posturas e las pazes segund que era tratado y ese dia el rrey de Granada fuese a su rreal; e otro dia partio dende e fue a posar çerca del rrio de Guadiaro. E el ynfante Abomelique fuese para Algezira.

E el rrey don Alonso mando poner sus engenios en la mar, porque los leuasen a Tarifa, e desçerco la villa; e fue posar a Puerto Llano, e quedo ay aquel dia. E estando el rrey de Castilla en aquel lugar, ansi como a la media noche, llego a el vn ome que le dixo que los hijos de Ozmin auian muerto en aquella noche a Mahomad aquel rrey de Granada. E ansi como lo dixo al rrey lo oyeron otros muchos de la hueste; e vinieron a la tienda del rrey, cuydando que el ynfante Abomelique no querria guardar aquella tregua, e consejauan al rrey que se fuese de alli aquella noche en guisa que fuese en Alcala de los Ganzules antes que amanesçiese. Y el rrey veyendo que si ansi lo fiziese que yria muy menguado de su honrra e los que con el estauan tomarian gran daño e peligraria mucha gente, no lo quiso fazer, e atendio fasta que fuese otro dia. E desque fue amanesçido e el dia claro, partio de alli e fue su camino adelante para Alcala de los Ganzules, e de ay fue su camino para Xerex, e dende ay fuese para Seuilla.

(148) Cuenta la ystoria que los hijos de Ozmin quando vieron aquellas vistas que ouo el rrey de Granada con el rrey de Castilla, e que estuuieron anbos los reyes gran pieça en habla, cuydaron que era en daño dellos. E desque el rrey de Granada fue sosegado en su rreal en vn valle qu'es çerca de Guadiaro, enbio por su alguazil para acordar con el por quales de sus lugares yria a la villa de Malaga, e otrosi como enbiaria aquellas gentes que alli auia traydo para sus lugares; e Abobete e Abraen el Beodo hijos de Ozmin, auiendo voluntad de matar a su rrey, hablaron con algunos que entendian que les hauian de ayudar, e dixeronles que aquella fabla e amistad que el rrey de Granada auia fecho con el rrey de Castilla que non les paresçia buena, e otrosi que el rrey de Granada traya vestidas rropas que el rrey de Castilla le diera, e que porque comiera con el e traya vestidas sus rropas, que era christiano.

E desque esta habla fue acabada, fueron se para el rrey, e dixeronle que el ynfante Abomelique les auia enbiado mensajero en que les enbiaua a dezir mucho mal del, que era malo e fijo de christiana, e que fiziera fabla con el rrey don Alonso que era contra su ley, e que tenia vendida la casa de Granada con todo el señorio suyo, por lo qual el enbiara cartas allen la mar al rrey Alboaçen

sword whose scabbard was completely covered with thin plates of gold and had on it many emeralds and rubies and sapphires and a large pearl. He also gave him a basinet [helmet] richly worked in gold, with many gems set around its rim, especially two rubies, one set above the other at the front, each as large as a chestnut; he further gave him many pieces of cloth of gold and of silk of the kind they make in Granada. King Alfonso responded by giving him many presents he had brought with him.

Once the agreement and the truce had been signed there that day the King of Granada returned to his camp, and next day he left there and went to stay near the Guadiaro river. Prince Abu Malik left for Algeciras.

Then King Alfonso ordered that his siege-engines should be put on ships and taken to Tarifa, where the siege was lifted. He went to Puerto Llano, and stayed there that day. While the King of Castile was there, at about midnight, a man came to tell him that the sons of Osmin had that night assassinated Muhammad, the King of Granada. When the man gave this news to the King, many other members of the army heard it too, and they came to the royal tent, believing that Prince Abu Malik was not disposed to keep to the truce, and advising the King that he should leave the place that night so as to reach Alcalá de los Gazules before dawn. However the King, considering that such a departure would be dishonourable for him and for his men, as well as being dangerous for many people, refused to do this, and waited till dawn. When day broke and there was plenty of light, he departed from there and went forward to Alcalá de los Gazules, and thence to Jerez and so on to Seville.

[148] The sons of Osmin, when they heard about the meeting between the King of Granada and the King of Castile, and that the two monarchs had spent a long time talking together, believed that this would be an adverse development for them. As soon as the King of Granada was at rest in his camp in a valley near the Guadiaro, he sent for his chief minister in order to determine with him the route he should follow to Málaga, and also what means he should use to send home all the men he had assembled. Then Abobete and Abraham 'the Sot', sons of Osmin, who were planning to murder the King, spoke to several people who were to help them, telling them that that friendly talk which the King of Granada had had with the King of Castile seemed to them to be a bad thing, and furthermore that the King of Granada was wearing clothes that the King of Castile had given him, concluding – because they had dined together and the King of Granada came away wearing clothing given him by King Alfonso – that the King of Granada must be a Christian.

When they had ended this discussion they went to the King, and told him that Prince Abu Malik had sent them a message in which he said many discreditable things about him: that he was an evil man and the son of a Christian woman, that he had had talks with King Alfonso which was contrary to his Law, and that he had sold the royal line of Granada together with all his lordship. On account of all this he [Abu Malik] had sent letters across the sea to

su padre en rrazon deste fecho; e quando lo el supiese, que a ellos culparia mucho que fueron con el a las vistas de los christianos; e que por esta rrazon que pasaria la mar e faria hueste sobre Granada, e que conquistaria el rreyno con quantos fuesen, e que por escusar este daño que podria acaesçer que los rrogaua de su parte e les mandaua so temor de la su espada del rey de Benamarin su padre que luego pusiesen rremedio en aquel fecho por que la casa de Granada, que Dios sienpre mantuuiera de luengo tienpo sobre quantas tierras los omes auian, no se perdiese.

E quando el rrey de Granada oyo esta rrazon, dixo contra Abrahen, que dezian el Beodo por quanto bebia vino y era el mayor de los hijos de Ozmin, que bien sabia el la fabla que fiziera con el rrey don Alonso; e que el se lo consejara. E dixo le Abrahen que no dezia verdad. E quando el rrey vido que lo desmentia su vassallo, ouo muy grande pesar; e con la saña que ouo, quisole echar mano de la barba. E quando esto vido Abraen, tiro vn espada de la vayna e firio al rrey con ella; e bien ansi lo fizieron los otros cavalle.os traydores a Dios y al mundo, los que mal siglo ayan sus animas. [...]

his father Abu'l Hassan about it; and when the Sultan heard about it, he would severely condemn those who went with the King of Granada to the talks held with the Christians, and would in consequence cross the sea and send an army against Granada, conquering the kingdom and all the people in it. In order to avoid this disaster which might befall them, he [Abu Malik] for his part begged them – and indeed ordered them, under the threat of the sword of his father the Marinid Sultan – that they should speedily seek to remedy the matter, in order that the royal house of Granada, which God had maintained in power longer than that of any other land, should not be destroyed.

When the King of Granada heard all this, he said to Abraham, the one they called 'the Sot' on account of his wine-drinking, who was the eldest of the sons of Osmin, that he knew perfectly well what had been the nature of the talks held with King Alfonso, and had advised him accordingly in them. Abraham said this was not true. When the King realized that his vassal was calling him a liar, he flew into a rage, and in that state tried to seize Abraham by the beard. At this Abraham drew his sword and struck the King with it, and the other knights – traitors to God and to man, whose souls should be damned for evermore – thereupon did the same. [...]

102

58. The Salado campaign (1340)

Following developments outlined in the introduction to text 57, Sultan Abu'l Hassan Ali, after securing his rule in N. Africa, began sending men and supplies into Spain in 1338. Under this new threat Alfonso XI appealed to the Pope, Benedict XII, for financial and spiritual support: the Pope sent a crusading banner and made concessions on tithes to the benefit of the Castilian Crown, this being the reason why after his victory Alfonso made his submission to the Pope and sent him a share of the booty, as in chapter 254.

The Christian forces concentrated in Seville in the late summer of 1340, Alfonso being joined by his father-in-law the King of Portugal, Afonso IV, with a thousand knights. The immediate object was to relieve Tarifa, besieged by the Muslims. The naval disaster described in chapter 245 occurred about 10 October. The royal army reached Peña del Ciervo on the coast on 29 October. On 30 October the Archbishop of Toledo said Mass for the army, read out the papal bull of the Crusade, and gave an inspiring sermon. Against great odds and in circumstances at times desperate for the Christians, they decisively defeated the Muslim forces of Morocco and Granada on the shore and around the estuary of the little river Salado, to the west of Tarifa, as described in chapters 250 and 251 of the chronicle (omitted here). In chapter 252 the writer compares this victory with that of Las Navas in 1212 (text 40), concluding that the Salado was 'de mayor milagro, et más de loar.'

The account of the booty won by the Christians (chapter 253) probably

(245) Dicho avemos que el Rey Albohazen, desque vio las galeas et las naves del Rey de Castiella en la guarda de la mar, que envió a decir a Joan Alfonso de Benavides et a los caballeros que estaban en Tarifa, que enviasen a él dos caballeros, et que fablaría con ellos algunas cosas que eran servicio del Rey de Castiella et suyo dél. Et los de Tarifa acordaron de enviar a él Muño Ruiz de Villamediana, et a Ruy López de Ribera, et que les diesen otros dos caballeros en rehenes. Et las rehenes dadas, fincó que otro día fuesen aquellos dos caballeros al Rey Albohazen oír lo que les quería decir. Et en aquella noche estando el Prior en la guarda de la mar con aquellas quince galeas et doce naves, veno tan grand tormenta en la mar, que perescieron las doce galeas de aquellas en la costa de la mar, et murieron y muchas gentes de los christianos, et los que escaparon vivos, fincaron todos en poder de los moros; et las naves non podieron estar allí, et corrieron con aquella tormenta, las unas fasta Cartagena, et las otras a Valencia en el regno de Aragón. Et escapó el Prior en una galea, et otras dos galeas con él.

Et el Rey Albohazen sopo esto en aquella noche; et en amanesciendo envió gentes de caballo et de pie que tomasen todos aquellos christianos que avían escapado de las galeas; et predicó a los sus moros, et díxoles, que Dios facía miraglos por el destruimiento de las flotas de los christianos, porque les él

does not exaggerate. The Sultan and the King of Granada – since 1333, Yusuf I – had been so confident of victory that they travelled with their harems and many children (an Arabic source credits the Sultan with having sired 1862 of them), and with substantial treasuries. In contrast, Alfonso's treasury was permanently empty. His need for money from the Pope and the Spanish Church had been very real, and during preparations for the campaign in Seville, he had pawned the crown jewels to pay for two weeks' food supplies for his army. After victory at the Salado, he had just enough time to replenish and repair Tarifa before returning via Jerez to Seville before his supplies again ran out.

The extracts are from the Crónica de Alfonso XI *(Biblioteca de Autores Espaoles, LXVI), for which see the previous text. This chronicle seems here to have a more compact and effective narrative than the* Gran crónica, *the latter being at this point almost too rich in literary developments, such as the lengthy prophetic dream of Fatima, wife of the Sultan, and the Sultan's boast to his court that he would enter Toledo, conquer all Spain, and occupy Europe according to a prophecy now about to be fulfilled.*

The Poema de Alfonso XI *has a lengthy section on this campaign, while in Portuguese there survive two fragments of a poem on the* Batalha do Salado; *these, and the relationship between all these texts, are discussed by Mercedes Vaquero in a paper in* Portuguese Studies, 3 (1987), 56-69, *with mention also of several Latin hymns celebrating the victory, now preserved in MSS of Coimbra and Toledo.*

(245) We said earlier that Sultan Abu'l Hassan, when he observed the galleys and ships of the King of Castile lined up [to defend Tarifa with its Christian garrison on the seaward side], asked Juan Alfonso de Benavides and his men inside Tarifa to send two knights out to him, since he had certain things to say of importance to the King of Castile and to the garrison. The Tarifa garrison agreed to send Muño Ruiz de Villamediana and Ruy López de Ribera to him, asking for two to be sent to them in return as hostages. When the hostages arrived, it was agreed that the two knights should be sent next day to hear what the Sultan wanted to say to them. That night as the Prior was on duty with his fifteen galleys and twelve ships, such a great storm blew up that twelve of the galleys sank and many Christians were drowned, while those able to reach the shore all fell into Moorish hands. The ships could not remain where they were, but ran before the storm, some to Cartagena, others as far as Valencia in the kingdom of Aragón. The Prior escaped on one galley, and two other galleys with him.

The Sultan learned of this the same night, and at dawn sent out horsemen and foot-soldiers to capture all those Christians who had escaped from the galleys. He preached to his Moors, telling them that God was working miracles in order to destroy the Christian fleet, so that he could then go on to occupy

podiese tomar la tierra. Et los moros tomaron las armas todas, et las otras cosas que estaban en aquellas galeas, et traxieron ante el Rey Albohazen todos los christianos que escaparon de las galeas; et los que quisieron renegar, et tornarse moros, escaparon la vida. Et en estos ovo uno que dixieron Sancho Ortiz, et era freyre de Sanct Joan, et hermano de aquel Prior; et renegó, et tornóse moro, et otros algunos con él; et otrosí los que non quisieron renegar, fueron luego descabezados. Et en estos fue tomado un escudero de linage de buenos caballeros, et diciánle Joan Alfonso de Salcedo; et al tiempo que le prisieron los moros, fizo mucho por se defender; et por la bondat que en él vieron los moros, ficieron mucho por lo tomar a vida, coydando que lo tornarían moro, et que se aprovecharían de la su bondat. Et desque lo llegaron ante el Rey Albohazen, preguntáronle, si quería renegar de la ley de los christianos, et creer en la ley de Mahomad; et él dixo que non, mas que creía en su ley así como verdadero christiano. Et el Rey Albohazen dixo que se tornase moro, et que le daría grande aver, et que lo faría señor de muchos caballeros, et si non que le mandaría luego descabezar. Et aquel Joan Alfonso dixo al Rey: 'Jesu-Christo murió por mí, e yo quiero morir por él, et faz lo que quisieres': et fue luego descabezado.

Et los que estaban en la villa de Tarifa, non sabiendo ninguna cosa del perdimiento de la flota, enviaron aquellos dos caballeros al Rey Albohazen. Et desque llegaron ante él, dixiéronle lo que él enviara decir a los de la villa, et que venían a oir lo que les dixiese. Et el Rey Albohacen, porque era perdida la flota del Rey de Castiella, dixo, que él non les enviara decir nada, et que los oiría, si alguna cosa le quisiesen decir de parte del Rey de Castiella, o de parte de los de la villa. Et ellos dixieron, que non le avian a decir nada, mas que mandase llamar al caballero que fuera a la villa con aquella razón, et que con él lo probarían: et llamáronlo. Et desque veno, dixo ante el Rey, que él fuera a decir a los de la villa lo que aquellos caballeros dicían. Et el rey díxoles que les non quería decir ninguna cosa, mas que comiesen allí con él, et que les daría algo de lo suyo así como era acostumbrado de dar a los estraños que venían a la su casa del Rey de Marruecos. Et este día era viernes, et traxieron luego delante de aquellos dos caballeros un atayfor lleno de gallinas menudas adobadas, et dixiéronles que comiesen. Et aquellos caballeros dixieron que non comerían allí, nin tomarían dél ninguna cosa, pues estaba allí así como enemigo de su Señor. Et el Rey mandó venir algunos christianos de los que avian renegado; et señaladamiente veno y aquel Sancho Ortiz, et mandáronle que comiese de aquella vianda; et comió de aquellas gallinas ante aquellos caballeros. Et ellos pidieron al rey mucho afincadamiente, que les mandase ir a la villa donde salieran. Et el Rey enviólos, porque le traxiesen sus rehenes.

Et desque las rehenes fueron salidas fuera de la villa, fizo ferir los atabales, et mandó que se armasen todos los de los sus reales, et que fuesen a combatir la villa. Et los que estaban en la villa de Tarifa apercibiéronse cada unos en sus quadriellas para se defender; ca ellos tenían la cava bien fonda, et bien limpia,

their land. The Moors then collected all the weapons and other things aboard the galleys, and brought all the Christians who had escaped alive from the galleys before the Sultan. Those who were willing to convert to Islam were granted their lives. Among these was one Sancho Ortiz, a friar of St John, a brother of the Prior's: he embraced Islam, and a few others did too. Those who were unwilling to apostatize were immediately beheaded. One of those captured was a squire of good family, named Juan Alfonso de Salcedo. Before being captured, he had fought bravely to defend himself, and since the Moors observed his bravery, they did all they could to capture him alive, thinking that he might convert to Islam and that they could make good use of his qualities. As soon as they brought him before the Sultan, they asked him if he would abandon Christianity and accept Islam: he answered that he would not, and that as a true Christian he believed in his Law. The Sultan told him that if he would convert, he would make him wealthy and put him in command of many soldiers, and that if he refused, he would be instantly beheaded. Juan Alfonso said to the Sultan: 'Jesus Christ died for me, and I am willing to die for Him, so do what you will.' Thereupon he was executed.

Those who were inside Tarifa, knowing nothing of the destruction of the fleet, sent the two knights to the Sultan. Once in his presence, they asked the Sultan what it was he wished to say to them. The Sultan, knowing of the loss of the fleet, now said that he had sent no message to them, but that he would listen to them if they wished to say anything to him on behalf of the King of Castile or on their own account. They replied that they had nothing to say to him, but asked that he should call the soldier who had gone to Tarifa with the message, since thereby they could prove the truth of the matter; and he was called. When he arrived, he confirmed to the Sultan that he had gone to Tarifa to say what the two Christian knights had reported. The Sultan repeated that he had nothing to say to them, but invited them to dine with him there, adding that he would make them some gift as was the custom when strangers came to the palace of the Sultan of Morocco. That day was Friday: they set before the two knights a deep dish full of spiced small chicken, and told them to eat. The two knights said that they would not eat any part of it, for to them the dish was like an affront to their Lord. The Sultan ordered that some of the Christians who had converted should be brought in, especially Sancho Ortiz, and they ordered him to eat some of the dish; and there before the two knights he ate the chicken. The knights then earnestly besought the Sultan to allow them to leave for Tarifa; and the Sultan, in order to have his hostages back, sent them off.

As soon as his hostages were safely outside the fortress, the Sultan ordered his drums to sound and all the men in his camp to arm and go off to attack Tarifa. Those inside the fortress formed up in their companies to defend themselves. They had dug the moat very deep, and kept it clear, and each night

porque de cada noche la afondaban, et la alimpiaban; et otrosí cada noche tornaban a la villa las piedras que lanzaban de día fuera contra los moros. Et como quier que ante desto les oviesen fecho muchos combatimientos, pero aquel fue el más afincado combatimiento que les ficieron, ca llegaron a dar de las lanzas a los que estaban en las barreras; et en un logar entraron los moros con los christianos, entre la barrera et el muro de la villa; pero los caballeros que eran dados por sobresalientes en los combatimientos, llegaron a aquel logar, et echaron a los moros fuera, feriendo en ellos, et matando muchos dellos: et porque los moros en aquel día rescibieron muy grand daño partiéronse del combatimiento. Pero porque en aquel día ovo muchos de los christianos feridos, fincaron escarmentados. Et los moros de allí adelante comenzaron a labrar la torre que querían facer cerca de la torre de Don Juan, la cual la estoria ha contado que los christianos ge la derribaron quatro veces. [...]

(253) Pues que el Rey don Alfonso de Castiella et de León, et el Rey de Portogal que venía con él, fueron tornados a Sevilla, los desta ciudat rescibiéronlos con muy grand placer, et ficieron muchas alegrías. Et el Arzobispo et el Cabildo de la sancta Iglesia de la ciubdat de Sevilla saliéronlos a rescebir con grand procesión, et los pendones que fueron tomados en aquella sancta batalla, en que fue vencido el Rey Albohacen et el Rey de Granada et de los otros moros de grandes solares et de grandes poderes que y vinieron, metiéronlos en la ciubdat baxos en los cuellos de los moros que traian cativos. Et los Reyes de Castiella et de Portogal, et los perlados, et los ricos-omes que venían con ellos, fueron a la Iglesia con la procesión: et ellos et todos los christianos que con ellos venian, dieron gracias a Dios de la mucha merced que les ficiera.

Et porque en el desbarate de aquellos reales fueron tomadas muy grandes quantías de doblas, que fueron falladas en el alfaneque del Rey Albohacen, et en las tiendas de los otros moros que eran y et en él, en que avían muchas doblas, que en cada una dellas avía tanto oro como en cient doblas marroquíes. Et otrosí fueron y tomadas muchas vergas de oro de que labraban aquellas doblas, et muchas argollas de oro et de plata que traían las moras en las gargantas, et a las muñecas, et a los pies, et mucho aljófar, et muchas piedras preciosas, que fue fallado en el alfaneque del Rey Albohacen. Et otrosí en este desbarato fueron tomadas muchas espadas guarnidas de oro et de plata, et muchas cintas anchas texidas con seda, con oro, et guarnidas de plata, et muchas espuelas, que eran todas de oro et de plata esmaltadas, et otras muchas que eran guarnidas de eso mesmo. Et otrosí fueron y tomados muchos paños de oro et de seda, et muchas tiendas que eran de grandes precios. Et otrosí fueron y presos et cativos muchos moros de grandes solares et de grandes quantías. Et porque todas estas cosas tomaron omes de poca valía, los caballeros pedieron al Rey por merced que non perdiese tan grand aver como allí era tomado, et que lo oviese para sí. Et por esto el Rey ante que partiese de la Peña del Ciervo, mandó saber deste aver; et veniendo en el camino para Sevilla, cobró mucho dello; pero algunos de los que

they dug it deeper and cleared it out. Each night they brought back inside the fortress the stones they had fired by day at the Moors. Before this time there had been a good deal of fighting, but it was now greatly intensified, since the Moors managed to use their spears against those behind the defences. At one point the Moors succeeded in pinning the Christians down between the outer defences and the town wall; but the knights, who had been outstanding in the fighting, fought their way to the spot and drove the Moors out, wounding and killing many of them. Then the Moors, having suffered great losses, withdrew from the fight. Even though many of the Christians were wounded too, it was the Moors who had the worst of it. After that the Moors began to build a siege-tower up against the tower of Don Juan, but the Christians – according to the account we are following – managed to destroy it four times. [...]

(253) After King Alfonso of Castile and León and the King of Portugal had returned to Seville, the people of the city received them with immense rejoicing, and made many demonstrations of it. The Archbishop and the Chapter of the Holy Church of Seville went out to greet them with a fine procession, and the banners which were captured in that sacred enterprise, in which Sultan Abu'l Hassan and the King of Granada and other Moors rich in estates and authority who were there were defeated, were brought into the city lowered and tied to the necks of Moorish captives. The Kings of Castile and of Portugal and the bishops and nobles who were with them all joined the procession to the cathedral, where they and the Christian people gave thanks to God for the great favour He had shown them.

Now when the enemy camps were sacked there was found a huge quantity of *doblas* in the Sultan's treasury and in the tents of the other Moors, each of these coins containing as much gold as there would be in a hundred Moroccan *doblas*. There were also found many bars of gold from which the *doblas* were made, and many gold and silver circlets of the kind Moorish women wear at their throats and wrists and feet, together with pearls and many precious stones that were discovered in the Sultan's treasury. Also in this rout were taken many swords decorated with gold and silver, and many broad sashes woven with silk and gold thread, and embroidered with silver, and spurs all enamelled with gold and silver. A great quantity of gold and silver cloth was also taken, together with valuable tents. Many Moors who owned large estates and great wealth were also taken prisoner. Since much of all this was taken by low-class persons, the knights begged the King not to lose the immense wealth that had been taken, but to gather it for himself. So the King, before he left Peña del Ciervo, ordered lists of all the booty to be drawn up. As he came on the road to Seville, a large part of it was recovered; but some of those who had taken it fled with it outside

lo ovieron tomado, fuxieron con ello fuera del regno a Aragón, et al regno de Navarra; et muchos dellos fueron a la ciubdat de Aviñón, do era entonce el Papa Benedicto. Et tanto fue el aver que fue levado fuera del regno, que en París, et Aviñón, et en Valencia, et en Barcelona, et en Pamplona, et en Estella, en todos estos logares baxó el oro et la plata la sesma parte menos de como valió; pero que el Rey Don Alfonso de aquello que él pudo aver, yuntólo todo, et púsolo en un palacio, las doblas a su parte, et las espadas a otro cabo, et las cintas a su parte, et los paños a otra parte, et las siellas, et los frenos, et las espuelas a otro cabo. Et todas las joyas así puestas, et todos los moros que pudo aver, mandólos poner en el corral delante aquel palacio atados en sogas, et el fijo del Rey Albohacen, et el fijo del Rey de Sujulmenza con ellos; et mandó llamar al Rey de Portogal et mostrógelo todo, et rogóle que tomase dende lo que quisiese. Et el Rey de Portogal tomó algunas de las espadas, et de las siellas, et de los frenos, et de las espuelas; et dixo, que de las doblas que non quería nenguna cosa. Et el Rey de Castiella rogóle mucho afincadamiente que tomase algunas de ellas; et porque non lo quiso facer, el Rey de Castiella diole el fijo del Rey de Sidjilmasa, et diole otros moros de los que tenía allí. Et el Rey de Portogal fue muy pagado de quanta honra le fizo el Rey de Castiella, et salió de Sevilla. Et el Rey de Castiella por le honrar, fueron amos a dos de consuno fasta en Cazalla. Et dende fuese el Rey de Portogal para su tierra, et el Rey de Castiella tornó a Carmona por algunas cosas que avía de librar. [...]

(254) Este noble Rey Don Alfonso era muy católico, et temía a Dios, et amaba mucho honrar la Iglesia. Et conosciendo la merced que Dios le avía fecho, et por honrar la sancta Iglesia de Roma, así como todo fiel christiano debe facer, envió al Papa con aquel Joan Martínez el su pendón que tovo consigo en el día de la sancta batalla, et algunos de los pendones que fueron tomados de los moros, et el caballo en que estido aquel día con sus sobreseñales; et otrosí envió de aquellos moros que cativó en la batalla, et de los caballos, et de las otras cosas que fueron tomadas en la hueste de los Reyes de Marruecos et de Granada, et envió pedir et rogar al Papa con este su mandadero, que pues él tenía comenzada con los moros tan alta guerra et tan grande, como non toviera ningún rey de los que fueron en Castiella nin en León desde muy luengos tiempos, que él quisiese facer alguna ayuda con que lo podiese mantener. Et aquel Joan Martínez fue al Papa con aquella mandadería; et desque llegó a Aviñón, do el Papa estaba, sopiéronlo muchos cardenales de los de la Corte, et saliéronlo a rescebir muy lexos de la villa. Et tantas fueron las gentes que lo salieron acoger, que en dos leguas ovieron que andar desde la mañana fasta la hora de la nona. Et él entró en Aviñón do estaba el Papa Benedicto, et levaba el pendón del Rey Don Alfonso de Castiella enfiesto; et delante del pendón iban los caballos que fueron tomados en la lid, et que el Rey enviaba al Papa, todos ensillados uno ante otro; et levábanlos omes de diestro, et cada uno dellos levaba una adarga et una espada del arzón colgada. Et luego cerca del pendón iba el caballo del Rey; et luego a pos el caballo iban veinte et quatro moros, que

the kingdom to Aragón and Navarre, and many of them went to Avignon where Pope Benedict was then residing. So great was the quantity of booty taken out of the kingdom that in Paris and Avignon, in Valencia and Barcelona, in Pamplona and Estella, gold and silver dropped by a sixth part of what it was really worth. King Alfonso brought together as much of the booty as he could, separating the coin, the swords, the sashes, the cloth, the saddles, the bridles, and the spurs. He ordered all the precious stones and the Moorish prisoners bound with ropes to be displayed in the courtyard in front of his palace, together with the son of the Sultan and the son of the King of Sidjilmasa; then he asked the King of Portugal to come and showed it all to him, inviting him to take as much as he wanted of it. The King of Portugal selected some of the swords, and the saddles, and the bridles, and the spurs; and said that he would not take any of the coin. Then the King of Castile urged him most strongly to take some of the coin; and since he was still unwilling to do this, the King of Castile gave him the son of the King of Sidjilmasa, together with others of the Moors he had there. The King of Portugal was highly pleased with the honour shown him by the King of Castile, and left the city; in order to show him proper respect, the King of Castile accompanied him as far as Cazalla. Thence the King of Portugal left for home, and the King of Castile went to Carmona to attend to certain business. [...]

(254) This noble King Alfonso was a good Catholic who feared God and greatly loved to be able to honour the Church. Aware of the favour which God had shown him, and in order to honour the Holy Church of Rome (as every good Christian should), he sent Juan Martínez to the Pope with the banner which accompanied him on the day of the battle, together with some of the banners which had been captured from the Moors, and the horse he rode that day together with its trappings. He also sent some of the Moors he captured in the battle, and some horses, and other things taken from the host of the Kings of Morocco and Granada. His messenger was to ask the Pope that since he [the King] had begun such an important and noble campaign against the Moors, greater than any undertaken for a very long time by any monarch who had ruled in Castile or León, the Pope should make available some form of aid with which he might continue the struggle. With this message Juan Martínez went to the Pope. As soon as he arrived in Avignon, where the Pope was, many cardinals of the papal curia heard of it and went out to greet him at some distance from the city. So great was the press of people who came out to greet him, that it took from early morning until mid-afternoon for him to cover two leagues. Then he entered Avignon bearing the banner of King Alfonso of Castile aloft. Before the banner there walked the horses that had been captured in the battle, one behind the other, all saddled; those in charge of them led them along on their right hands, each horse having an oval shield and a sword hanging from the saddle-bow. Next, close to the banner, walked the King's horse. After the horse marched twenty-four Moors carrying each a banner from among those that had

levaban veinte et quatro pendones de los que fueron de los moros baxos en los cuellos. Et desque este mandadero del Rey de Castiella llegó ante el Papa, acogióle muy bien, et ovo con él muy grand placer. Et el Papa decendió de la siella en que estaba, et trabó con la mano del pendón del Rey Don Alfonso, et comenzó decir así: 'Vexilla regis prodeunt, fulget Crucis mysterium.' Et los cardenales, et los arzobispos et obispos, et la otra clerecía que y estaban, todos comenzaron a cantar aquel hymno, et el comienzo del hymno dice así en romance: 'La señal del Rey paresce, el misterio de la Cruz resplandece.' Et acabado este canto, el Papa mandó llamar para otro día muy grand consistorio, et muy público. Et como quiera que ante desto avía él fecho facer muchas procesiones, et dado muchas gracias a Dios al tiempo que sopo que los christianos vencieran a los moros; pero en aquel día fizo facer muchas procesiones, et otorgó muchos perdones a todos aquellos que gradesciesen a Dios la merced que avia fecho a los christianos; et él dixo la misa ese día, et predicó, diciendo, que esta sancta batalla era semejante a la que ficiera el Rey David, en que tiró el freno del tributo de la mano de los Filisteos, et que firió al Rey Adajer fijo de Loat Rey de Sabá, de la encontrada de Emate; et otrosí que firió a Sirio Rey de Damasco, et que les mató siete mill caballeros et quarenta mill peones et que les tomó muchas armas, et muchos collares, et otros muchos algos; et así como el Rey David venciera aquellos dos Reyes, así este muy noble Rey Don Alfonso venciera los Reyes de Marruecos et de Granada, et les matara muchas gentes, et les tomara todo el algo que allí tenían; et que tiró de la mano de aquellos Reyes moros el freno del tributo que coydaban aver sobre los christianos, así como lo ovieron la otra vez, quando España fue en poder de los moros. Otrosí dixo, que este reconoscimiento que el Rey de Castiella enviaba a la Iglesia de Roma, era semejante de un fecho que acaesció en la estoria de los Macabeos, en que dixo, que el Rey Antiaco, fijo de Demetrio, envió a Simón soberano sacerdote en Hierusalem ofrendas et dones en reconoscimiento del grand sacerdocio; et que este muy noble Rey Don Alfonso, conosciendo la merced que Dios le ficiera, et aviendo fiuza que de allí adelante le faría muchas más mercedes en el persiguimiento de la guerra de los moros, que así como fiel christiano et verdadero enviaba estonce sus donas a el teniente-logar del soberano sacerdocio; et que aquí se podía provar lo que era dicho, que por los Reyes et por los Príncipes christianos avía poder la Iglesia de Roma. Et como quiera que esto decía por los Reyes et Príncipes del mundo, pero que más especialmente se podía decir por los Reyes de Castiella et de León, et mucho más por este muy noble Rey Don Alfonso de Castiella et de León, que desde la su mocedad comenzó el persiguimiento de la guerra de los moros, poniendo el su cuerpo a muchos trabajos et a muchos peligros por servicio de Dios, et por acrecentamiento de la fe católica; et que en esta sancta batalla, que fue vencida cerca de Tarifa, se puso el Rey a tan grandes trabajos, et en aventura de tan grand peligro, yendo él con muy pocos a pelear con tan grand muchedumbre de los moros. Et sobre esto puso otras muchas autoridades de la ley vieja et de la

belonged to the Moors, tied to their necks. When the messenger from the King of Castile arrived before the Pope he was well received by him. The Pope came down from his seat and took King Alfonso's banner into his hands, saying: 'Vexilla regis prodeunt, fulget Crucis mysterium.' The cardinals, archbishops and bishops, and all the other clergy who were there, all began to sing the hymn whose first line in the vernacular is 'La señal del rey paresce, el misterio de la Cruz resplandece'. When the singing was over, the Pope ordered that next day a great public consistory should be held. Even though the Pope had held many processions, and had given thanks to God ever since he knew that the Christians had defeated the Moors, on that day he none the less held new processions, and granted pardons to those who were disposed to thank God for the favour He had shown the Christians. On that day he said Mass and preached as follows: This holy battle was comparable to that which King David fought, in which he cast off the burden of tribute to the Philistines, or the battle in which he smote Hadarezer the son of Rehob, King of Zobah unto Hamath; or that in which he smote Syrus King of Damascus, killing seven thousand of their horsemen and forty thousand foot-soldiers, and took from them many weapons and many necklaces and much other booty. Just as King David vanquished those two kings, so did this most noble King Alfonso vanquish the Kings of Morocco and Granada, and killed many of their people, and took all the property they had with them there; and he tore from the hands of those Moorish rulers the burden of tribute which they were intending to impose upon the Christians, just as they had imposed it in former times, when Spain as in the power of the Moors. Furthermore he said that this recognizance which the King of Castile was sending to the Church of Rome was similar to an incident in the story of the Maccabees, when King Antiochus, son of Demetrius, sent to Simon the high priest in Jerusalem offerings and gifts in recognition of the high priesthood. The most noble King Alfonso, aware of the favour which God had shown him, and trusting that henceforward He would grant him many more mercies in the prosecution of the war against the Moors, as a loyal and true Christian was now sending his gifts to the person who occupied the place of the high priest, providing proof of what had been said, that the Church of Rome owed its power to Christian kings and princes. Although this was said about all the world's rulers, it was especially said of the Kings of Castile and León, and most particularly of this noble King Alfonso of Castile and León, who in his youth began the attack on the Moors, placing his person in great toils and in many dangers for the service of God and the furtherance of the Catholic faith. In this holy battle, which was fought and won near Tarifa, the King exposed himself to great troubles, and possibly to great danger, going as he did with very few men to fight such an immense army of Moors. Concerning this the Pope cited many other authorities from the Old

112

nueva. Et todos los que allí estaban con el Papa dieron muchas gracias a Dios, et grandes loores por quanta merced avía fecho a los christianos en aquella batalla. Et el Papa otorgó al Rey más gracias de las que ante le avía otorgado para aquella guerra que avía con los moros. [...]

Testament and the New. All those who were with the Pope gave thanks to God, and praised Him for the favour he had shown the Christians in that battle. The Pope granted the King more indulgences than he had given him before for the war he was continuing against the Moors. [...]

59. Market forces impose peace with the infidel (1360)

At times in the 13th and through much of the 14th century the Aragonese were on terms of peace and even of alliance with Muslim Tunis. There were frequent diplomatic contacts, the Aragonese were able to maintain a consulate in Tunis, and for a time (text 48) the Dominicans maintained their school of Arabic there. The chief interest of the two nations in all this was trade, so beneficial to the prosperity of both. Efforts were made to exclude other nations – the Castilians in particular – from this profitable business. In the present document, signed in Tunis on 15 January 1360, an existing treaty is renewed for ten years. Francisco Sacosta, ambassador of Peter IV of Aragón, had evidently travelled to Tunis to negotiate with representatives of the Sultan Abu Ishak Ibrahim. The treaty was witnessed by many Tunisians and by

[...] Item et si forte aliquod lignum seu ligni aut aliquod stolum uel apparatum dominationis illustrissimi et excelsi domini Regis Petri veniret in Nobili Ciuitate Tunisii, uel in eius constrictu, placet nobis quod possint habere refrigerium cum eorum peccunia. Et quod nullus audeat eis contradicere aquam.

Item si aliquis sarracenus nobilis ciuitatis predicte iret in dominio illustrissimi et excelsi domini Regis Petri, sit securus tam de persona quam de rebus, et quod nichil sit sibi petitum nisi tamen quod est de iure consuetum, eundo stando et redeundo.

Item si aliquis ueniret de dominio illustrissimi et excelsi Regis Petri in Ciuitate Tunisii uel in eius constrictu, idem per similem modum tractabitur. Et quod dominacio Ciuitatis Tunisii teneatur facere fundachos in Ciuitate pro mercatoribus.

Item quod teneatur dare predictis mercatoribus Cameras pro eorum statu, et potecas pro mercancias custodienda, et quod teneat eis conductis, et quod non habitent cum eis alique naciones sine uoluntate et consensu eorum.

Et quod illustrissimus et excelsus dominus Rex Petrus possit infra Nobilem Ciuitatem Tunisii et eius constrictu ponere consulos ubi mercatores habitant, et quod dicti consuli faciant iustitiam omnibus uassallis illustrissimi et nimis excelsi domini regis Petri, et quod nullus se intromictat nisi dominus consul.

Et quod dictus dominus consul habeat son dret consuetum, et etiam de omnibus mercatoribus.

Et quod nullus Sarracenus nec nullus iudeus Nobilis Ciuitatis Tunisii non possit esse captus nec sclauum, in dominio illustrissimi et excelsi principis domini Regis Petri, a die date presencium usque ad decem annos completos. Et si forte infra istud tempus aliquis esset captus uel seruum, quod statim debeat esse liber. Similiter etiam si aliquis de dominio illustrissimi et excelsi domini Regis Petri esset captus non ualeat esse sclauum nec captiuum, in dominatione Nobilis Ciuitatis Tunisii et eius constrictu, ab illa hora que ista pax facta fuit usque ad decem annos completos. Et si forte infra istud tempus aliquis esset captus seu

*eighteen Christians, including one Franciscan friar; the rest were presumably
merchants and residents. The Latin version is a translation of an Arabic
original, its enormous preamble being taken up with incredibly flowery
phraseology about the two monarchs and with invocations to the Deity – jointly
uttered by the signatories – to favour both equally.*

*The fundacho of the text is in others alfundicum, the fonduk or elsewhere
the khan, defined by Burns as 'at once a public inn, goods depository, mail
drop, ... exhibit hall'. When overseas, it was an important part of a trading
concession, becoming 'a diplomatic enclave protecting and serving the European
merchant community within an Islamic city'.*

*The text occupies six printed pages as reproduced (with notes about the
circumstances and date, and a facsimile) by I. de las Cagigas in Hespéris, 18
(1934), 65-77. On the background, see the full study by Dufourcq.*

[...] If perchance any ship or ships or any fleet or vessel of any kind from
the lands of the most illustrious and noble King Peter should come to the city of
Tunis or lands in its jurisdiction, we grant that its crew should be able to buy
food supplies with their own money. Also that nobody should dare to deny them
water.

If any Muslim fom the noble city aforementioned should go to the lands of
King Peter, let the safety of his person and his possessions be guaranteed; no
charge should be levied from him beyond that allowed by customary law, whether
he is going or staying or returning.

If anyone should come from King Peter's lands to Tunis or lands in its
jurisdiction, he will be treated in like manner. The government of the city of
Tunis is obliged to provide *fonduks* in the city for the merchants.

The same government is obliged to provide for the aforesaid merchants
rooms in keeping with their status, and warehouses for the storage of their goods,
and means of transport for them; and will also ensure that people of other
nations do not live with them except with their full agreement.

King Peter shall be able to establish consulates wherever his merchants
reside in the city of Tunis and lands in its jurisdiction, and the aforesaid consuls
shall dispense justice to all the vassals of King Peter, none being involved with
the administration of justice except his worship the consul.

The aforementioned consul should enjoy his rights under customary law, and
the same applies to the merchants.

No Muslim or Jew of the city of Tunis shall be a captive or a slave in the
lands of King Peter, from the present date for a period of ten full years. If
perchance within this period anybody is captured or enslaved, he should be set
free at once. The same applies to anyone from the lands of King Peter: if
anyone is captured he must not be enslaved or held captive in the lands of the
city of Tunis and lands in its jurisdiction, from the moment this peace is signed
for ten full years. And if perchance within this period anyone is captured or

116

captiuus, quod statim debeat liberari. Et quod possit in domum suam reddire si
uellet. [...]

Petrus Florentini ex Imperiali Auctoritate publicus ubique notarius, predicta
manu propria scripsi, et publicaui. Et per viam turcimanni de linga Sarracenica
in linga latina presentem cartam copiaui, et solito meo signo signaui. [...]

held as a captive, he should be set free at once, and allowed to go home if he so wishes. [...]

I, Peter the Florentine, public and general notary by Imperial Authority, with my hand wrote and issued this. I have copied the present letter after it was translated from Arabic into Latin by the [Muslim] translator, and I have sealed it with my customary seal. [...]

60. The Moor, noble knight and lover (about 1410)

Various versions of the famous tale of El Abencerraje y la hermosa Jarifa
*are known from the middle years of the 16th century, both printed and
manuscript. The most attractive version is that of Antonio de Villegas'
miscellany the* Inventario, *known in a printing of 1565 (whose licence to print
had been applied for, however, in 1551). The fullest study of the problems,
with editions of the various texts, is that by Francisco López Estrada (Madrid,
1957); our extract is from this, pp. 311-15. Readers may wish to acquaint
themselves with the fine version of the story which Lope de Vega wrote as a
play,* El remedio en la desdicha, *reflecting as they do so that this would have
made a splendid basis for an operatic libretto.*

*Rodrigo de Narváez was no figure of fiction but a solidly historical person
who occupies two pages in Fernando de Pulgar's* Claros varones de Castilla *(in,
for example, Brian Tate's edition, pp. 55-57). He was governor of the fortress
of Antequera from 1410 until his death in 1424. Descendants held the same
post until 1472, and again from 1529, a fact probably not unconnected with the
emergence of the story in print a little later; a link may also be suspected with a
noble Aragonese family, the Ximénez de Embún, which protected* moriscos *from
the Inquisition. The 'gentil moro' of the story is Abindarráez, a member of the
famous clan of the Abencerrajes (Banu Serraj) of Cordova and Granada which
– as Abindarráez tells Rodrigo de Narváez after his capture   had suffered
much under suspicion of having plotted against the King of Granada. This*

Dize el cuento que en tiempo del Infante don Fernando, que ganó a
Antequera, fue un cavallero que se llamó Rodrigo de Narváez, notable en virtud
y hechos de armas. Este, peleando contra moros, hizo cosas de mucho esfuerço,
y particularmente en aquella empresa y guerra de Antequera hizo hechos dignos
de perpetua memoria, sino que esta nuestra España tiene en tan poco el
esfuerço, por serle tan natural y ordinario, que le paresce que cuanto se puede
hazer es poco; no como aquellos romanos y griegos, que al hombre que se
aventurara a morir una vez en toda la vida le hazían en sus escriptos immortal y
le trasladavan en las estrellas. Hizo, pues, este cavallero tanto en servicio de su
ley y de su Rey, que después de ganada la villa le hizo alcaide della para que,
pues avía sido tanta parte en ganalla, lo fuesse en defendella.

Hízole también alcaide de Alora, de suerte que tenía a cargo ambas fuerças,
repartiendo el tiempo en ambas partes y acudiendo siempre a la mayor
necessidad. Lo más ordinario residía en Alora, y allí tenía cincuenta escuderos
hijosdalgo a los gages del Rey para la defensa y seguridad de la fuerça; y este
número nunca faltava, como los immortales del rey Darío, que en muriendo uno,
ponían otro en su lugar. Tenían todos ellos tanta fee y fuerça en la virtud de su

aspect of the story probably derived from the fact that in 1482, after what had been virtually a civil war in Granada, most of the clan who had been on the losing side were executed in what is called the 'Hall of the Abencerrajes' in the Alhambra palace. The clan figures romantically in Ginés Pérez de Hita's Guerras civiles de Granada: historia de los bandos de Zegríes y Abencerrajes *of 1595, but real romantics should turn to Chateaubriand's* Les Aventures du dernier Abencerraje. *There is a modern study by L. Seco de Lucena Paredes,* Los Abencerrajes, leyenda e historia *(Granada, 1960).*

The chief interest of the tale lies in the intensity of the idealization of their Moorish enemies (from whom, however, danger was still to come at the time the story was written, in the Alpujarra rebellion) by Spanish writers: a process which in a way had begun in the person of Avengalvón (text 24) and which is well analysed by López Estrada in the work mentioned. Their gentlemanly class was not only thought chivalrous on the Christian model; they were also dashing in their persons – as in our extract – and noble lovers too, for Abindarráez's pain is owed more to separation from his lady, Jarifa, than to the indignity of being captured by Christians. In a way, the story is a defence of religious tolerance, since Narváez accepts the two Moorish lovers as equals and as friends, 'aunque las leyes son diferentes' ['although our two faiths are different']. Already in the 13th century in Valencia, newly conquereu by the Aragonese, there is ample evidence that Christian knights recognized a corresponding knightly class among the Muslims of the region, as documented by Burns, pp. 116-19.

The story goes that in the time of Prince Ferdinand [Fernando 'de Antequera', Regent from 1406 to 1412 during the minority of John II of Castile], he who captured Antequera [1410], there was a knight by the name of Rodrigo de Narváez, outstanding in courage and warlike deeds. This man did great things in battle against the Moors, and especially in the Antequera campaign his mighty deeds would be worthy of everlasting fame, were it not that this Spain of ours holds courage in such small esteem, it being so natural and everyday, that it seems to her that all one may do is of little account. It was otherwise among the Romans and Greeks, for the man who exposed himself to death once in a lifetime was immortalized in their writings and raised to the stars. This man, then, did so much in the service of his faith and of his King that, when Antequera was taken, the King made him governor of it so that he could do as much in defence of the town as he had done in winning it. The King made him governor also of Alora, so that he had both fortresses in his charge, and he divided his time between the two according to which had the greater need. For the most part he lived in Alora, having fifty nobly-born squires there at the King's expense to ensure the defence and safety of the fortress. This number never changed, for if one died, another was put in his place, as with the Immortals of King Darius. All of them had such faith in the courage of their commander that no

capitán, que ninguna empresa se les hazía difícil, y ansí no dexavan de ofender a sus enemigos y defenderse dellos; y en todas las escaramuças que entravan, salían vencedores, en lo cual ganavan honra y provecho, de que andavan siempre ricos.

Pues una noche, acabando de cenar, que hazía el tiempo muy sossegado, el alcaide dixo a todos ellos estas palabras:

'Parésceme, hijosdalgo, señores y hermanos míos, que ninguna cosa despierta tanto los coraçones de los hombres como el continuo exercicio de las armas, porque con él se cobra experiencia en las proprias y se pierde miedo a las agenas. Y desto no ay para que yo traya testigos de fuera, porque vosotros sois verdaderos testimonios. Digo esto porque han passado muchos días que no hemos hecho cosa que nuestros nombres acresciente, y sería dar yo mala cuenta de mí y de mi oficio si, teniendo a cargo tan virtuosa gente y valiente compañía, dexasse passar el tiempo en balde. Parésceme, si os paresce, pues la claridad y seguridad de la noche nos combida, que será bien dar a entender a nuestros enemigos que los valedores de Alora no duermen. Yo os he dicho mi voluntad; hágase lo que os paresciere.'

Ellos respondieron que ordenasse, que todos le seguirían. Y nombrando nueve dellos, los hizo armar; y siendo armados, salieron por una puerta falsa que la fortaleza tenía, por no ser sentidos, porque la fortaleza quedasse a buen recado. Y yendo por su camino adelante, hallaron otro que se dividía en dos. El alcaide les dixo:

'Ya podría ser que, yendo todos por este camino, se nos fuesse la caça por este otro. Vosotros cinco os id por el uno, yo con estos cuatro me iré por el otro; y si acaso los unos toparen enemigos que no basten a vencer, toque uno su cuerno, y a la señal acudirán los otros en su ayuda.'

Yendo los cinco escuderos por su camino adelante hablando en diversas cosas, el uno dellos dixo:

'Teneos, compañeros, que o yo me engaño o viene gente.'

Y metiéndose entre una arboleda que junto al camino se hazía, oyeron ruido. Y mirando con más atención, vieron venir por donde ellos ivan un gentil moro en un cavallo ruano; él era grande de cuerpo y hermoso de rostro, y parescía muy bien a cavallo. Traía vestida una marlota de carmesí y un albornoz de damasco del mismo color, todo bordado de oro y plata. Traía el braço derecho regaçado y labrada en él una hermosa dama, y en la mano una gruessa y hermosa lança de dos hierros. Traía una darga y cimitarra, y en la cabeça una toca tunezí que, dándole muchas bueltas por ella, le servía de hermosura y defensa de su persona. En este hábito venía el moro mostrando gentil continente y cantando un cantar que él compuso en la dulce membrança de sus amores, que dezía:

> Nascido en Granada,
> criado en Cártama,
> enamorado en Coín,
> frontero de Alora.

undertaking seemed too difficult for them; and they emerged victorious from every skirmish, winning honour and profit, so that they were always wealthy.

One evening, as they were finishing supper, the night being very calm, the governor spoke to them all as follows:

'It seems to me, gentlemen, that nothing so stimulates men's hearts as the frequent practice of arms, since in that way one acquires experience of one's own weapons and loses fear of those of the enemy. There is no need for me to quote evidence of this from outside, since you are all witnesses to its truth. I say this because many days have passed without our doing anything that might enhance our reputations, and it would be to give a poor account of myself and my command if, having under me such a valiant company, I should let time pass uselessly away. So – if you are agreeable – since the calmness of the night and the moonlight beckon us out, I think we should go and let our enemies know that the defenders of Alora are not asleep. I have told you my wish; tell me what you think.'

They answered that he should give his orders and that everyone would follow him. Narváez named nine men and told them to arm. When this was done, they went out through a hidden doorway in the fort, so as not to be heard, to prevent any risk to the castle. As they went along they found that the track divided into two. The governor said to them:

'It could be that if we all go along one path, our prey will go along the other. You five go along this branch, and I with the other four will go along that one. If it should chance that one group meets enemies too numerous for them, blow your horn and the other group will come to help you.'

As the five squires were going along their track talking about this and that, one of them said:

'Quiet, comrades: I think I hear people coming.'

They concealed themselves in a copse beside the track, and heard noises. Looking closely, they could see a gallant Moor on a roan horse coming towards them. He was tall and handsome, and looked a fine figure as he rode. He wore a bright red jacket and a damask burnous of the same colour, all embroidered with gold and silver. He rode with his right arm bared and on his shirtsleeve there was worked the portrait of a beautiful lady. In his hand he held a thick and elegant two-edged lance. He carried a shield and a scimitar, and on his head wore a Tunisian turban which, wound many times round his head, served as both adornment and defence for his person. So dressed, the Moor rode along with a cheerful mien, singing a song he had composed in sweet celebration of his love, which went like this:

> Born in Granada,
> raised in Cártama,
> fell in love in Coín
> not far from Alora.

61. La Higueruela: three perceptions (1431)

John II of Castile succeeded his father Henry III in 1406, aged only a few months; the country was governed by regents until he came of age. He was a sensitive, learned, and artistically gifted man, but he lacked willpower and political instincts and for most of his reign was content to leave government to his Constable (chief minister), Alvaro de Luna, who became virtual dictator. John II seems also to have been a singularly unmilitary man, a disadvantage in a period when European 'chivalry' was attaining a height of showy, egotistical decadence. Pope Martin V hopefully issued a crusading bull for him on 8 October 1421, but this did not stimulate any quick response. The 1431 expedition to Granada assembled nearly all the nation's military power in what was plainly a massive and well-planned operation, but it seems to have had little artillery (two big cannon with female names – compare 'Big Bertha' – are mentioned in a variant version of our ballad text (b)) and no siege equipment. The intention was thus not to take Granada and end the war, but to weaken the economy by seizing or destroying crops and chopping down trees, and to exploit weakness within the state caused by dynastic rivalries and dissension; in particular to place on the throne of Granada the pretender 'Abenalmao' as a tame vassal of Castile. The unspoken objective was doubtless to give proper chivalresque employment in the field to the energetic but increasingly turbulent barons of Castile: the chronicle accounts are full of tedious lists of them and their ostentatious deeds.

Ridwan Bannigas (Reduán Vanegas), vizier of the former King of Granada Muhammad VIII who had been put to death by his rival Muhammad IX ('el Izquierdo') in late March 1431, secretly left Granada and proposed to John II at his base in Cordova that he should place on the throne of Granada the pretender Yusuf Ibn al-Mawl, known to the Christian chroniclers as Abenalmao. He was the grandson of King Muhammad VI 'el Bermejo' who had been killed by the Castilian King Peter 'the Cruel' in 1362. This was agreed; Abenalmao presented himself in the royal camp, now outside Granada, and did homage to John II. The main points of their pact were that Abenalmao would pay a heavy annual tribute, would free all Christian prisoners held in Granada and prevent any converting to Islam, and – most extraordinarily, one might think – that Abenalmao or his son would attend the Castilian Cortes (parliament).

The Christian army camped outside Granada on 28 June 1431. After two days of skirmishing, the main action was joined – not altogether intentionally, it seems from the Christian accounts – on 1 July. After the Christian victory the army devastated the area around the city, but could achieve nothing more, and withdrew to Cordova and thence to Toledo, where it disbanded after a magnificent victory parade and service of thanksgiving. Abenalmao with Castilian support entered Granada and was proclaimed King on 1 January 1432, as Yusuf IV, and he ratified the pact with John II on 27 January. However,

support for him in the realm was far from total: Muhammad IX's men returned, and Yusuf (Abenalmao) was captured and executed in April 1432.

Our three texts offer differing perceptions of these events. Text (a) is the asic chronicle account from the Crónica del Halconero de Juan II, *edited by uan de Mata Carriazo (Madrid, 1946), chapters 89-91. The royal falconer was Pedro Carrillo de Huete, an eye-witness to the events described. According to him, the Castilian army consisted of 10,000 cavalry and 50,000 infantry, a further force being added to this when the contingent from Seville appeared. Parallel accounts may be found in the* Crónica de D. Juan II *printed in* Biblioteca de Autores españoles, vol. LXVIII, *and in* El Vitorial: Crónica de D. Pedro Niño.

Text (b) is a famous ballad known in various versions printed in the middle and late years of the 16th century. The version selected is that of Ginés Pérez de Hita, Guerras civiles de Granada (1595), *as adapted in* Spanish Ballads *edited by Colin Smith (Oxford, 1964). An earlier version of equal interest is that published and translated by Roger Wright in this series, No. 62. Some doubt attaches to the identity of the Moor who explains the sights of the city to King John; it is usually taken that the Abenámar of the ballad is Abenalmao the Pretender, especially since the latter, as a descendant of al-Ahmar 'the Red', may well have had this dynastic name among his titles (Aben al-Ahmar 'descendant of the Red': Bénichou), and after all the chronicles say that the Pretender was in the company of King John. However, there was at this period another noble Granadine Moor who is precisely named as Abenámar in the chronicle of El Halconero in connection with events of 1436. What matters much more than all this is the extraordinary evocation of the splendours of Granada, its famous buildings complete after the work of the 14th and early 15th centuries, and viewed for the first time by bedazzled Christians. There are illogicalities in the text, as critics have pointed out, but if one can manage to share King John's admiring gaze (as any modern tourist surely can) his declaration of love for the city as a desirable bride becomes natural enough. The conceit according to which the female city is seen as the spouse of her male ruler is said to be typical of Arabic verse, and Arabic influence is by no means to be rejected in the rhetoric with which the siege of Seville was described (text 47), though hardly likely to have been present in the equation of the Empress with Toledo under siege in 1139 (text 32). For an excellent study of the genesis of this ballad, see P. Bénichou,* Creación poética en el romancero tradicional *(Madrid, 1968), pp. 61-92), with full bibliography.*

Text (c) is an extract from Juan de Mena's allegorical poem El laberinto de *Fortuna, completed in 1444 (edited by J. G. Cummins (Salamanca, 1968)). The poem is very uneven but at times, as here, rises to a height of epical grandeur. The poet's purpose was to persuade John II to undertake a moral regeneration of himself and his people; in stanza 152 he specifically uses the example of the 1431 campaign to insist that all efforts should be directed*

124

against the Moors and not put into 'querellas' and 'quistiones', that is, civil disturbance and disputes between barons, which were indeed the permanent curse of John II's reign. No literary historian seems to have noticed that the poet, although within his imaginative construct and within his allegorical dream-journey apparently viewing scenes of military history depicted in the palace of Fortuna, may have been viewing a perfectly tangible object. Soon after La Higueruela, John II ordered a huge strip of canvas to be painted with a series of scenes from the campaign, and this hung for at least two centuries in the Alcázar (fortress-palace) of Segovia. Philip II ordered a complete copy to be made by two Italian painters, Granelio and Fabricio, for the Sala de las

(a)

(89) Este día, estando en este rreal, pasóse al Rey vn ynfante moro que se llamaba Abenalmao, fijo del rrey Mahomat, el qual de derecho, después de la muerte del rrey Chiquillo, era rrey de Granada. E al Rey plogo mucho dello, e rreçibiólo muy bien.

(90) Juebes que fueron 28 de junio del año de 31, entró el Rey en la vega de Granada, a vna legoa de la çibdad, e asentó su rreal çerca de vn pueblo que se llama Elvira. E el rreal se asentó en Majarachuchit.

E los moros, como bieron que la hueste entraua en la Vega e tan çerca se ponían de la çibdad, pusiéronse todos en vatalla a rrayz de las huertas de la çibdad. E eran en número de cuatro mill de a cauallo e cien mill peones. Esto fazían ellos con esfuerço de muchas azequias que ende abía.

Esto todo asy pasado, el domingo que fue primero día de julio, año de 31, que por la devinal graçia el señor Rey don Jhoan estando en su rreal, envió mandar al su maestre de Calatraua, don Luys de Guzmán, que no enbargante que era fiesta, que le mandava que porque corría peligro luego fuese a fazer allanar las acequias, porque mejor podiesen pelear con los enemigos de la sancta ffe. E el maestre puso luego en obra el mandamiento del Rey, e fue a fazer allanar las asequias.

E asy estándolo continuando, salieron los moros a él, e aquexáronle tanto, que ovo demandar socorro al Rey. E el Rey envió luego allá a socorrerlo a los condes don Enrrique, conde de Niebla, e don Pedro de Estúñiga, conde de Ledesma, e don Garçi Fernández Manrrique, conde de Castañeda. E como fueron, posiéronse luego en par de la vatalla del maestre.

E los moros desque esto vieron, salió luego toda la morisma, así de cauallo como de pie, e ordenaron sus vatallas. E como los condes vieron que la vatalla querían dar, luego en este punto le fizieron saber al Rey, al rreal. E salió luego el condestable don Albaro de Luna en el avanguarda, e luego en pos dél el Rey nuestro señor con su vatalla rreal.

E todos puestos en el canpo, e todas sus vatallas ordenadas, rreynante la debinal graçia, e con la ayuda del apóstol Santiago, començóse la vatalla en el canpo, el qual se llama Andaraxemel. E fueron vençidos los moros e desvara-

Batallas in the Escorial, where as a fresco it occupies the complete length of one wall and may still be admired and studied in detail. Diego de Colmenares describes the original – in his day, moth-eaten and torn – and the Escorial copy in his Historia de ... Segovia *published in 1637 (2nd edition (Madrid, 1640), p. 337), adding a reference to stanza 148 of Mena's* Laberinto.

A precisely parallel exercise could be undertaken with three perceptions of the ill-fated expedition which D. Enrique de Guzmán, Conde de Niebla, undertook against Gibraltar in 1436. The chronicles mentioned have accounts; in the ballad* Dadme nuevas, caballeros *John II or his Queen asks for news of the Count; and in Mena's* Laberinto, *stanzas 159-86 evoke the tragic episode with a wealth of omens and counter-omens.*

(a)

(89) That day there came to the King at his headquarters a Moorish Prince named Abenalmao, son of King Muhammad, who by rights, after the death of the ruler we called 'Chiquillo' ('Titch'), was King of Granada. The King was delighted about this, and received him very warmly.

(90) On Thursday, 28 June 1431, the King entered the *vega* of Granada, about a league from the city, and established his camp near a village called Elvira. The camp was at Majarachuchit.

The Moors, seeing our army enter the *vega*, and establish themselves so close to the city, all formed up in companies among the market-gardens of the city. They numbered 4,000 horsemen and 100,000 infantry. They did this behind the protection of the numerous irrigation-channels there.

After this, on Sunday, the first of July, 1431, King John at his headquarters sent a message to order – even though it was Sunday – the Master of Calatrava, Don Luis de Guzmán, to go and fill in these irrigation-channels, in view of the danger they represented, and in order that our men should be able to get to close quarters with the enemies of the Faith. The Master at once carried out the King's order, and went off to fill in the channels.

While this was being done, the Moors came out against him, and pressed him so hard that the Master had to send to the King for help. The King sent Don Enrique, Count of Niebla, and Pedro de Estúñiga, Count of Ledesma, and Garci Fernández Manrique, Count of Castañeda, to help him. When they arrived, they placed themselves beside the Master's company.

As soon as they observed this, the whole Moorish force came out, cavalry and infantry, and formed up in companies. When the Counts saw that they were disposed to attack, they at once sent a message to the King at his headquarters. Then Don Alvaro de Luna went into the van, and after him his Majesty the King with his royal company.

Everybody being thus positioned in the field, and all the companies formed up, divine protection and the aid of the Apostle St James being assured, the

tados, e muertos dellos diez o doçe mil moros; tanto que duró el alcanze dellos fasta Maxaçad, que es çerca de las puertas de Granada.

La batalla se començó entre nona e vísperas, e sobrevino çedo la noche, si no muchos más se destruyeran de los enemigos de la fe. En este logar que se llama Andaraxemel podía ser media legoa de Granada la batalla.

Después de asy fecha la vatalla, estobo el Rey en el canpo fasta que se quería poner el sol. E desque ya fue toda la batalla rronpida, e syendo el Rey çertificado que los moros eran ya ençerrados en la çibdad de Granada, mandó a Pero Carrillo, su falconero mayor, que fuese al rreal, a su capillán mayor e a los otros capillanes, e que mandase que fuesen a rreçebirlo con la proçesión fasta la puerta del palenque, por donde avía salido la vatalla.

(91) Este santo acto en este sancto día pasado, el señor Rey dixo al ynfante Benalmao que le mandaba e mandó que dende en adelante él se llamase rrey de Granada, que él quería, con el ayuda de Dios e de su patrón Santiago, de le entregar e apoderar el rreyno. E que él lo toviese por su mandado, porque él e los sus moros fuesen súbditos a él e a su mandado. E por le más ondrar, diole vn pendón que tenía de la su devisa de la Vanda, en señal de ondra e señorío en que lo entendía poner.

(b)
'¡Abenámar, Abenámar,
moro de la morería,
el día que tú naciste
grandes señales había!
Estaba la mar en calma,
la luna estaba crecida;
moro que en tal signo nace
no debe decir mentira.'
Allí respondiera el moro
bien oiréis lo que decía:
'No te la diré, señor,
aunque me cueste la vida,
porque soy hijo de un moro
y una cristiana cautiva;
siendo yo niño y muchacho
mi madre me lo decía,
que mentira no dijese
que era grande villanía:

battle began. The place is called Andarajemel. The Moors were defeated and routed, some ten or twelve thousand of them being killed; and the pursuit lasted as far as Majazad, which is close to the gates of Granada city.

The battle had begun between nones and vespers, and night came on quickly; had this not been so, many more of the enemies of the Faith would have been destroyed. This place called Andarajemel was about half a league from the city.

After the battle, the King remained in the field till sunset. As soon as the fighting had finished completely, and the King being assured that all the Moors were now shut up inside Granada city, he ordered his head Falconer, Pedro Carrillo, to go to his camp and speak to his principal chaplain and the other chaplains, ordering them to come and receive him in procession at the gate of the stockade, through which his royal company had earlier gone out.

(91) This blessed triumph being thus won on this holy day, our lord the King told Prince Abenalmao, and so ordered it, that thenceforward he should be titled King of Granada, for he wished – with the help of God and St James – to establish him as ruler of the kingdom. Also that the Prince should hold the kingdom as his fief, in order that the Prince and his Moors should be subject to him [King John] and to his commands. In order to honour the Prince more, the King gave him a banner bearing the device of the Sash, as a mark of distinction and of the dignity to which he, the King, intended to raise him.

(b)

'Abenámar, Abenámar,
Moor of Muslim lands,
on the day that you were born
there were great omens!
The sea was calm,
the moon was full;
the Moor born under such a sign
ought not to tell a lie.'
    Then the Moor replied
– you shall hear what he said –:
    'I'll not lie to you, my lord,
even if it costs me my life,
for I am the son of a Moor
and of a captive Christian woman;
when I was a little boy
my mother said to me
that I should never tell a lie
for it's an evil thing to do;

por tanto pregunta, rey,
que la verdad te diría.'
  'Yo te agradezco, Abenámar,
aquesa tu cortesía.
¿Qué castillos son aquéllos?
¡Altos son y relucían!'
  'El Alhambra era, señor,
y la otra la mezquita;
los otros los Alixares
labrados a maravilla;
el moro que los labraba
cien doblas ganaba al día,
y el día que no los labra
otras tantas se perdía.
El otro el Generalife
huerta que par no tenía;
el otro Torres Bermejas,
castillo de gran valía.'
  Allí habló el rey don Juan,
bien oiréis lo que decía:
  'Si tú quisieses, Granada,
contigo me casaría:
daréte en arras y dote
a Córdoba y a Sevilla.'
  'Casada soy, rey don Juan
casada soy, que no viuda;
el moro que a mí me tiene
muy grande bien me quería.'

(c)

(145)   Allí vi pintadas por orden los fechos
de los Alfonsos, con todos sus mandos,
e lo que ganaron los reyes Fernandos,
faziendo más largos sus regnos estrechos;
allí la justiçia, los rectos derechos,
la mucha prudençia de nuestros Enriques,
porque los tales tú, Fama, publiques,
e fagas en otros semblantes provechos.

(146)   Escultas las Navas están de Tolosa,
triumpho de grande misterio divino,
con la morisma que de Africa vino,
pidiendo por armas la muerte sañosa.

so ask me, your Majesty,
and I will tell you the truth.'
    'I thank you, Abenámar,
for this courteous reply.
What castles are those
so tall and shining bright?'
    'That is the Alhambra, my lord,
and next to it the mosque;
over there, Los Alijares,
wondrously built;
the Moor who worked on them
earned a hundred gold pieces a day,
and on the day he did not work
he forfeited the same sum.
Over there, the Generalife,
a garden that has no peer;
and there, Torres Bermejas,
a most worthy castle.'
    Then King John spoke up,
– you shall hear what he said –:
    'If you so wish, Granada,
I will marry you:
I'll give you as a dowry
Cordova and Seville.'
    'I am married already, King John,
married, and not a widow;
the Moor who is my master
loves me very greatly.'

(c)

(145) There I saw depicted in order the deeds of the Alfonsos, with all their commanders, and all that the Ferdinands conquered, extending the narrow lands of their kingdoms; also the acts of justice, righteous rulings, and the great prudence of our Henrys, [depicted] in order that you, Fame, should make them known, and should extend their benefits to others.

(146) There is depicted the Navas de Tolosa battle, a triumph owed to a great divine mystery, won against the Muslims who had come from Africa as they

Están por memoria también gloriosa
pintadas en uno las dos Algeziras;
están por espada domadas las iras
de Almofaçén, que nos fue mayor cosa.

(147)   Cresçian los títulos frescos a bueltas
de aqueste rey nuestro muy esclaresçido,
los quales abrían allende cresçido
si non recresçieran algunas rebueltas,
las quales por pazes eternas disueltas
presto nos vengan a puerto tranquilo,
porque Castilla mantenga en estilo
toga y oliva, non armas con peltas.

(148)   Con dos quarentenas e más de millares
le vimos de gentes armadas a punto,
sin otro más pueblo inerme allí junto,
entrar por la vega talando olivares,
tomando castillos, ganando lugares,
faziendo por miedo de tanta mesnada
con toda su tierra tenblar a Granada,
tenblar las arenas fondón de los mares.

(149)   Mucha morisma vi descabeçada
que más que reclusa detrás de su muro
nin que gososa de tiempo seguro
quiso la muerte por saña d'espada;
e mucha más otra por pieças tajada
quiere su muerte tomarla más tarde;
fuyendo non fuye la muerte covarde,
que más a los viles es siempre llegada.

(150)   Como en Çeçilia resuena Tifeo,
o las ferrerías de los milaneses,
o como gridavan los sus entremeses
las saçerdotiças del tiemplo lieo,
tal vi la buelta d'aqueste torneo;
en tantas de bozes prorrompe la gente
que non entendía sinon solamente
el nombre del fijo del buen Zebedeo.

sought a cruel death in battle. Then – as a reminder that is also glorious – the two actions at Algeciras are painted together; the wrath of Abu'l Hassan, who posed the greater threat to us, was placated by the sword [i.e., at the Salado, 1340: text 58].

(147) New titles to fame of this famous King of ours grow apace more numerous; and these would have increased still further had it not been for the outbreak of certain revolts; may these now be settled in everlasting peace and may we soon be brought into a safe harbour, in order that Castile should keep in fashion the toga and the olive [symbols of peace], not weapons and shields.

(148) With more than forty thousand men-at-arms we saw him ready for the fray, and without any other unarmed people there invade the *Vega* [rich flat land of Granada], chopping down olive-trees, capturing castles, taking villages, and, with the fear spread by such a large force, making the whole land of Granada quake and the sands at the bottom of the sea shiver.

(149) I saw many Moors lying headless, men who had not taken refuge behind their walls and who did not enjoy a safe enough time [to escape] but went to their deaths in the wrath of the sword; and I saw many other Moors slashed with wounds who chose to try to defer their deaths; but the coward cannot flee death by fleeing, for it comes most surely to the base.

(150) Just as Typhaeus [in mythology, one of the Titans who stormed Jupiter's heaven, and was buried under Mount Etna] booms in Sicily, or the Milanese iron-foundries resound, or as the priestesses of the Bacchic temple chant their liturgies, [such was the sound] as I watched the return from that battle; the people shouted so loudly that all I could make out was the name of the son of good Zebedee [i.e., St James, Patron of Spain].

(151)   E vimos la sombra d'aquella figuera
donde a desoras se vido criado
de muertos e pieças un nuevo collado,
tan grande que sobra razón su manera;
e como en arena de momia se espera,
súbito viento levanta grand cumbre,
así del otero de tal muchedumbre
se espanta quien antes ninguno non viera.

(152)   ¡O virtuosa, magnífica guerra!
En ti las querellas bolverse devían,
en ti do los nuestros muriendo bivían
por gloria en los çielos y fama en la tierra,
en ti do la lança cruel nunca yerra
nin teme la sangre verter de parientes;
revoca concordes a ti nuestras gentes,
de tales quistiones y tanta desferra.

(151) And we saw the shade of that fig-garden where untimely there was seen to arise a new hillock of corpses and severed limbs, so high that it seemed unbelievable; and just as in the land of mummies [Egypt] one may expect that a sudden wind will raise up a high hill, in this case anyone who had not seen it before would be amazed at a mound of this magnitude.

(152) Ah, noble and virtuous war! All disputes should be forgotten and all effort devoted to you, in which our men by dying lived on in glory in heaven and fame here on earth; to you, when the cruel lance never misses its aim and does not hesitate to shed the blood of relatives; call back our people from such dissension and confusion so that they may dedicate themselves to you [the just war against the Moors].

62. A heretic flees to Granada (1443)

Alonso de Mella was born in Zamora, and became a Franciscan. He seems to have been in trouble with the ecclesiastical authorities from an early date (perhaps 1434), but had powerful protectors, Pope Eugenius IV, no less, and his brother Juan, Bishop of Zamora and later a Cardinal. We hear of him and others in deep trouble in the Basque Country from 1442, especially at Durango, near Bilbao: a grave heresy, presumably stimulated by Franciscan preaching, was spreading. Its nature is not precisely known, but it probably corresponded to heretical movements of the time led by Wycliffe in England and Hus in Bohemia, involving the free interpretation of the Bible against established authority, doubts about the sacrament of marriage, etc. The Church and the civil power united to suppress the movement, and there were public burnings in Valladolid and Santo Domingo de la Calzada in Old Castile. Fray Alonso de Mella and others fled to Granada, and Fray Alonso died there, evidently

[...] Propter omnes supra dictas causas, o domine, stantes nos supradicti in dicto regno, et diligenter perscrutantes et examinantes fidem quam sarraceni tenent et credunt, reperimus dictos sarracenos non esse infideles, sicut illuc dicitur, quinymmo reperimus eos esse catholicos et fideles et credentes in solum verum Deum, creatorem celi et terre, quem cum tanta fide, timore, humilitate, reverentia et devotione adorant et honorant in omnibus suis factis et dictis. Et placeret Deo, quod illi qui dicunt se christianos timerent eum, crederent, adorarent et honorarent cum tanta reverentia et timore. Item reperimus dictos sarracenos credentes et confitentes omnia sancta facta et dicta Ihesu Christi, quem, multo amplius quam christiani, in suis verbis et factis honorant, credentes de ipso quod secundum rationem potest et debet creditum esse. Reperimus etiam eos dispositos audire et auscultare omne illud quod secundum rationem potest verificari; secundum quas rationes in eis repertas veraciter cognoscimus Deum non esse duntaxat Deum christianorum, sed esse Deum omnium illorum qui recte credunt in eum, et per digna opera adimplent mandata sua. Et quod Deus non est acceptor personarum, cum sit pater omnium et sit illi cura de omnibus (Sap. 6.8) nam oculi omnium respiciunt in eum, qui non vult mortem peccatoris (Ez. 33.11), nec delectatur in perditione morientium. [...]

unrepentant.

Soon after arriving in Granada (probably in 1443) Fray Alonso wrote a long letter to Juan II of Castile. This is eloquent, powerfully reasoned, highly respectful, and full of biblical references in support of his attitude. He asked that a committee composed of 'providos et honestos religiosos' ('knowledgeable and worthy clerics') should be formed to review his ideas and proposals, and he sought also an audience with the King at which he could explain himself, to be followed by a public debate. The committee was to consider 'id quod secundum rationem debat credi et recepi' ('that which according to reason should be believed and accepted'): proof, if any were required, of the dangerous ground he was treading.

The letter with other relevant materials was found in the Vatican archives. Its full text is published as an appendix to the paper by Darío Cabanelas in Al-Andalus, *15 (1950), 233-50, and the above information is extracted from this.*

[...] For all the reasons mentioned above, your Majesty, we the aforementioned being in this kingdom [of Granada] have been carefully examining and inquiring into the faith which the Muslims hold and profess. We find that the Muslims are not unbelievers [infidels], as is said at home, but rather we found them to be sincere believers in the one true God, creator of heaven and earth, the God whom with such faith, fear, humility, reverence, and devotion they worship and honour in all their deeds and words. May it please God that those who call themselves Christians should fear, believe, worship, and honour Him with equal reverence and awe. Then again, we found that the Muslims believe and accept all the holy deeds and words of Jesus Christ, whom, much more than do the Christians, they honour in their words and deeds, believing in those things which according to reason can and should be believed about Him. We found them also disposed to hear and listen to everything which in reason can be verified. According to the reasoning which we observed in them we truly recognized that God is not merely the God of the Christians, but the God of all those who properly believe in Him, and who by worthy deeds do His bidding. Also, that God makes no distinction of persons, but is the Father of all and is concerned with everybody who turns his eyes towards Him (Wisdom of Solomon 6.8), and who does not wish the death of any sinner (Ezekiel 33.11), nor does He take any pleasure in the damnation of the dying. [...]

136

63. Christmas festivities in Jaén (1463)

Miguel Lucas de Iranzo rose from humble beginnings to positions of great power under Henry IV of Castile, as royal favourite, general, grandee, and eventually Condestable – chief minister – and governor of the important frontier city of Jaén. This rise and these activities created many enemies for Miguel Lucas among the clans of great barons in the often anarchic circumstances of the reign of the ineffectual Henry IV; but Miguel Lucas had his admirers too, among them Pedro de Escavias, mayor of neighbouring Andújar, who wrote the chronicle of the Constable's deeds from 1458 to 1471. The writer, about whom little is known, was as remarkable as his subject, for his text is a document of extraordinary interest for its direct observations of the life of the times, and it is anything but a dry political record; Pedro de Escavias evidently stood very close to Miguel Lucas and had access to documentary evidence he needed, possessing also a lively style. The Constable's end was as dramatic as much of his life: he was murdered by a crossbowman at the start of Mass in the cathedral of Jaén, in March 1473, apparently because of popular resentment about favour he had shown to the conversos, *the converts from Judaism, by then numerous and often in positions of economic and professional power in many Spanish*

Venidas las fiestas de la Natiuidad de Nuestro Señor Jesucristo del año del Señor de mill & quatroçientos & sesenta & tres años, como todos conosçiesen quel deseo del dicho señor Condestable fuese exerçitarse, después de los fechos tocantes a la guerra, en conbites & salas, fiestas & juegos de cañas, & otros actos de plaçeres onestos, do lo suyo con todos pudiese gastar, buscauan envençiones tocantes a esto.

Y el domingo que fue segundo día de pascua, después de comer, se acordaron doçientos caualleros de los más prinçipales y mejor arreados de su casa & de la çibdad de Jahén, la meytad de los quales fueron en ábito morisco, de baruas postizas, & los otros cristianos.

E los moros fingieron venir con su rey de Marruecos, de su reyno, y trayan delante al su profeta Mahomad, de la casa de Meca, con el Alcorán e libros de su ley, con grant çirimonia, en vna mula muy enparamentada; y en somo, vn paño rico en quatro varas, que trayan quatro alfaquíes. E a sus espaldas venía el dicho rey de Marruecos, muy ricamente arreado, con todos sus caualleros bien ajaezados, & con muchos tronpetas e atabales delante.

E desque fue aposentado, enbió con dos caualleros suyos vna carta bermeja al dicho señor Condestable. Los quales, desde la puerta de su posada, le fiçieron saber cómo estauan allí dos caualleros del rey de Marruecos, que le querían façer reuerençia & dar vna carta que del rey su señor le trayan. A los quales el dicho señor mandó responder que entrasen. E luego descaualgaron de sus cauallos, y entraron en vna sala de su posada, muy bien guarneçida de gentiles paños

cities, and the targets of much mob violence at the time in Cordova and other Andalusian towns.

In the text which follows, the festivity so elaborately planned and executed is best analysed in terms of drama without a stage. Royal and noble households throughout Europe indulged this taste at the time and for centuries to come. Miguel Lucas, who had often fought the Moors of Granada from his base in Jaén, is here shown triumphing over them again in the 'juego de cañas' (a simulacrum of combat, on horseback, with great formalities; as in Aeneid V.585) *as a prelude to the voluntary conversion of the 'Moors'. The letter from the 'King of Morocco' had evidently been prepared with some care, since it imitates certain features of Arabic discourse. Not all the Moors in Jaén were actors dressed up for the part. At Carnival before Lent the following year, Miguel Lucas entertained the Moorish military governor of Cambil and several gentlemen of the entourage of the King of Granada over several days, providing for their delight more 'cañas', a torchlight tour of the city, mummers, night music and dancing, a performance involving a noted madman, and a splendid open-air banquet: 'Fue cosa por çierto que a todos bien paresçió, mayormente a los moros, que diçien vnos a otros* axudy.'

The extract is from Juan de Mata Carriazo's edition, Hechos del Condestable Miguel Lucas de Iranzo *(Madrid, 1940), chapter 10, pp. 98–100.*

At the time of the celebration of the birth of Our Lord Jesus Christ in 1463, since everyone knew that our lord the Constable wished to enjoy some relaxation after his warlike activities, that is to say in gatherings of different kinds, festivities, and contests with *cañas,* and other pleasurable and respectable diversions, in which he could employ his resources to the benefit of all, they began to devise ways in which they might do this.

On Sunday, the second day of the Christmas season, after a meal, two hundred of the chief and best-equipped knights of the Constable's household and of the city of Jaén organized themselves so that half should appear in Moorish dress, with false beards, and half as Christians.

The Moors pretended to arrive with their King of Morocco, newly come from his realm; they were preceded by the prophet Muhammad, from his abode in Mecca, and by the Koran and other books of their Law, all with great ceremony, on a richly-caparisoned mule; over it there was a richly-worked cloth supported on four poles, each carried by a holy man. Behind these came the King of Morocco richly dressed, with all his knights elegantly equipped, together with drums and trumpets.

When the King was settled in his place, he sent two of his knights with a letter on red parchment to the Lord Constable. These two, at the door of the Constable's lodging, announced to him that they were two knights of the King of Morocco, and that they wished to greet him and hand him a letter they were bringing from their King. The Lord Constable asked them to enter. They

françeses; do lo fallaron con la señora condesa su muger, él y ella muy ricamente vestidos, & bien aconpañados de muchos caualleros & escuderos, e dueñas & donçellas, de su casa & de la dicha çibdad.

E como llegaron a él, después de le aver besado las manos, diéronle vna carta bermeja, que deçía en esta manera:

'El rey de Marruecos, beuedor de las aguas, paçedor de las yeruas, defendedor de la ley de Mahomad, guárdelo Dios con su mano la grande, saludes sobre vos el valiente y esforçado & noble cauallero don Miguel Lucas, condestable de Castilla (hónrrelo Dios, anpárelo Dios). Fago vos saber cómo oyendo la grant destruyçión & derramamiento de sangre que vos, onrrado cauallero, avéys fecho en los moros del rey de Granada mi tío, delantero de los muchos trabajos, sofridor de los grandes miedos, guerreador contra los muchos cristianos (defiéndalo Dios, esfuérçelo Dios de su esfuerço). E veyendo quel nuestro Mahomad así nos oluida & el vuestro Dios así vos ayuda, yo soy venido, con acuerdo & consejo de todos los mayores & más prinçipales caualleros de mi reyno, por ver la çirimonia de vuestra ley, que tanto nos es ofensiua. E porque si a vos plaçerá de mandar que oy vuestros caualleros cristianos con los mis moros jueguen las cañas, e si en aquesto como en la guerra vuestro Dios vos ayuda a leuar lo mejor, luego el nuestro profeta Mahomad & los libros de nuestra ley que conmigo mandé traer serán de mí e de mis moros renegados. E por mí e por ellos desde aquí me someto a ser a vuestra ordenança & mandado, & de vos conosçer vasallaje, & de reçebir vuestra cristiandad en el río o do deuamos ser bautizados. Esforçado señor y noble Condestable, ónrrevos Dios, anpárevos Dios con su onrra & su esfuerço.'

La carta leyda, el dicho señor Condestable respondió a los dichos caualleros que le plaçía de buena voluntad. E luego caualgó, & mandó que todos los caualleros, que estauan en punto, viniesen a jugar las cañas con los dichos moros. El qual juego se fizo en la plaça de Santa María, por espaçio de más de tres oras; tan porfiado, que ya los cauallos no se podían mouer, do andauan muchos braçeros & muy desenbueltos caualleros.

E después que ovieron jugado las cañas, el rey de Marruecos, con todos sus moros, leuando su profeta Mahomad & su Alcorán delante, llegó al señor Condestable, & fízole vn razonamiento so la forma siguiente:

'Muy noble señor Condestable: Yo he visto & bien conoçido que no menos en el juego de las cañas que en las peleas vuestro Dios vos ayuda, por do se deue creer que vuestra ley es mejor que la nuestra. Y pues así es, yo & mis moros renegamos della y de su Alcorán, y del nuestro profeta Mahomad.'

Y diçiendo e façiendo, dieron con él & con los libros que trayan en tierra. E con muy grandes alegrías & gritas, & con muchos tronpetas e atabales, fueron con el dicho señor Condestable por toda la çibdad fasta la Madalena. Y en la fuente della lançaron al su profeta Mahomad, y a su rey derramaron vn cántaro de agua por somo de la cabeça, en señal de bautismo; & él & todos sus moros le besaron la mano. E de allí toda la cauallería & grant gente de pie de onbres &

dismounted and went into a hall of the palace, richly decorated with elegant French tapestries, where they found the Lord Constable seated with the Countess his wife, both richly attired, in the company of many knights and squires and ladies and maids of their household and of the city.

As soon as they entered they kissed the Constable's hands and gave him the red parchment, whose text was as follows:

'The King of Morocco, water-drinker and grass-grazer, defender of the Law of Muhammad (may God protect him with His powerful hand), sends greetings to you, most valiant and brave and noble knight don Miguel Lucas, Constable of Castile (may God honour and protect him). I would have you know that news has reached us of the immense destruction and bloodshed which you, honoured sir, have caused to the Moors of the King of Granada, our uncle, he who has been the foremost in all exertions, the sufferer of so much fear, the warrior against so many Christians (may God defend him and give him strength of His strength). Seeing that our Muhammad so forgets us and that your God so aids you, I have come, with the agreement and on the advice of all the important knights of my realm, to view the ceremonies of your Law, which is so offensive to us. If it should please you to order that today your Christian knights should engage in a contest of *cañas,* and if it should happen that in this as in battle your God helps you to win, then I and my Moors will abandon our prophet Muhammad and the books of our Law which I ordered to be brought with us. And for myself and for them, from this moment I shall submit to your orders and will do homage to you, and I will receive your Christian faith in the river or wherever we should be baptized. Brave Lord, noble Constable: may God honour you, support you, and give you strength.'

When the letter had been read, the Lord Constable replied to the two knights that he was pleased to assent. He rode off, ordering all his knights – who were already prepared – to take part in the *cañas* contest against the Moors. This took place in the square before the Cathedral of St Mary, lasting fully three hours, and it was so hard-fought that eventually the horses could scarcely move, and there was a great press of foot-soldiers and unhorsed knights.

After this contest the King of Morocco, and all his Moors, bearing [the figure of?] their prophet Muhammad and their Koran, approached the Lord Constable and addressed him as follows:

'Most noble Lord Constable: I have seen and realized that in the *cañas* contest as in battle your God aids you, and hence it is to be believed that your Law is superior to ours. This being so, I and my Moors renounce that Law and the Koran and our prophet Muhammad.'

So saying, they dashed [the figure of?] Muhammad and the books they were carrying to the ground. Then, with merry shouts, and much playing of trumpets and drums, they paraded round the city with the Constable as far as La Magdalena. Into the fountain in that square they threw their prophet Muhammad, and poured a pitcherful of water over their King's head, as a sign of

niños vinieron a la posada del dicho señor Condestable, con mucho plaçer & alegría, dando gritos & boçes; do a todos generalmente dieron colaçión de muchas frutas & vinos.

baptism; and he and all his Moors kissed the Constable's hands. Thereafter all the riders and a mass of people on foot, men and boys, proceeded to the Constable's lodging amid great jubilation and a deal of shouting; and there everybody was served a collation of divers fruits and wine.

64. Life on the Granadine frontier (1465)

A number of our earlier texts dealt with Christian captives in Muslim hands and the efforts made, especially with divine aid, to release them. In the later medieval centuries the problem continued on a great scale, its resolution being often aided by treaties which ordered the release of all prisoners (held in Christian as well as Muslim lands, of course) and by the creation by both sides of the office of alfaqueque, *the ransomer. Since his name is Arabic (al-fakkak, 'envoy' and 'redeemer of captives'), the suggestion for his creation may have come from the Moors in the first place. He is first mentioned in Castile in the Partidas II.3.1-3 (text 53), where his qualities and duties are listed in detail; but he had appeared much earlier in Aragón, as* exea *and* almotalefe – *again, both words of Arabic origin – in the town charter of Belchite of 1116 (Brodman). His task was to arbitrate and conduct negotiations about the return of prisoners and loot, reparations for damage 'improperly' caused, etc., and for these purposes he enjoyed safe-conduct on both sides of the frontier. What is said in the following extract about Jaén presumably applied along much of the Granadine frontier at the time. Indeed, despite the presence in Granada of a large number of long-term Christian prisoners (text 66), much of the hostile*

En tanto que la guerra entre el señor Condestable y el maestre de Calatraua pasaua, los moros leuaron algunos cristianos & otras cosas de la çibdad de Jahén. Y por tanto, para façer prendas por ellos, mandó a çiertos caualleros de su casa que fuesen a correr a tierra de moros.

Los quales, a veynte & dos de nouiembre, corrieron a Montexícar, de donde troxieron diez o doçe moros y çiertas bestias & cabras & paños y otras cosas. Y como llegaron con ello a Jahén, luego lo mandó poner todo en secrestaçión y en buena guarda. Y en tanto mandó a vn alhaqueque que fuese a la çibdad de Granada, y mandó a su alguaçil mayor que escriuiese al alguaçil mayor de Granada, façiéndole saber cómo aquellos moros y cosas avía traydo por prendas de çiertos cristianos que de la çibdad de Jaén, en paçes, avían leuado; todo lo qual estaua depositado y a buen recabdo. Y el dicho señor Condestable no lo avía consentido vender fasta ver su respuesta, si querrían boluer los dichos cristianos que avían leuado.

Y dende a ocho días, saliendo su merçed por la puerta Noguera, con todos los caualleros que en la dicha çibdad tenían acostamientos del rey nuestro señor, a resçebir alarde dellos, con sus tronpetas y atabales, llegaron con el dicho alhaqueque que avía ydo a Granada vnos seys caualleros moros y otros algunos de pie, mucho onbres de pro, que venían al dicho señor de parte del rey de Granada sobre las dichas prendas. A los quales mandó aposentar bien e darles todas las cosas que para su despensa avíen menester.

activity along this border seems to have consisted at the time of the taking of persons and cattle for purely temporary bargaining purposes. Both peoples in the frontier areas – many of them agriculturally or pastorally rich, and thickly populated – must have lived in constant fear: while their superiors bargained and jousted and at times were richly entertained by their enemies (as in the previous text), ordinary farmers and travellers might be subject to the kind of disturbance and loss here illustrated. There are fascinating studies of the situation by J. W. Brodman, 'Municipal ransoming law on the medieval Spanish frontier', Speculum, 60 (1985), 318–30, and J. de Mata Carriazo, 'Relaciones fronterizas entre Jaén y Granada el año 1479', Revista de Archivos, Bibliotecas y Museos, 61 (1955), 23–51, reprinted in his collected essays En la frontera de Granada (Seville, 1971), pp. 239–64; see also A. García Valdecasas in La Corónica, 16 (1987–88), 108, with bibliography.

The extract is taken from the same source as the preceding, p. 303. The chronicle does not say what the outcome of the negotiations was, but to judge by the friendly way in which the Constable received the Moors, it was satisfactory to both parties.

While the war between the Lord Constable and the Master of Calatrava was going on, the Moors carried off some Christians and booty from the city of Jaén; and so, in order to secure something that might be held as a pledge against their return, the Constable ordered certain knights of his household to make a raid into Moorish territory.

These knights raided Montejícar on the 22nd November, returning with ten or twelve Moors and some horses and goats and cloths [i.e. valuable brocades or silks] and other items. When they arrived with this in Jaén, the Constable ordered that it should all be placed in safe-keeping. He then ordered that an arbitrator should go to Granada, with a letter written by his chief secretary to the chief secretary of Granada, informing him that he had taken those Moors and those goods as surety against the return of certain Christians whom they, the Moors, had taken from the city of Jaén, then on terms of peace with Granada, he having placed both persons and goods in safe-keeping. He added that he would not allow persons and goods to be sold until he knew what reply Granada would make, that is to say, whether the Moors would return the aforementioned Christians they had taken away.

A week later, the Lord Constable went out by the Noguera gate, with all the knights of the city who were in the pay of our lord the King, and he reviewed them to the sound of trumpets and drums. Thereupon there arrived in the company of the arbitrator who had gone to Granada some six Moorish knights and a few others on foot, all very worthy people, these having come from the King of Granada to discuss the matter of the sureties. The Constable ordered that the visitors should be properly lodged and given everything needful for their comfort.

65. Granada on the eve of surrender (1491)

The survival of the Kingdom of Granada for some two hundred years longer than in some ways might seem logical was owed to many factors: the military support it could call on from N. Africa in the 14th century, the strength of its economy and armies, the allegiance of its seemingly contented citizenry; the fact that while Castile had the resources for a final push it usually lacked the willpower to unite and use them; the large sums which the Moors often paid in tribute, accepting formal vassalage to the Castilian monarchs; and, one might cynically add, the convenience of an adjacent state which offered a welcome and a career to disaffected Castilian gentlemen (texts 44, 50). Once the Catholic Monarchs had secured Isabel's succession firmly by winning the war against her rival Juana (1479) and had resolved many domestic matters at the Cortes of Toledo in 1480, the final effort against a desperate enemy in often difficult terrain could be begun. The capture of Alhama in February 1482 marked the start, but it took ten years of fighting to secure the final objective. In these years Granada was progressively weakened by dynastic rivalries and other jealousies, and no help came from Africa.

En todo el tiempo que los Reyes Católicos estubieron en la ciudad de Sancta Fe, siempre truxeron tratos con el rey moro de Granada para que les dexase la ciudad y se fuese a las Alpuxarras, las quales le davan de juro de heredad para sí y para sus descendientes, con más otras rentas y juros en el dicho reino. Y dilatávase esta cosa porque la reina su madre siempre contradecía con toda su posibilidad para que no se concertase con los Reyes Católicos ni desamparase su reino, aconsejándole que aguardase la postrera fortuna y muriese rey.

Y a esta causa siempre el rey moro se guardava quando hablava en los tratos que traía con los Reyes que la reina su madre no lo supiese. La qual se decía Çetí, y hera de nación cristiana, y avía sido cativa quando los moros robaron a Cieça, que es una villa del reino de Murcia. Y como en aquel tiempo era pequeña, con halagos y otros medios que tubieron con ella la hicieron tornar mora; y salió de buen jesto y mujer de bien, y el rey Muley Bulgazen se casó con ella. Lo qual se tubo a muy gran cosa, porque entre los moros era tenida en mucho, porque el Rey o otro qualquier cavallero pudiese casar con cristiana que se ubiese tornado mora.

Esta reina salió de muy grande y valeroso ánimo, y como dicho tengo siempre fue en contradecir a su hijo para que no dexase el reino, sino que muriese rey, como avían hecho sus antepasados. Pero créese que después ella fue en aconsejarle lo contrario, para que lo hiciese, por cierta cosa que aconteció. Y fue que como los Reyes Católicos tubiesen hecha la ciudad de Sancta Fee, y acordasen de dexar jente en ella y levantar su real hasta otro

There are many accounts of the last days of Granada, and the story has been sentimentalized in later writings, in pictures, etc. The following is taken from the Crónica de los Reyes Católicos *by Alonso de Santa Cruz, finished in manuscript in 1550; it is edited by Juan de Mata Carriazo (Seville, 1951, 2 vols). The section is Book I, chapter 3 (pp. 39–43 of vol. I), which has the virtue of depicting – imaginatively, with its direct speech, but perhaps with relative authenticity – the human aspect of the tragedy. The King of Granada was Abu Abd Allah, known in Spanish as 'Boabdil' and as 'el Rey Chico', the latter being a version of Arabic* al-Zaquir *'the little one', presumably a reference to his stature. His mother is said to have been named originally Isabel de Solís, a Christian, daughter of the governor of Bedmar near Jaén; she converted to Islam under the name of Turayya, 'Zoraya' (or in our text, 'Cetí'), and achieved great influence. King 'Muley Bulgazen' who married her was Abu'l Hassan, for long a rival and enemy of Boabdil; he finally abdicated in 1485.*

During the whole time that the Catholic Monarchs were in the encampment at Santa Fe, they engaged in negotiations with the Moorish King of Granada with the intention that he should abandon the city and go to the Alpujarras, he being guaranteed a perpetual income there for himself and his descendants, together with other rents and interest in that region. But this matter was delayed because the Queen-Mother always prevented him by all means in her power from reaching an agreement with their Majesties, or from leaving his kingdom; she advised him to wait to see what fate would bring, and wanted him to die a king.

For this reason the Moorish King was always careful in his dealings with our Monarchs that his mother should not find out about them. This lady was called Cetí, and was by origin a Christian, having been captured when the Moors attacked Cieza, a town in the kingdom of Murcia. She was small at the time, and by means of blandishments and by other methods applied to her they secured her conversion to Islam. She turned out to be a woman of fine appearance and of worth, and King Abu'l Hassan married her. This was considered a startling event, because among Moors it was thought exceptional that the King or any other nobleman should marry a Christian who had converted to Islam.

This Queen turned out to have a strong will of her own, and as I have said, she persistently opposed her son so that he should not abandon the kingdom and should die a king, as his ancestors had done. But it is said that later she advised him in a contrary sense, that is, urging him to do it [i.e. negotiate with the Christians], because of something which happened. It was this way. When the Catholic Monarchs had built Santa Fe, and had agreed to garrison it and remove their headquarters from it till the following summer, certain noblemen voiced their opinions about the matter, advising his Majesty that he, before raising the siege, should set out in force to approach the city, and that the Christian knights

la ciudad, y que los cavalleros cristianos travasen escaramuça con los moros, ꞏ
verano, ubo algunos pareceres de cavalleros sobre ello, que aconsejavan al Rey
para que Su Alteza, antes de levantar el real, saliese poderosamente a dar vist:
ahiciesen por apartarlos de la ciudad lo más que se pudiese; y así apartado
tornasen sobre ellos, no cuydando de matar ni de robar, se cuydase de entrar po
las puertas de la ciudad, aunque fuesen rebueltos con los moros, y que muries
quien muriese.

El qual acuerdo y consejo se determinó el executar otro día, y no se tub
en ella tanto secreto que no lo viniese a saber un mudéxar que se avía salido de
Albaycín con Çibulcoçia Avencerraje, y venido al real. El qual al tiempo que s
bolvían las vatallas al real, que era casi puesto el sol, se quedó atrás
disimuladamente, y dixo a un moro todo lo que avia pasado en el real, para que
se lo dixese al Rey, porque todos estubiesen sobre aviso. Y así el moro lo dixo
al rey, el qual dio parte a sus cavalleros de ello; y se acordó con ellos de salir
otro día de la ciudad con la más jente que pudiese, y dar la batalla a los
cristianos, y morir todos antes que recebir tal afrenta, que una ciudad tan grande
se entrase así.

Y con este acuerdo se levantó otro dia de mañana, y adovó su cuerpo como
suelen hacer los moros quando se ponen en peligro de muerte; y pidió sus armas
y se armó, estando presente la madre y la mujer y hermana. Y después de
armado, pidió a su madre la mano para se la besar, y dixole que le diese su
bendición; y abrazó a la hermana y la besó en el pescuezo, y a su mujer abrazó
y besó en el rostro, y lo mismo hiço a una hija suya. Todo lo qual
hordinariamente solia hacer todas las veces que salía a la batalla. Y aquel día
añadió una habla, diciendo a la madre y a todas las otras que le perdonasen
algunos enojos que les avía dado. De lo qual se escandaliçó la reyna, y turbada
le dixo:

'¿Qué novedad es ésta, hijo mío?'

Y el rey le respondió:

'No es ninguna, pero es rraçón que yo haga esto.'

Y en diciendo esto, la madre se asió del hijo, y le conjuró le dixese adónde
yva, y qué era lo que quería hacer. Y diciendo esto començó a llorar; y
viéndola así, las otras dueñas començaron de hacer lo mismo, y era el alarido en
toda la casa tan grande, que parecía que le tenían muerto. Todavía la madre
asida de su hijo; y no le quiso soltar hasta que le dixo lo que avia savido que se
avía concertado en el real de los cristianos. A lo qual respondió la reyna:

'Pues hijo, ¿a quién encomendáis a la triste de vuestra madre y mujer y
hijos y hermanos, parientes y criados, y toda la ciudad, y los otros pueblos que
os son encomendados? ¿Qué cuenta daréis a Dios de ellos, poniéndolos en tan
mal recado como los ponéis, dando la horden que dáis para que todos muramos a
espada y lança, y los que quedaren sean cavtibos? Mirad bien lo que hacéis, que
en las grandes tribulaciones an de ser los grandes consejos.'

should skirmish with the Moors, trying to draw them away from the city as far as they could; and when they had been drawn off, the Christians should turn back to attack them, not intending to kill or take booty, but trying to get in through the gates of the city, even though they would be all mixed up with the Moors; and this without regard to the casualties that might be suffered.

This advice was accepted, and it was agreed that the move should be made next day; but it was not kept as secret as it should have been, and the matter became known to a *mudéjar* [Muslim living under Christian rule] who had left the Albaicín with Zibulcocia Abencerraje and had come to the royal camp. This man, at a time when the troops were returning to headquarters, at about sunset, stayed behind and hid himself, and told another Moor all that had happened in the royal camp, in order that everybody in the city should stay alert. This Moor reported the matter to the King, and it was agreed that the following day they should ride out from the city with as many men as they could assemble, all disposed to die rather than suffer such an insult, that such a great city should be entered in the way proposed.

On this understanding, the King of Granada rose early next day, and made his person ready in the way that Moors do when facing danger of death. He called for his weapons and armed himself, with his mother and wife and sister present. When he was armed, he asked his mother for her hand so that he could kiss it, and asked her to give him her blessing. He embraced his sister and kissed her on the neck, and embraced and kissed his wife on the face, as he did his daughter also. All this was what he normally did each time he was going out to battle. That day he added a short speech, in which he asked his mother and the others to forgive him for certain annoyances he had caused them. At this the Queen was alarmed, and said to him in distressed tones:

'What new thing is this, my son?'

The King answered:

'It is nothing new, but I have a reason for what I did.'

As he said this, the mother clutched her son, and begged him to tell her where he was going, and what he was proposing to do. As she spoke she began to weep; the other women, seeing her like this, began to weep too, and the uproar in the house was so great that it seemed they were bewailing the King's death. The mother continued to clutch her son, and refused to let go until he told her what he had learned about the plan made in the Christian camp. To this the Queen replied:

'So, my son: to whom do you commend the defence of your poor mother and wife and children and brothers and sisters, relatives, servants, the whole city, and all the towns that have been under your rule? What account will you give of them to God, leaving them in such an evil state as you do, giving orders as you do which will have the effect of letting us all die by sword and spear, while any who do survive will be prisoners? Consider well what you do, for great good counsel comes when great tribulations demand it.'

El rey respondió:

'Señora, muy mejor es morir de una vez que viviendo morir muchas.'

La madre le respondió:

'Verdad es, hijo, lo que decís, si solamente vos muriésedes y todos se salvasen, y la ciudad se libertase. Mas tan gran perdición es muy mal hecho.'

Y el rey respondió:

'Dexadme, señora, que los cavalleros me esperan.'

Su madre le replicó:

'Vive Dios, que no os dexe hasta que me prometáis de no poneros oy en lugar peligroso, y de tener vuestra jente no se aparte de las puertas de la ciudad.'

Y no le soltó de las manos hasta que en el [tahalí] que llevaba le juró de lo hacer así. Porque aquel era juramento que el rey y los grandes de los moros hacían.

Saliendo el rey al campo, mandó tener la jente para que lo acordado en el real de los cristianos no viniese a efecto. Y esto fue la causa, como he dicho, para que muchos pensasen que la reina de allí adelante fuese en aconsejar al rey que tomase algún medio con los Reyes Católicos, para que ellos y los de la ciudad y pueblos fuesen libres para poderse pasar en Africa. Aunque sólo esto no fuera causa para que se efetuara el concierto, sino sucediera aver tanta hanbre en la ciudad que hera conpasión de ver las moras con sus hijos en los brazos dar voces por las calles, con la gran necesidad y miseria que padecían.

Y como el común de la ciudad se viese padecer tanto travajo, se juntavan en quadrillas dando voces, diciendo que el rey devía hacer partido con los cristianos; donde no, que ellos lo harían, pues tanto les inportava. Todo lo qual iba a oídos de su rey, que no poco lo sentía. Y sin esto, fue aconsejado el rey de muchos moros viejos que tenían grande experiencia en cosas de guerra, que devía hacer partido con los Reyes; traiéndole a la memoria muchas cosas para que no lo dexase de hacer.

Entre los quales era aver perdido tanta cavallería y tantas ciudades y villas y lugares del reino, y acrecentarse cada día el exército de los cristianos y el suyo disminuirse. Sobre todo, que la multitud de hombres viejos y mujeres y niños que avía en la ciudad, los quales por no tener bastimentos no podían sufrir la hambre; y que a esta causa vendrían a desanparar la ciudad y irse al real de sus enemigos, por cuya causa la ciudad se tomaría, y todos vernían a ser cautibos y muertos. Y que de su parecer debería con buena voluntad açetar el partido, porque haciéndolo ansí tendrían los Reyes Católicos respeto a su dinidad, y lo tratarían como amigo; y de otra manera no podrían todos dexar de ser muertos y presos.

The King replied:

'My lady, it is much better to die once than to live on while dying a thousand deaths.'

His mother answered:

'What you say is true, my son, if only by your death everyone else could be saved and the city could keep its freedom. But the ruin you will bring upon us all is an evil thing.'

To this the King rejoined:

'Leave me, my lady; my knights await me.'

His mother exclaimed:

'For God's sake, I will not let go of you until you promise me that you will not put yourself in any place of danger, and that you will order your men not to separate themselves from the city gates.'

She would not let his hands go until he swore on the sword-belt he was wearing that he would do so; for such was the way of swearing which the King and the chief men among the Moors had.

When the King reached the field, he ordered his men to stay where they were so that the plan made in the Christian camp should not prove effective. This was the reason, as I said, why many should think that the Queen thenceforward was advising the King that he should reach some kind of accommodation with the Catholic Monarchs, in order that the royal family and the inhabitants of the city and the towns should be free to cross over into Africa. Yet this alone was not sufficient cause for the accommodation to be reached, for it was also the case that there was such hunger in the city that it was sad to see the Moorish women with their babies in their arms crying out in the streets, so great was their need and their suffering.

Since the common people in the city were suffering so badly, they gathered in groups to shout out that the King should reach an agreement with the Christians; and if he did not, they would, since it was a desperate matter for them. All this reached the King's ear, and he was much grieved by it. Even without this, the King was advised by many old Moors who had a great deal of experience in military matters to reach an accommodation with their Majesties; they reminded him of many things which urged him along this path.

Among these was the fact that he had lost so much of his cavalry and so many cities and towns and villages of his realm, and the fact that the Christian army was getting larger day by day while his own was diminishing. Above all, they said that the mass of old men and women and children in the city had no supplies of their own and could no longer bear the hunger; for this reason they would abandon the city and go over to the enemy camp, thus allowing the city to be captured, and all of them to be taken prisoner or killed. Further, that in their view the King should accept such an accommodation gracefully, for in this way their Majesties would respect his dignity, and treat him as a friend; if this were not done, they would surely all end up dead or imprisoned.

Lo qual oído por el rey, le pareció buen consejo, y lo tubo en mucho; y determinó que de allí adelante se hablase en partido con los Reyes Católicos. Y para esto envió secretamente unos alfaquíes moros a Sus Altezas, suplicándoles señalasen algunos de los suyos con quien tratasen de las condiciones de la paz.

When the King heard this he thought it good advice, and resolved that thenceforward he would negotiate a pact with the Catholic Monarchs. For this purpose he secretly sent several of the religious leaders to their Highnesses, asking them to nominate some of their own people with whom they might discuss terms for peace.

66. An Austrian traveller in Spain (1494-95)

Hieronymus Münzer was born about 1460 in Feldkirch (Austria). He trained and practised as a doctor and developed a strong interest in geography and astronomy, publishing several works. With three companions he travelled through France, Spain, Portugal, and Germany, aided throughout by safe-conducts and letters of recommendation from the powerful, and he afterwards wrote his account of what he saw in his Itinerarium, *which long remained in manuscript. He was in Spain from 17 September 1494 to 9 February 1495; he seems not to have spoken Spanish, but presumably one of his companions did. His observations show a keen perception, a feeling for landscape, and a doctor's special interest in botany, agriculture, and foods; he had a fair political awareness, and an intense religiosity which led him to visit every church, monastery, and shrine on his route. His observations on Granada and its region, so recently taken under Christian control, are particularly*

Malicam fortissimam fecerunt situs loci, portus maris et fortissima duo castella. Rex autem integris mensibus sex terra marique eam obsedit omnemque meatum prohibuit, ad tantamque famem eos compulit, ut vigili supra muros in die darentur onzie due panis, et pauperes et alii panem ex lignis et corticibus superioribus (quorum corneum mollescunt) dactilorum pulverizatis facere pulsi sunt. Tandem quinque milia Sarracenorum et mulieres eorum circa littus maris exiverunt versus montana occidentis maritima, que plena erant Sarracenis. Exercitus autem Regis Ferdinandi hoc prohibuit et multos interfecit aliosque ad civitatem intrusit. Ultimo se in graciam Regis dederunt, qui quinque milia hominum singulos ad unum vendit, hominem unum pro 30 ducatis, ea condiccione, ut quisque emptus se 30 ducatis redimere possit. Potitus autem civitate castellum quindecim diebus restitit. Se tandem etiam dedit.

Multa essent scribenda, quomodo quidam Sarracenus sanctus ab eis reputatus Malicam exiverat et in exercitum Regis veniens quendam comitem don Alfarum de Portugalia (quem in Madril vidi et allocutus sum, cuius fratrem Ferdinandum Rex Portugallie capite truncavit) letaliter vulneravit credens hunc Regem fuisse. Qui in minimas partes a Christianis discerptus est.

Olim ante annos septingentos, dum Machometiste Malice potirentur, omnes Christianos ad unum interfecerunt. Iuravit hoc Rex idem facere; sed pro sua clemencia et humanitate eos ut captivos vendidit.

Item in diebus Ianuarii anno 1494 (sunt iam 10 menses) tantus erat terre motus in Malica, qui multas turres et edificia corruere fecit. Item terra in portu maris ita inflata erat, ut multe naves in sicco starent, quousque ex alato vento terra resiliret.

interesting, and he devotes many pages to this, giving a sympathetic account of surviving mosques, Moorish customs and dress, etc., with special praise at several points for the achievements of Moorish agriculture and for gardens which took his eye. Despite this generous attitude, he was no romantic and was well aware of the horrors of the recent fighting and the bitterness of the religious conflict, as the extract shows. The harshness of the treatment of Málaga was exceptional; profits from the sale of its population into slavery were exceptional too, since it is recorded that more than 56 million maravedís accrued to the Castilian Crown.

The section of the Itinerarium *which concerns Spain and Portugal is published by L. Pfandl in* Revue Hispanique, *48 (1920), 1–144, with commentary and notes continuing to p. 179; our extract – chapter 9, section 3, in Puyol's text – is taken from this. There is a Spanish translation, with notes, by J. Puyol (Madrid, 1924), and this version was republished by J. García Mercadal in his* Viajes de extranjeros por España y Portugal *(Madrid, 1952), pp. 327–417. It would be well worth reissuing in popular form.*

The situation of the place, its seaport, and two mighty castles, made Málaga an exceptionally strong city. However, the King of Spain besieged it for six whole months [in fact, four; from 7 April to 18 August 1487] by sea and by land, preventing the entry of supplies, and causing the inhabitants such hunger that the watchmen on the walls received no more than two ounces of bread daily, and the poor and others were reduced to making bread from wood and the bark of the upper parts of palm-trees, which they softened and ground up. Eventually five thousand Moors and their womenfolk tried to flee from the city along the shore into the mountains to the west, which were still occupied at the time by Moors; but King Ferdinand's army stopped them, killing many and forcing the rest back into the city. Finally Málaga surrendered unconditionally to the King, who sold five thousand of its people one by one as slaves, at 30 ducats each, but allowing anyone able to purchase his freedom for a like sum to do so. The castle held out for two weeks longer, but eventually it too surrendered.

Much might be written about a certain Muslim, considered by them to be a holy man, who emerged from Málaga and penetrated the King's camp, where he seriously wounded Count Alvaro of Portugal, believing him to be the King; the soldiers cut him to pieces. (In Madrid I met and spoke to this nobleman, whose brother Ferdinand had his head cut off on the orders of the King of Portugal.)

The King of Spain, knowing that 700 years before the Moors had ordered all the Christians of Málaga to be killed, down to the last man, swore to do the same to them; but in his clemency and humanity he sold them as slaves instead.

In January 1494 – some ten months ago – there was a powerful earthquake in Málaga, which caused many towers and buildings to fall. In the harbour area the earth moved to such an extent that many vessels found themselves on dry land as though carried by a violent wind.

Potitus item Malica pernotati sunt ei 752 Christiani captivi, qui tanta fame erant extenuati, ut Rex brodiis pullorum et aliis ad sanitatem eos reduceret. Inter quos erat quidam Almanus ex Turego, Heinricus Murer, qui 4 annis durissima servitute gravatus erat. Inter ceteros captos exivit senex barbatus, qui se 48 annis captum dixit. Ad quem Regina: 'Quid cogitasses, si primo anno captivitatis tibi dictum fuisset: redemptor tuus ut nos nondum natus est?' Ad que tristis respondit: 'Pre dolore mortuus fuissem.' Exeuntes autem captivi cum cruce parva lignea magno ullulatu clamaverunt: 'Advenisti redemptor mundi, qui liberasti nos ex tenebris inferni.' Prostrarunt autem se Rex et Regina in terram magno fletu dicentes: 'O crux, ave, spes unica! Non nobis, sed nomini tuo sit gloria!' O quantus luctus mixtus gaudio aderat. Item 9 Christiani capti et fidem renegantes devicta Malica exuti et preacutis arundinibus transfixi sunt a Rege christianissimo usque ad mortem. Et erant 2 Lumbardi et 7 Hispani ex Castilia. Missilibus autem arundinis mortui corpora igne cremata sunt. O christianissime Rex, laudes tuas in eternum cantabo!

When Málaga fell, there were found 752 Christian captives, nearly dead from hunger; the King ordered them to be given chicken broth and other food to bring them back to health. Among these was one German-speaker from Zurich, Heinrich Murer, who had been imprisoned for four years in brutal conditions. From among the others there emerged a bearded old man who said he had been a prisoner for 48 years. The Queen asked him: 'Did you ever think that it might be said, in your first year of captivity, that he who was to save you [King Ferdinand] was not at that time born?' The poor fellow answered: 'I would have died of grief.' Other prisoners emerged carrying a small wooden cross and cried out loudly: 'You have come, Redeemer of the world, and have freed us from the depths of hell.' The King and Queen prostrated themselves on the ground and cried among their tears: 'Oh Cross, our sole hope! Glory be not to us but to Thy Name!' There was great sadness mingled with joy. When Málaga was taken, nine Christians who had apostatized were captured, and on the orders of the King were shot to death with arrows; these were two Lombards and seven Castilians. After this execution their bodies were burned. Oh most godly King, I will sing your praises for evermore!

156

67. The King of Tlemcen becomes King Ferdinand's vassal (1512)

For centuries Spanish rulers had dreamed of carrying the war against the Muslims onto N. African soil. An early instance, at least in the literary record, is found in lines 2493-2504 of the Poema de mio Cid (text 24), when the hero, having won Valencia and defeated the effort of King Búcar to recover it, says that in Morocco there is fear he might attack them; the Cid prudently remarks that he has no such intention, but will exact tribute from the Moroccans (though this in itself much overstates the reality of the matter). Alfonso X hoped to carry the war to Africa, and in 1252 and 1255 the Pope exhorted the Spanish bishops to help such a 'crusade'. In 1260 Castilian forces took and briefly held Salé in Morocco, but this was virtually the end of the endeavour until the Portuguese took and occupied several Moroccan towns, beginning with Ceuta in 1414. After the capitulation of Granada the possibility of such an invasion came to the fore. By the treaty of Tordesillas in 1494 Morocco and W. Africa were to be for Portugal, the coast east of Morocco for Spain; Pope Alexander VI accepted this division and granted crusading indulgences for Christians going to fight there.

'En el Nombre de Dios piadoso, apiadador poderoso sobre lo visible, al muy alto y muy poderoso e esclarecido Rey mayor en el mundo, cuyo estado, linaje y grandeza es más antigua que de ningún Príncipe, tan excelente y tan liberal, que sus obras manifiestan las obras de su Persona, que ya por el mundo son divulgadas, el cual es de mayor estimación y reputación que ningún Príncipe, pasado [o] de nuestro tiempo; grave para ser temido, regidor gracioso, benigno para que todos le osen demandar mercedes, D. Fernando Rey de Aragón, de las dos Sicilias, de Jerusalén y de todas partes a do envía su poder, y la muy alta e muy poderosa y esclarecida Reyna e Señora Doña Juana, Reyna de Castilla, de León, de Granada, la más verdadera Reyna e Señora de todas las que viven, por ser mejor en sus pasados de mayores estados.
El Siervo de Dios Muley-Baudala-Abdali, Rey de Tremezen. Beso las manos de V.A. y me humillo por mi Embaxador, ante vro. acatamiento, y pongo debajo de vro. servicio mi persona y mi tierra, y envío[o]s mi obediencia y mi voluntad pura para estar y permanecer en vro. servicio, en público y en secreto, y téngome por ser vro. siervo en más que ningún Rey de los moros, por la esperanza que tengo de vtra. grandeza; mi obediencia y la paz y concordia de V.A. comienzan agora, e por ello doy a Dios y a V.A. muchas gracias; tengo por perdido todo el tiempo que no he estado en vro. servicio, agora prometo de conservarlo, cuanto en mí esté, plegue a Dios de poner su mano para conservarlo en V.A. de voluntad, para que reciba mi obediencia y le sea aceptada y agradable. Recibí una carta de V.A. que me alumbró para las cosas justas de toda paz y concodia, y en ella vi el amor que V.A. me tiene, y la voluntad que tiene a mis cosas, en aceptar mi servicio, por lo cual doy a Dios muchas gracias,

Queen Isabel's dying wish (1504) is said to have been for a continuation of war against the Muslims in N. Africa. Andalusian nobles such as Diego Fernández de Córdoba and the Duke of Medina Sidonia, who had been active in the final stages of the war against Granada, led expeditions, and it is these factors which enable one to consider war in N. Africa as a natural extension of the Peninsular campaign concluded in 1492. It was naturally important also to subdue Muslim power in N. Africa and prevent aid and encouragement being sent to the now subject Moors, moriscos, of Granada, particularly in view of the rebellion these staged in 1500-01 in the Alpujarras and elsewhere. In 1506 the Spaniards extended their hold on Melilla (held since 1494), and took Oran in 1509, Bougie and Tripoli in 1510. In January 1512 the ruler of Tlemcen in what is now Algeria saw the need to submit to King Ferdinand. The following text, whose original was presumably in Arabic, is preserved together with a description of the ruler's embassy by Andrés Bernáldez, a cleric of Seville, in his Historia de los Reyes Católicos *concluded in manuscript form in 1513. It is chapter 229 of the edition by the Bibliófilos Andaluces (Seville, 1870, 2 vols).*

One wonders what – among so much diplomatic jargon and high politics – became of the little girl.

'In the Name of merciful God, powerful protector of all that we see, to the most high and powerful and famous King, greatest in this world, whose estate, lineage, and greatness are more anciently founded than those of any other ruler; so excellent and so liberal that his deeds show forth the qualities of his person, now amply known throughout the world, and who stands in higher esteem and repute than any other Prince either of the past or of the present; grave in order to be feared, a gracious ruler, kindly so that all may venture to ask favours of him, Ferdinand, King of Aragón, of the Two Sicilies, of Jerusalem, and of all regions to which he extends his power. Also to the most high and powerful and famous Queen and Lady Joan, Queen of Castile, of León, of Granada, the truest Queen and Lady of all those alive on account of the quality of her ancestors' blood.

Muley Baud'Ala Abd-'Ali, King of Tlemcen, Servant of God. I kiss your Highness's hands, and in the person of my ambassador I humble myself before you, begging your attention. I place my person and my realm at your service, and send you my allegiance and my sincere wish to be and to remain in your service, in public and in secret. I consider myself your servant to a greater extent than any other Moorish ruler, on account of all that I hope for from your greatness. My allegiance and wish for peace and concord from you start now, and for that I give thanks to God and to your Highness. I consider all the time that I have not spent in your service as wasted, and now I promise to maintain that service, as far as it lies in my power; may it please God to use His hand in order to maintain your Highness's goodwill in maintaining it, so that you may receive my allegiance and so that it should be acceptable to you. I received a

que conozco ha odío lo que le he rogado, y más veo el efecto que esperaba, así como el dador es infinito es mi placer infinito cuando vide la carta de V.A. en que parece acepta mi servicio.

Muy poderoso Señor: envío a V.A. dos cosas que le son debidas, los christianos que estaban cautivos, e aquí se hallaron, que es cosa Santa e agradecida de Dios, para este mundo, e para el otro, que vos como su Rey justo sois obligado a pedillo, e otro presente temporal, que como a persona Real se debe, de todos los otros Reyes menores; no es tan grande como mi voluntad, mas es señal que todo lo que queda es de V.A.

El Alcayde Mohamad de Lubdi es persona de linaje e de virtud, sabio e entendido en todas las cosas de generosidad e nobleza, antiguo criado mío: por fidelísimo y de buen consejo envíole, porque para enviar ante vra. grandeza no se podía escoger persona más fiel. Suplico a V.A. que lo mande oyr y crea del todo lo que de mi parte le digere, y si demás de lo que acá sabemos a V.A. pertenece otra cosa de que le podamos servir, con él me lo envie a mandar.'

La sobre dicha carta vino al Rey D. Fernando en el mes de enero del año del Nacimiento de Ntro. Redemptor Jesuchristo, de 1512 años, y con ella le envió en presente las cosas siguientes:

Estando el Rey en Burgos, ciento y treinta christianos que estaban cautivos en su reyno, e veinte y dos caballos, encubertados de cubiertas de grana y los botones de abajo de la barriga de oro, e a el pecho; más un juego de ajedrez de oro, tabla y trebejos, e cada un trebejo atado con una cadenita de oro, con pollos reciennacidos, e una gallina morisca, india, pintada pardilla, que cantaba muy maravillosamente, e un león manso pequeño e una doncella pequeña, blanca como nieve, e muy hermosa, de sangre Real, e muy vestida de terciopelo, e con una cadena de oro, e muchas manillas de oro, e muchas piedras preciosas; e más, sesenta mil doblas, e otras muchas cosas, lo cual todo envió con el dicho su Embaxador, de Orán, e vinieron con todo ello en salvamento al Puerto de Cartajena, e dende fueron a Burgos, donde por el Rey fueron bien recibidos.

letter from your Highness which explained to me matters properly concerning peace and concord, and in that letter I could perceive the love you bear me and your goodwill towards my affairs, as you accept my service; for this I thank God, for I know that He has granted what I asked, and furthermore I can see the consequences I was hoping for; just as the Giver is infinite, so was my pleasure infinite when I saw the letter in which your Highness accepts my service.

Most powerful Master: I send you two items which are properly yours. One is the Christians who were here as prisoners. To release them is a holy act and one pleasing to God, both in this world and in the next, and you as their just King were obliged to ask for their release. The other present is a material one, of the kind proper to a royal personage, one greater than all the other lesser monarchs. It is not so large as I might wish, but is a sign that all the rest is yours also.

My minister Muhammad de Lubdi is a man of birth and good qualities, wise and experienced in all matters concerning generosity and nobility, and he has been for many years a servant of mine. I send him to you as an exceptionally loyal and sensible person, and none better could have been chosen to send to your Highness. I beg your Highness to listen to him and believe everything that he will say to you on my behalf. If there is any further matter of which we might be unaware here but in which we could serve you, send me instructions about it through him.'

This letter reached King Ferdinand in January 1512. With it there arrived a present the record of which is as follows:

There came to the King while he was in Burgos 130 Christians who had been held prisoner in Tlemcen; and 22 horses dressed in scarlet cloths, the bosses of the girths under their bellies being of gold, and those at their breasts also; then, a chess-set all of gold, both board and pieces, each piece being attached by a little golden chain; then, newly-hatched chicks, and a Moorish or Indian bird, greyish like a guinea-fowl, which sang most wondrously; then, a small tame lion; then, a tiny girl as white as snow, very lovely, of the blood-royal, richly dressed in velvet, wearing a gold chain and gold bangles and many precious stones; and finally, 60,000 gold pieces, and much else besides, all of which the King sent from Oran with the ambassador mentioned earlier. They all reached Cartagena safely, and went from there to Burgos, where they were graciously received by King Ferdinand.

68. Oppression and protest (1566)

The terms on which Granada capitulated in 1492 were generous, and were maintained for some years under the tolerant Archbishop of Granada, Fr Hernando de Talavera. The arrival of the severe Fr Francisco Jiménez de Cisneros in 1499 put an end to this: forced conversion of the Muslims by mass baptism began, and this, with other acts, caused a rebellion of the moriscos *in the Alpujarras in 1500, speedily suppressed. New measures began to affect the large population of* moriscos *in Aragón in 1526, and in the same year Charles V on the advice of lawyers and clerics imposed measures designed to force the Granadine* moriscos *to conform to Christian usages in such matters as language, clothing, and bathing, but he was bought off by a contribution of 80,000 ducats to his treasury. Philip II's zeal for the faith was not to be so easily deflected. His* Pragmática *(proclamation) of 17 November 1566 was effective from 1 January 1567. Every aspect of life was to be affected in the effort to make the* moriscos *good Christians – they were this in name only, most retaining their Muslim faith and practices – and good Spaniards. After three years all use of Arabic was to be prohibited; Castilian dress was to be worn, and women were not to cover their faces; Moorish names were to be dropped; Christian customs should apply at weddings and all other festivities, Moorish dancing and musical instruments being banned; bathing habits should be abandoned and bath-houses be destroyed; and so on.*

[...] No se fundaron los vaños sino para linpiarse de qualquier çuçidad pública con la demasiada calor que ay en ellos y con el agua caliente que ay en ellos; saca el sudor de los cuerpos en que salen las tales zuçidades y los malos umores; y los vañeros lávanlos ansí en rrascallos con sus uñas y otras cosas de lana sobre cortesas que se dizen 'almohaças', y manos de palmas y piedras de mar con que les linpian la pranta del pie y calcañal dél, y con labarse. Pues que lo que se puede dezir que en los vaños pasan algunos pecados mortales, ansy a cristianos como a los nueuamente convertidos: de mugeres hablo, que en yr a los dichos vaños se conçiertan con sus galanes, para que en los dichos vaños se junten con ellos: esto no se puede averiguar por ninguna vía; porque estando las mugeres en los dichos vaños, ansy cristianas viejas como nueuas, según tan muncho número de mugeres y vañeras que las lavan, y durante las dichas mugeres en el vaño, no entra ningún varón por la puerta dél; pues, siendo esto ansy, no determino cómo se puede dezir que se juntan en el vaño para hazer los tales pecados. Pues, podemos dezir que algunas de las dichas mugeres viejas y nueuas tengan este mal pensamiento para juntarse con sus galanes; mejor aparejo ternán en yr a sus visitas, ansí en visitar yglesias, como en jubileos y farsas donde se topan las mugeres y honbres unos con otros, y ternían mejor aparejo en consertar posada de dejamiento donde se junten; y creo que por algunas de las

The Granadine moriscos were a cowed subject population but could not silently accept the destruction of their whole way of life. The most senior of their leaders, Francisco Núñez Muley (an old man, who says he had been a page-boy to Hernando de Talavera in 1502) addressed to Pedro de Deza, the newly-appointed president of the Audiencia (High Court) of Granada, a lengthy and considered, if somewhat repetitive protest against the Pragmática, *commenting point by point. He was not without support among Christian authorities, but the objections had no effect; in despair, the* moriscos *rose in revolt (text 69).*

Several differing texts of Núñez Muley's protest are known. The most authentic seems to be that published by K. Garrad in Atlante, 2 (1954), *198-226; our extract is taken from this, pp. 217-18. It is also in* Revue Hispanique, 6 (1899), 205-39. *An excellent short book on all these matters, covering essential cultural and anthropological aspects, is Julio Caro Baroja's* Los moriscos del Reino de Granada *(Madrid, 1957; 2nd edition, 1976). On Muslim bathing habits in S. Spain, the theme of our extract, see Ariè, pp. 392-96; a Granadine theologian in a book of 1638 recalled that the* moriscos *had been accustomed to bath (or bathe) 'even in December', evidently an unnatural practice. Garrad in a note sums up Church objections: 'the public baths ... afforded an opportunity for practising Mohammadan rites, in which ablution is the customary preliminary to prayer, and ... they were centres of illicit sexual intercourse.'*

[...] The baths were not built for any reason other than for people to clean themselves of dirt with the great heat and warm water there is in them; this causes the body to sweat, and in the sweat dirt and unhealthy humours leave the body. The bath attendants clean the bathers partly by scraping them with their nails and with pads of wool mounted on pieces of bark which they call 'almohazas', also with bunches of palm-leaves and stones from the sea [pumice?] with which they rub the soles of the feet and heels; and people wash themselves. As for the baths being places for mortal sins, concerning both Old Christians and recent converts: with regard to women, and the charge that they go to the baths to make assignations with their lovers and indeed to make love there, there is no way in which this could be proved, for while the women – both Old and New Christians – are using the baths, there are far too many other women around, and female bath-attendants washing them [for this to be possible]; and while the women are bathing, no man is allowed in; and this being so, I do not see how anyone can say that they get together in the bath-houses to commit such sins. We might allow that some of the women, both Old and New Christians, do indeed want to meet their lovers, but they would manage this more readily by going on social calls, or visiting churches, or going to religious festivities and plays where men and women are mixed up together, and there they would find more opportunity for making assignations at some lodging-house where they could

causas susodichas el señor Alçobispo avía mandado que las 'Salues' en quaresma se hiziesen muy tempranas antes de la oraçión, por escusar algunas de las causas susodichas. Pues podemos dezir que sy los dichos vaños se quitasen y que no los ubiese, pues çerrar que nadie no labase su cuerpo en su casa ni fuera della ni en rrío ni en arroyo, pues ¿qué harían los enfermos o las personas que tubiesen neçeçidad de linpiarse de las tales suziedades susodichas? Aurá quien pueda dezir '¿Qué hazen los de Castilla de los vaños?' Puédese rresponder que tienen libertad para se lauar donde quisyeren, y con esto pueden pasar sin los dichos vaños. Pues estas livertades no las tienen los naturales deste rreyno por ninguna vía; e por las causas arriba dichas de las suziedades y personas que trabajan en ellos, más que en otros rreynos a causa de los edifiçios de aguas ansy suzias como linpias; mayormente que en toda Castilla auía vaños, y en el tiempo de la sagrada escritura avía vaños; y no se dexaron de auellos en Castilla, sino a causa que los vaños afloxan los mienbros y venas de los honbres para la guerra; pues en este rreyno los naturales no son gente de guerra para los afloxar, y tienen en esto más neçeçidad de los vaños por las causas arriba declaradas. […]

get together. I think that for one of these reasons his Grace the Archbishop ordered that in Lent the 'Salva Regina' should take place very early, before the Oration, in order to avoid such problems. We may ask: if the baths were to be suppressed, and closed, and it were decreed that nobody could wash his body in his house or outside it or in a river or a stream, what would the sick do, or those people that need to wash off the dirt I mentioned before? [The writer earlier specifies kinds of activity that make people dirty: handling fish, metal-working, etc.]. Some may say: 'What do the Castilians do about washing?' The answer might be that they are free to wash wherever they want, and so can manage without baths of our kind. But the people of this kingdom do not in any way enjoy such liberty, and yet need to wash for the reasons outlined above, connected with the dirty kinds of work they do, this need being greater than in other regions; [and moreover we have here] bath-houses and a system of drains. It should be specially noted that baths used to exist in Castile, and in biblical times there were baths also [John 5.2]]; and they were abolished in Castile only because bathing weakens the limbs and sinews of men for war [perhaps a reference to the – legendary? – decree of Alfonso VI after the defeat at Uclés in 1108, according to which all baths were to be destroyed]; but in this kingdom there are no warlike people who could be weakened in this way, and they need their baths for the reasons given above. [...]

69. The Alpujarra rebellion (1568-70)

The rebellion – for the background to which, see text 68 – lasted about a year and a half. Of the three chief accounts of it which exist, that of Diego Hurtado de Mendoza is both the closest to the events in time and also that by the closest observer, and the Guerra de Granada *has rightly enjoyed the status of a classic as both prose and historiography. Hurtado de Mendoza (c. 1500–75) was a member of a branch of the great Mendoza family which established itself in Granada; he had a varied and distinguished career as diplomat, soldier, scholar, and poet, in sum an excellent representative of Renaissance man. His special*

(a)

Siguiéronse luego ofensas en su ley, en las haciendas, y en el uso de la vida, así en cuanto a la necesidad, como cuanto al regalo, a que es demasiadamente dada esta nación; porque la Inquisición los comenzó a apretar más de lo ordinario. El Rey les mandó dejar la habla morisca, y con ella el comercio y comunicación entre sí; quitóseles el servicio de los esclavos negros a quienes criaban con esperanzas de hijos, y el hábito morisco en que tenían empleado gran caudal; obligáronlos a vestir castellano con mucha costa, que las mujeres trajesen los rostros descubiertos, que las casas acostumbradas a estar cerradas, estuviesen abiertas; lo uno y lo otro tan grave de sufrir entre gente celosa. Hubo fama que les mandaban tomar los hijos, y pasarlos a Castilla; vedáronles el uso de los baños, que eran su limpieza y entretenimiento; primero les habían prohibido la música, cantares, fiestas, bodas, conforme a su costumbre, y cualesquier juntas de pasatiempo. Salió todo esto junto, sin guardia, ni provisión de gente; sin reforzar presidios viejos, o afirmar otros nuevos. Y aunque los moriscos estuviesen prevenidos de lo que había de ser, les hizo tanta impresión, que antes pensaron en la venganza que en el remedio. Años había que trataban de entregar el reino a los príncipes de Berbería, o al turco; mas la grandeza del negocio, el poco aparejo de armas, vituallas, navíos, lugar fuerte donde hiciesen cabeza, el poder grande del Emperador, y del Rey Felipe su hijo, enfrenaba las esperanzas, e imposibilitaba las resoluciones especialmente estando en pie nuestras plazas mantenidas en la costa de Africa, las fuerzas del turco tan lejos, las de los corsarios de Argel más ocupadas en presas y provecho particular, que en empresas difíciles de tierra.

qualifications to write about the revolt and its suppression were that he knew Granada and the moriscos *intimately, while of the revolt itself he says 'parte de la cual yo vi y parte entendi de personas que en ella pusieron las manos y el entendimiento'. He wrote his account in 1571–75; it circulated a good deal in manuscript (some 34 MSS are known) and was published only in 1627, that is, after passions had cooled and after those mentioned in it – not always favourably – had died. There are many modern editions; our extracts are taken respectively from pp. 108–9 and 228–30 of the Castalia edition by B. Blanco–González (Madrid, 1970), and are self-explanatory.*

(a)

Then there followed offences against their faith, against their properties, against their way of life, both as to very basic matters and as to the lighter side (to which this people is overmuch given); and the Inquisition began to press them harder than was normal. The King ordered that they give up using Arabic, which meant the end of intercourse and communication among themselves. They were stopped from having Negro slaves in their service, brought up by them in the hope that they would produce children. They were forced to give up their Moorish dress in which they had invested a lot of money, and were ordered to dress in Spanish style at great expense. The women were forced to leave their faces uncovered, and houses normally kept closed were ordered to be opened up, both matters most hard to be borne by a jealous people. It was rumoured that their children were to be taken from them to be brought up in Castile. The use of the baths, that had served for both cleanliness and entertainment, was forbidden to them. Earlier, a ban had been placed upon their music and songs, traditional weddings, and any gathering of a leisure kind. All this happened at one blow without planning or provision of persons to oversee it all: old prisons were not strengthened, and no new ones were built. And although the Moors were forewarned about what was to come, in the event it came as such a profound shock that they thought rather of vengeance than of any remedy. Years before they had tried to hand the kingdom over to the rulers of Barbary, or to the Turk; but the sheer scale of the operation, their scant supply of weapons, food stocks, ships, their lack of a fortress where they might establish their headquarters, the great power of the Emperor [Charles V] and of his son Philip [II], checked all their hopes, and also prevented them taking any decisions; especially as we had our fortresses in a state of alert on the African coast, and the Turkish forces were so remote, and the corsairs of Algiers were more occupied in taking prizes and in gain for themselves than in dubious operations on land.

166

(b)

Mandó el Rey que todos los moriscos habitantes en Granada saliesen a vivir repartidos por lugares de Castilla y el Andalucía; porque morando en la ciudad no podían dejar de mantenerse vivas las pláticas y esperanzas, dentro y fuera. Había entre los nuestros sospechas, desasosiego, poca seguridad: parecía a los que no tenían experiencia de mantener pueblos oprimiendo o engañando a los enemigos de dentro y resistiendo a los de fuera, estar en manifiesto peligro. Con tal resolución ordenó don Juan a los veinte y tres de junio que encerrasen todos los moriscos en las iglesias de sus parroquias; ya era llegada gente de las ciudades a sueldo del Rey, y se estaba con más seguridad. Puso la ciudad en arma: la caballería y la infantería repartida por sus cuarteles; ordenó al marqués de Mondéjar que subiendo al Albaicín se mostrase a los moriscos, y con su autoridad los persuadiese a encerrarse llanamente. Recogidos que fueron de esta manera, mandáronles ir al Hospital Real fuera de Granada un tiro de arcabuz. Anduvo don Juan por las calles con guardas de a caballo y guión; violos recoger inciertos de lo que había de ser de ellos; mostraban una manera de obediencia forzada, los rostros en el suelo con mayor tristeza que arrepentimiento; ni de esto dejaron de dar alguna señal, que uno de ellos hirió al que halló cerca de sí, dícese que con acometimiento contra don Juan, pero lo cierto no se pudo averiguar porque fue luego hecho pedazos. Yo que me hallé presente diría que fue movimiento de ira contra el soldado, y no resolución pensada. Quedaron las mujeres en sus casas algún día, para vender la ropa y buscar dineros con que seguir y mantener sus maridos. Salieron atadas las manos, puestos en la cuerda, con guarda de infantería y caballería por una y otra parte, encomendados a personas que tuviesen cargo de irlos dejando en lugares ciertos del Andalucía, y guardarlos; tanto porque no huyesen, como porque no recibiesen injuria. Quedaron pocos mercaderes y oficiales, para el servicio y trato de la ciudad: algunos a contemplación y por interés de amigos. Muchos de los mancebos que adivinaron la mala ventura huyeron a la sierra, donde la hallaban mayor; los que salieron por todos tres mil y quinientos, el número de mujeres mucho mayor. Fue salida de harta compasión para quien los vio acomodados y regalados en sus casas: muchos murieron por los caminos, de trabajo, de cansancio, de pesar, de hambre, a hierro, por mano de los mismos que los habían de guardar, robados, vendidos por cautivos.

(b)

The King ordered that all the Moors living in [the city of] Granada should leave and be settled in the villages of Castile and Andalusia, the reason being that if they stayed in the city intercourse between them and hence their hopes would be sustained, both among themselves and more widely. Among our people there existed suspicion, unease, a feeling of insecurity; to those unaccustomed to keeping a people in subjection or playing a double game with enemies at home while holding off those abroad, it seemed that they were in obvious peril. With all this in mind Don John [of Austria] ordered on 23 June [1570] that all the Moors should be shut up in their parish churches. Now new men had arrived from the city militias, paid by the King, and people felt more safe. Don John ordered the city to be put into military readiness, with the cavalry and the infantry in their barracks. He ordered the Marquis of Mondéjar to go up through the Albaicín and show himself to the Moors, so that with his authority he could persuade them to shut themselves in the churches without trouble. Once they were rounded up in this way, the Moors were ordered to proceed to the Royal Hospital which stands at a distance of an arquebus shot outside Granada. Don John went around the streets accompanied by mounted guards and a banner. He saw the Moors gathered together, unsure of what was to become of them. They showed a kind of grudging obedience, with their faces cast down more in sadness than repentance; but there was still some small sign of resistance, for one of them wounded the soldier he found close to him, it was said with a mind to attack Don John, but the truth could not be ascertained because he was instantly cut to pieces. I who was present would say that it was a movement produced by anger against the soldier, without any considered intention. The women stayed in their homes another day or so, in order to sell off clothing and try to get money together so that they could follow and maintain their husbands. They all left with their hands tied and attached to a rope, guarded on both sides by cavalry and infantry, entrusted to persons who were charged with the duty of leaving them in groups in designated villages of Andalusia, and with the duty of guarding them: partly so that they should not escape, partly so that they should receive no harm. A few merchants and craftsmen remained, in order to maintain services in the city; a few others stayed, protected by friends. Many of the young men who guessed what their fate was to be fled to the mountains, where a worse one awaited them. Those who left were in all 3,500 men, and the number of women was much higher. It was an exodus that aroused great pity in anyone who had earlier seen them comfortable and at ease in their homes; many died along the roads, of their labours, of exhaustion, of grief, of hunger; or they were killed or robbed or sold as slaves by the very people charged with protecting them.

70. The galley-slave (1583)

The perpetual menace of the pirates based on the Barbary coast became more serious in the second half of the 16th century with the presence of the Turks who were ever more active in the central and western parts of the Mediterranean. Dragut in line 5 of our text was a much-feared Turkish captain.

Amarrado al duro banco
de una galera turquesca,
ambos manos en el remo
y ambos ojos en la tierra,
un forzado de Dragut
en la playa de Marbella
se quejaba al ronco son
del remo y de la cadena:
'Oh sagrado mar de España,
famosa playa serena,
teatro donde se han hecho
cien mil navales tragedias,
pues eres tú el mismo mar
que con tus crecientes besas
las murallas de mi patria,
coronadas y soberbias,
tráeme nuevas de mi esposa,
y dime si han sido ciertas
las lágrimas y suspiros
que me dice por sus letras;
porque si es verdad que llora
mi cautiverio en tu arena,
bien puedes al mar del sur
vencer en lucientes perlas.
Dame ya, sagrado mar,
a mis demandas respuesta,
que bien puedes, si es verdad
que las aguas tienen lengua;
pero, pues no me respondes,
sin duda alguna que es muerta,
aunque no lo debe ser,
pues que vivo yo en su ausencia.
Pues he vivido diez años
sin libertad y sin ella,

Luis de Góngora (1561-1627), the greatest poet of his time, caught the essence of what must have been a not uncommon aspect of this menace, in the ballad form of which from his earliest writing days he was a master. The text is that of the Chacón manuscript of the poet's work, published by R. Foulché-Delbosc (New York, 1921, 3 vols), I, pp. 51-52, here modernized.

Chained to the hard bench of a Turkish galley, with both hands on his oar and both eyes fixed on the land, one of Dragut's prisoners off the coast of Marbella groaned to the harsh noise of the oar and the chain:

'Ah, sacred seas of Spain, and famous peaceful shore, place which has witnessed a hundred thousand maritime tragedies, since you are the same sea which with your waves kisses the walls of my native land so proud with their battlements, bring me news of my wife, and tell me if the tears and sighs she expresses in her letters have been sincere; for if it is true that she weeps on your sands for my captivity, you can readily rival southern seas with shining pearls [the wife's tears = drops of sea-water].

Give me, oh sacred sea, a reply to my questions; you are well able to, if it is true that waves have tongues; but, since you do not answer, doubtless she is dead; yet it cannot be so, since I still live without her.

Since I have lived ten years without freedom and without her, forever

siempre al remo condenado,
a nadie matarán penas.'
  En esto se descubrieron
de la religión seis velas,
y el cómitre mandó usar
al forzado de su fuerza.

condemned to row, hardships will never kill anybody.'

At this there were sighted six ships of our navy, and the commander of the slaves ordered the prisoner to pull hard.

71. The final chapter (1609?)

In September 1582 the Consejo de Estado, meeting in Lisbon, resolved to seek what the 20th century would sadly recognize as the 'final solution', by expelling the moriscos, *just as the Jews had been expelled in 1492. (An even more 'final' solution was proposed by some: 'embarcar a los moriscos en naves a las que se daría barreno en alta mar.') It was clear to the authorities that the* moriscos, *most of them Christian in name only, would cling to Islam and that any true conversion or cultural assimilation would take centuries; also that the danger of attack by their N. African and Turkish* coreligionaries, *for whom the* moriscos *constituted a potential and in a few cases an active 'fifth column' of allies, continued to be very real all along Spain's south coast. To these factors must be added the popular prejudices against them which are illustrated in our extract.*

The 1582 decision was a preliminary one only. The nation debated the question passionately. The moriscos *were not without their defenders, especially the great lords of Aragón and Valencia whose estates were so profitably worked by their Muslim subjects, and a few churchmen who held that their nominal Christian status protected them. Eventually the decision was made and the expulsion took place, region by region, from 1609 to 1614. Fr Jaime Bleda, who had written powerfully in favour of it, remarked that Philip III was thereby 'el postrero, y supremo conquistador de los moros de España', completing the 'Reconquest'. No count was made of numbers, but it is reasonably calculated*

Berganza: [...] Así, determiné soltarme, como lo hice, y saliéndome de Granada, di en una huerta de un morisco, que me acogió de buena voluntad, y yo quedé con mejor, pareciéndome que no me querría para más de para guardarle la huerta, oficio, a mi cuenta, de menos trabajo que el de guardar ganado; y como no había allí altercar sobre tanto más cuanto al salario, fue cosa fácil hallar al morisco criado a quien mandar, y yo amo a quien servir. Estuve con él más de un mes, no por el gusto de la vida que tenía, sino por el que me daba saber la de mi amo, y por ella la de todos cuantos moriscos viven en España. ¡Oh, cuántas y cuáles cosas te pudiera decir, Cipión amigo, desta morisca canalla, si no temiera no poderlas dar fin en dos semanas! Y si las hubiera de particularizar, no acabara en dos meses; mas en efeto habré de decir algo; y así, oye en general lo que yo vi y noté en particular desta buena gente. Por maravilla se hallará entre tantos uno que crea derechamente en la sagrada ley cristiana; todo su intento es acuñar, y guardar dinero acuñado, y para conseguirle trabajan y no comen; en entrando el real en su poder, como no sea sencillo, le condenan a cárcel perpetua y a escuridad eterna; de modo que ganando siempre y gastando nunca, llegan y amontonan la mayor cantidad de dinero que hay en España. Ellos son su hucha, su polilla, sus picazas y sus comadrejas; todo lo llegan, todo lo esconden y todo lo tragan. Considérese que

that some 300,000 persons were involved.

Cervantes wrote much about Moors and moriscos, *and had plenty of direct experience of both. He fought at Lepanto in 1571, and on returning from military service in Italy he was captured by pirates and spent five years as a prisoner in Algiers (1575-80); after that he lived much in S. Spain. In our passage from the story* El coloquio de los perros, *the dog Berganza (in reviewing the vices and defects of the various masters he has served) echoes all the popular hostility to the* moriscos. *The story was published in Cervantes'* Novelas ejemplares *in 1613; it is often held to have been written between about 1602 and 1606, that is, in the heat of the debate on the question, but Márquez Villanueva (see below) is surely right to hold that Cipión's reply, with its confident prophecy by hindsight, shows that at least this passage was composed in or after 1609. It is obviously wrong to take Berganza's diatribe as an expression of Cervantes' own views, as has often been done by critics (including, it seems, M. de Riquer in* Modern Language Review, *74 (1979), xxi-xxxv); the dog says of himself that 'a cuatro razones que digo, me acuden palabras a la lengua como mosquitos al vino, y todas maliciosas y murmurantes'.*

On the expulsion, an essential source is P. Boronat y Barrachina, Los moriscos españoles y su expulsión *(Valencia, 1901, 2 vols). For this aspect of Cervantes, the best study is that of F. Márquez Villanueva,* Personajes y temas del 'Quijote' *(Madrid, 1975), pp. 229-335, with full bibliography; see also J. Salazar Rincón,* El mundo social del 'Quijote' *(Madrid, 1986), pp. 201-10.*

Berganza: [...] I therefore resolved to get free, and I did; I left Granada and found myself on a Moor's farm, where he greeted me warmly, and I found I was better off, for it appeared that he wanted me only to guard the farm, a better job, in my book, and less demanding, than that of guarding flocks. And since there was in this case no arguing about wages, it was easy to find a servant for the Moor to order about, and for me to find a master to serve. I spent more than a month with him, not from any pleasure that I took in that lifestyle, but from a wish to find out about my master's way of life, and through that, the way of life of all the Moors we have in Spain. Ah, friend Cipión, what things could I tell you about these Moorish dogs, if I were not afraid of being unable to make an end of them in a fortnight! And if I were to go into detail about them, I wouldn't finish in two months. Yet I must tell you something; so listen to what I saw in general terms and noted in detail about these good people. It would be a wonder to find one among so many who adheres fully to the Christian faith. All their efforts go into making money, and putting money aside, and to get it they work and hardly eat; once a few coppers come into their hands, they condemn them to life imprisonment and everlasting darkness, so that by always earning and never spending, they pile up the greater quantity of all the money there is in Spain. Where money is concerned, they are its money-box, and are as busy as maggots in old clothes, or magpies and weasels: they gather it, hide it, swallow it

ellos son muchos y que cada día ganan y esconden, poco o mucho, y que una calentura lenta acaba la vida como la de un tabardillo; y como van creciendo, se van aumentando los escondedores, que crecen y han de crecer en infinito, como la experiencia lo muestra. Entre ellos no hay castidad, ni entran en religión ni ellas; todos se casan, todos multiplican, porque el vivir sobriamente aumenta las causas de la generación. No los consume la guerra, ni ejercicio que demasiadamente los trabaje; róbannos a pie quedo, y con los frutos de nuestras heredades, que nos revenden, se hacen ricos. No tienen criados, porque todos lo son de sí mismos; no gastan con sus hijos en los estudios, porque su ciencia no es otra que la de robarnos. De los doce hijos de Jacob que he oído decir que entraron en Egipto, cuando los sacó Moisén de aquel cautiverio salieron seiscientos mil varones, sin niños y mujeres; de aquí se podrá inferir lo que multiplicarán las déstos, que, sin comparación, son en mayor número.

Cipión: Buscado se ha remedio para todos los daños que has apuntado y bosquejado en sombra; que bien sé que son más y mayores los que callas que los que cuentas, y hasta ahora no se ha dado con el que conviene; pero celadores prudentísimos tiene nuestra república, que considerando que España cría y tiene en su seno tantas víboras como moriscos, ayudados de Dios hallarán a tanto daño cierta, presta y segura salida. [...]

up. Think how numerous these people are, and how every day they make money and hide it away, sometimes a little, sometimes a lot: a slow fever can end a life just as surely as typhus can. As their population grows, so does the number of those that hide money away, and this will go on indefinitely, as experience shows. Chastity is unknown among them, and not even their womenfolk become nuns; they all marry and multiply, for their sober style of life enhances their capacity for breeding. War does not diminish their number, nor do they take violent exercise of the sort that might wear them down. They rob us right and left, and on the produce from our estates, which they sell back to us, they become wealthy. They keep no servants, since they are servants to themselves. They spend nothing on education for their children, for the sole branch of learning which interests them is learning how to steal from us. There were twelve sons of Jacob, as I have heard tell, that went to Egypt, but when Moses led them out of that captivity, there were six hundred thousand men, and then all the women and children, and from this one can deduce how greatly these Moors will multiply, since they are incomparably more numerous than the Israelites.

Cipión: Some solutions have been proposed for all the evils that you have noted and sketched in, and I well know that the evils are greater and more numerous than those you have mentioned; but till now nobody has come up with the right answer. However, our nation has wise men who watch over it, and who, knowing as they do that Spain raises and holds in its bosom so many viperish Moors, will, with God's help, find a quick and certain remedy for these evils. [...]

72. Postscript: Sancho Panza meets an old friend (1614)

What follows, from Part II (published in 1615) of Don Quixote, *chapter 54, requires little introduction. The studies mentioned in the note to the previous text are fully relevant here too, and there are many others. One may briefly note that the meeting of Sancho and Ricote somewhere in Aragón has been pure chance. Ricote's name is richly significant in several ways: one, not now immediately apparent, is that there was a Valle de Ricote in Murcia which had an old-established* morisco *population of some 2,500 adults in 1614, so*

[...] Finalmente, al acabársele el vino fue principio de un sueño que dio a todos, quedándose dormidos sobre las mismas mesas y manteles; solos Ricote y Sancho quedaron alerta, porque habían comido más y bebido menos; y apartando Ricote a Sancho, se sentaron al pie de una haya, dejando a los peregrinos sepultados en dulce sueño, y Ricote, sin tropezar nada en su lengua morisca, en la pura castellana le dijo las siguientes razones:

'Bien sabes, ¡oh Sancho Panza, vecino y amigo mío!, cómo el pregón y bando que su Majestad mandó publicar contra los de mi nación puso terror y espanto en todos nosotros; a lo menos, en mí lo puso de suerte, que me parece que antes del tiempo que se nos concedía para que hiciésemos ausencia de España, ya tenía el rigor de la pena ejecutado en mi persona y en la de mis hijos. Ordené, pues, a mi parecer, como prudente (bien así como el que sabe que para tal tiempo le han de quitar la casa donde vive y se provee de otra donde mudarse), ordené, digo, de salir yo solo, sin mi familia, de mi pueblo, y ir a buscar donde llevarla con comodidad y sin la priesa con que los demás salieron; porque bien vi, y vieron todos nuestros ancianos, que aquellos pregones no eran sólo amenazas, como algunos decían, sino verdaderas leyes, que se habían de poner en ejecución a su determinado tiempo; y forzábame a creer esta verdad saber yo los ruines y disparatados intentos que los nuestros tenían, y tales, que me parece que fue inspiración divina la que movió a su Majestad a poner en efecto tan gallarda resolución, no porque todos fuésemos culpables, que algunos había cristianos firmes y verdaderos; pero eran tan pocos, que no se podía oponer a los que no lo eran, y no era bien criar la sierpe en el seno, teniendo los enemigos dentro de casa. Finalmente, con justa razón, fuimos castigados con la pena del destierro, blanda y suave, la más terrible que se nos podía dar. Doquiera que estamos lloramos por España; que, en fin, nacimos en ella y es nuestra patria natural; en ninguna parte hallamos el acogimento que nuestra desventura desea; y en Berbería, y en todas las partes de Africa donde esperábamos ser recebidos, acogidos y regalados, allí es donde más nos ofenden y maltratan. No hemos conocido el bien hasta que le hemos perdido; y es el deseo tan grande que casi todos tenemos de volver a España, que los más de aquéllos (y son muchos) que saben la lengua como yo, se vuelven a ella, y dejan allí sus mujeres y sus hijos desamparados, tanto es el amor que la tienen; y agora

*exemplary and loyal that they hoped to escape expulsion; but very late in the
day and by just one casting vote in the Consejo de Estado, they were banished
with the rest.*

*The tale of Ricote continues in chapters 63 and 65. Ricote has recovered
his treasure – which in our text might be thought illusory, or symbolic – and in
extraordinary circumstances in Barcelona is reunited with his daughter, Ana
Félix, whose story (like others in our series) is again a virtually ready-made plot
for a Rossinian opera.*

[...] Eventually they finished the wine and most fell asleep with their heads
on the tables. Only Ricote and Sancho stayed awake, since they had eaten most
and drunk least. Ricote drew Sancho aside, and they sat together at the foot of
a beech-tree, leaving the pilgrims sleeping soundly. Ricote, without once lapsing
into his native Arabic, said the following to Sancho in pure Castilian:

'You know, Sancho, old friend and good neighbour, that the proclamation
which his Majesty issued against my people filled all of us with terror; at least, it
did in my case, to the extent that long before the expiry of the period that was
set for us to leave Spain, the full harshness of the punishment was felt personally
by me and by my children. I resolved, since it seemed sensible – just as a man
who knows that on a certain date the house he lives in will be taken from him,
and he provides himself with another to which to move – I resolved, I say, to
leave the village by myself, without my family, and go and find a place to which
I might take them, in good time and without the urgency felt by the others when
they had to leave. I could easily see, as all our elders could see, that the
proclamation was not merely a threat, as some said, but laws of a definite kind,
which would be put into force in due time. It was learning of the base and
stupid plans which our people were making which drove me to this conclusion –
so base and stupid, indeed, that it seemed to me his Majesty was divinely
inspired when applying his brave decision –; not that we were all blameworthy,
since there were amongst us some firm and true Christians, but they were few,
and unable to oppose the non-Christians, and it made no sense to bring up a
serpent in one's bosom by allowing one's enemies to live in one's home.
Eventually, and rightly, we were punished by the sentence of expulsion, a light
and gentle sentence, but the most fearsome that could have been awarded us.
Now wherever we are we weep for Spain, for, after all, we were born there and
it is our native land. Nowhere do we find the welcome which our misfortune
merits, and in Barbary, and in all those parts of Africa where we hoped to be
received and welcomed and attended to, that is where they most insult us and
mistreat us. We never knew how well off we were until we lost it all. So great
is the urge that nearly all of us feel to return to Spain, that most of those – and
they are many – who know the language, as I do, come back to Spain, leaving
their wives and children abroad and unprovided for, so strong is the love they
bear her. Now I indeed feel the truth of the old adage, that love of country is

conozco y experimento lo que suele decirse: que es dulce el amor de la patria. Salí, como digo, de nuestro pueblo, entré en Francia, y aunque allí nos hacían buen acogimiento, quise verlo todo. Pasé a Italia, y llegué a Alemania, y allí me pareció que se podía vivir con más libertad, porque sus habitadores no miran en muchas delicadezas: cada uno vive como quiere, porque en la mayor parte della se vive con libertad de conciencia. Dejé tomada casa en un pueblo junto a Augusta; juntéme con estos peregrinos, que tienen por costumbre de venir a España muchos dellos, cada año, a visitar los santuarios della, que los tienen por sus Indias, y por certísima granjería y conocida ganancia. Andanla casi toda, y no hay pueblo ninguno de donde no salgan comidos y bebidos, como suele decirse, y con un real, por lo menos, en dineros, y al cabo de su viaje salen con más de cien escudos de sobra, que trocados en oro, o ya en el hueco de los bordones, o entre los remiendos de las esclavinas, o con la industria que ellos pueden, los sacan del reino y los pasan a sus tierras, a pesar de las guardas de los puestos y puertos donde se registran. Ahora es mi intención, Sancho, sacar el tesoro que dejé enterrado, que por estar fuera del pueblo, lo podré hacer sin peligro, y escribir o pasar desde Valencia a mi hija y a mi mujer, que sé que están en Argel, y dar traza cómo traerlas a algún puerto de Francia, y desde allí llevarlas a Alemania, donde esperaremos lo que Dios quisiere hacer de nosotros; que, en resolución, Sancho, yo sé cierto que la Ricota mi hija y Francisca Ricota mi mujer son católicas cristianas, y aunque yo no lo soy tanto, todavía tengo más de cristiano que de moro, y ruego siempre a Dios me abra los ojos del entendimiento y me dé a conocer cómo le tengo de servir. Y lo que me tiene admirado es no saber por qué se fue mi mujer y mi hija antes a Berbería que a Francia, adonde podía vivir como cristiana.'

A lo que respondió Sancho:

'Mira, Ricote, eso no debía estar en su mano, porque las llevó Juan Tiopieyo, el hermano de tu mujer; y como debe de ser fino moro, fuese a lo más bien parado; y séte decir otra cosa: que creo que vas en balde a buscar lo que dejaste enterrado; porque tuvimos nuevas que habían quitado a tu cuñado y a tu mujer muchas perlas y mucho dinero en oro, que llevaban por registrar.'

'Bien puede ser eso', replicó Ricote, 'pero yo sé, Sancho, que no tocaron a mi encierro, porque yo no les descubrí dónde estaba, temeroso de algún desmán; y así, si tú, Sancho, quieres venir conmigo y ayudarme a sacarlo, yo te daré docientos escudos con que podrás remediar tus necesidades, que ya sabes que sé yo que las tienes muchas.' [...]

sweet. As I said, I left our village, and went to France, and although they made us welcome enough there, I wanted to see more. I went to Italy, and then to Germany, and there I thought one could live in greater freedom, since its people are not given to hair-splitting distinctions; everybody lives as he chooses, and in most parts there is freedom of conscience. I rented a house near Augsburg [Bavaria; where in 1555 Charles V recognized the rights of the German Protestants]. Then I joined up with these pilgrims, who have the habit of coming to Spain every year to visit the shrines, to the extent that they reckon these shrines to be their Indies, where benefits and profits are sure to be made. They travel through the whole country, and are able to leave every town well topped up with food and drink, as the saying goes, and with at least a few coppers in their pockets. At the end of their journey they can show a profit of more than a hundred *escudos,* which they change into gold coin and keep in the hollow part of their pilgrims' staves, or sewn into patches of their capes, or they use some other crafty contrivance that they know about, and take it all out of the country and into their own lands, in spite of the guards at the frontier posts and in the ports, where they are searched. My plan now, Sancho, is to unearth the treasure I left buried, which I can do without any danger since it was outside the village, and then to write or get a message from Valencia to my daughter and my wife, who I know are in Algiers, and then contrive to bring them to one of the French ports, and take them from there to Germany, where we shall wait to see what God wants to do with us. You see, Sancho, I know for sure that my daughter Ricota and my wife Francisca Ricota are good Christians, and even though I myself am not, I still have more of the Christian than the Moor about me, and I perpetually pray to God that He will open the eyes of my understanding and tell me how I should serve Him. I was puzzled that my wife and daughter went to Barbary rather than to France, where they might have lived as Christians.'

To all of this Sancho replied:

'Look, Ricote, that decision was not in their hands, for it was Juan Tiopieyo, your wife's brother, who took them away; no doubt he was a real good Muslim, and so went off to the best place. I can tell you something else too: it's no good your going looking for what you buried, because we heard that they took a lot of pearls and money in gold from your brother-in-law and your wife when they searched them.'

'That may be so', answered Ricote, 'but I know, Sancho, that they can't have touched my cache, because I didn't tell them where it was, being fearful as I was that something might happen to it. So if you want to come with me, Sancho, and help me dig it up, I'll give you two hundred *escudos* for you to attend to your needs, and I know you're not short of those.' [...]

180

INDEX

Modern Editors and Scholars

Almqvist, Kurt II: 13
Alvar, Carlos II: 13
Arié, Rachel II: vii, 161
Bartholomaeis, V. de I: 85
Bénichou, P. II: 123
Biglieri, A.I. II: 55
Blanco-González, B. II: 165
Boronat y Barrachina, P. II: 173
Brodman, J.W. II: 142, 243
Burns, Fr Robert I. II: vii, 5, 60, 61, 115, 119
Cabanelas, Dario II: 135
Campo Jesús, Luis del II: 7
Cantarino, V. II: 61
Cardaillac, Louis II: vii
Caro Baroja, Julio II: 161
Castro, Américo I: vi, xii, 80
Catalán, Diego II: 97
Charlo Brea, Luis II: 3
Clissold, S. I: 115
Colbert, E.P. I: 43
Coll, J.M. II: 60, 61
Collins, Roger I: xii
Cossio, J.M. de II: 39
Coulet, J. I: 39
Craddock, J.R. II: 83
Cummins, J.G. II: 123
d'Alverny, M.T. I: 167
Dalché Gautier, P. I: 14
Dameto, Juan I: 145
Daniel, Norman I: xii, 31, 167; II: 75
Defourneaux, Marcelin I: xii, 85
Deyermond, A. I: 19
Dufourcq, Charles-Emmanuel II: vii, 39, 61, 115
Fernández, Juan Gil I: 24
Férotin, M. I: 89
Ferreiro, A. I: 85
Fletcher, R.A. I: 80
Foulché-Delbosc, R. II: 169
Gaiffier, B. de II: 75
Ganivet, Angel I: vi
Garcia Gallo, A. II: 83
Garcia Mercadal, J. II: 153
Garcia Valdecasas, A. II: 143
Garrad, K. II: 161

Gil, J. I: 43
Glick, Thomas F. I: ix, xii
González Ruiz-Zorrilla, Atilano I: 51
González, Julio II: 15
Goytisolo, Juan I: xii
Hillgarth, J.N. I: xii; II: 68, 87
Hodgkinson, J. I: 121
Huici Miranda, A. I: xii; II: 15
Joset, J. II: 93
Kedar, B.Z. I: xii, 167; II: 27, 75
Kendrick, T.D. I: 80
Kritzeck, J. I: 167
La Fuente, Vicente de II: 61
Lacarra, María-Eugenia II: 3
Las Cagigas, Isidro de I: xii; II: 115
Lomax, Derek W. I: viii, xii, 1
López Estrada, Francisco II: 118, 119
Mackay, Angus I: xii
Macpherson, I.R. II: 94
Mandach, A. de I: 33
Márquez Villanueva, F. II: 173
Martínez, Salvador I: 169
Mas Latrie, M.L. II: 87
Mata Carriazo, Juan de II: vi, 123, 137, 143, 145
Menéndez Pidal, R. I: 3, 9, 104, 115, 125
Meredith Jones, C. I: 33
Moxó, Salvador de II: vii
Muldoon, James II: vii, 27
Nykl, A.R. I: 108
O'Callaghan, J.F. I: xii
Oliver Asín, J. II: 93
Pérez de Urbel, Dom Justo I: 51
Pfandl, L. II: 153
Puyol, J. II: 153
Rey, Agapito II: 79
Riquer, M. de II: 173
Salazar Rincón, J. II: 173
Sánchez Belda, L. I: 139
Sánchez Dragó, F. I: v
Sánchez-Albornoz, C. I: xii
Seco de Lucena Paredes, L. II: 119
Simonet, F. I: xii, 43
Smith, Colin I: 49, 121; II: 3, 123
Soldevila, Ferran II: 49
Southern, R.W. I: xii

Texts

182

Themes

Persons

(Note: names consisting of more than one element are listed under the first name)

Places

Printed and bound by CPI Group (UK) Ltd, Croydon, CR0 4YY

09/06/2025

14685957-0004